BETH MOORE

LifeWay Press®
Nashville, Tennessee

Published by LifeWay Press®
© 2002 • Beth Moore
Fourth printing December 2004

ISBN 0-6330-9667-9

This book is the text for course CG-0815 in the subject area Bible Studies
in the Christian Growth Study Plan.

Dewey Decimal Classification Number: 248.84
Subject Heading: GOD \ CHRISTIAN LIFE \ FAITH

Unless otherwise indicated, Scripture quotations are from the Holy Bible, *New
International Version*, copyright © 1973, 1978, 1984 by International Bible Society.

Scripture quotations identified KJV are from the *King James Version*.

Scripture quotations identified AMP are from *The Amplified New Testament*
© The Lockman Foundation 1954, 1958, 1987. Used by permission.

Scripture quotations identified NASB are from the NEW AMERICAN STANDARD
BIBLE, © Copyright The Lockman Foundation, 1960, 1962, 1963, 1968, 1971, 1972,
1973, 1975, 1977, 1995. Used by permission.

Scripture quotations identified CEV are from the Contemporary English Version
Copyright © 1991, 1992, 1995 American Bible Society. Used by permission.

To order additional copies of this resource, write to LifeWay Church Resources
Customer Service; One LifeWay Plaza; Nashville, TN 37234-0013; fax (615) 251-5933;
phone toll free (800) 458-2772; e-mail customerservice@lifeway.com; order online
at www.lifeway.com; or visit the LifeWay Christian Store serving you.

Printed in the United States of America

Leadership and Adult Publishing
LifeWay Church Resources
One LifeWay Plaza
Nashville, TN 37234-0175

To my beloved church family at Houston's First Baptist Church—
I am nearly overcome with emotion as I attempt to find words to
express my gratitude and love for you. You have been everything
that constitutes a true church "home" to me for over twenty years.
You have loved and supported me and given me a safe place to
make mistakes so I could grow. You have been my constant during
a time of such change in my ministry life. A place of normalcy
and stability, you have been my harbor.

With deepest affection I dedicate this particular Bible study to you
because you are a church that has an undeniable history of believing
God. We have seen some miracles together, haven't we? Not bad for
a bunch of Baptists. God is good … and patient.

I wouldn't trade you for the world. Thanks for everything.

With much love,

Beth

CONTENTS

ABOUT THE AUTHOR
BETH MOORE

Beth Moore realized at the age of 18 that God was claiming her future for full-time ministry. While she was sponsoring a cabin of sixth-graders at a missions camp, God unmistakably acknowledged that she would work for Him. There Beth conceded all rights to the Lord she had loved since childhood. However, she encountered a problem: although she knew she was "wonderfully made," she was "fearfully" without talent.

Beth hid behind closed doors to discover whether a beautiful singing voice had miraculously developed, but the results were tragic. She returned to the piano from which years of fruitless practice had streamed but found the noise to be joyless. Finally accepting that the only remaining alternative was missions work in a foreign country, she struck a martyr's pose and waited. Yet nothing happened.

Still confident of God's calling, Beth finished her degree at Southwest Texas State University, where she fell in love with Keith. After they married in December 1978, God added daughters Amanda and Melissa to their household.

As if putting together puzzle pieces one at a time, God filled Beth's path with supportive persons who saw something in her she could not. God used individuals like Marge Caldwell, John Bisagno, and Jeannette Cliff George to help Beth discover gifts of speaking, teaching, and writing. Seventeen years after her first speaking engagement, those gifts have spread all over the nation. Her joy and excitement in Christ are contagious; her deep love for the Savior, obvious; her style of speaking, electric.

Beth's ministry is grounded in and fueled by her service at her home fellowship, First Baptist Church, Houston, Texas, where she serves on the pastor's council and teaches a large Sunday School class. Beth believes that her calling is Bible literacy: guiding believers to love and live God's Word.

Beth loves the Lord, loves to laugh, and loves to be with His people. Her life is full of activity, but one commitment remains constant: counting all things but loss for the excellence of knowing Christ Jesus, the Lord (see Phil. 3:8).

Beth's previous Bible studies have explored the lives of Moses, David, Paul, Isaiah, and Jesus. In *Believing God* she invites you to explore the heart of Christianity–faith. May you be blessed by your journey, as were those who joined her from all over the world for the original Internet study and those who worked with Beth to bring you *Believing God*.

INTRODUCTION

I am so thrilled about the faith-walk the two of us are about to take together that my heart rate is nearly aerobic, and this is only the warm-up! One reason I'm so out of breath is that I've been on this journey for almost five years, and recently, God instructed me to run back, get you, and bring you along. I so hope you'll come!

While I was writing *Breaking Free: Making Liberty in Christ a Reality in Life*, the study I consider to be my life message, God began challenging me through a Scripture we used in that series. Isaiah 43:10 says,

> "You are my witnesses," declares the Lord,
>   "and my servant whom I have chosen,
> so that you may *know* and *believe* me
>   and understand that I am He." (emphasis mine)

God confronted me with the truth that though I had believed in Him for many years, I had hardly begun to believe Him. He made something clear to me that He has sent me forth to say to you: God is so much more than we have yet acknowledged and experienced. He is capable of tremendously more than we have witnessed. I have become utterly convinced that we see so little primarily because we believe Him for so little. Here's the great news: God wants to change all that!

God began challenging me in every situation with these kinds of questions: "Beth, are you going to believe Me on this or not? What does My Word have to say? Who and what will you choose to believe?" The two most consistent words He has spoken to me in the past five years have been "Believe Me!" Though my new faith-walk is still a little wobbly and awkward, I have witnessed and participated in the activity of God more in the past 5 years than in the preceding 40 put together!

God not only challenged me personally, but He also began preparing me to be an ambassador of this message: The bride of Christ in our generation is nearly paralyzed by unbelief. Particularly in America! God is calling His bride to a fresh and lavish anointing of faith. He wants to put a fresh belief in our systems! We have been assigned to this world during vital days on the kingdom calendar. We have dropped our shield; therefore, we have never been more vulnerable to defeat. God is calling His church to draw the sword of the Spirit (the Word of God) and lift high the shield of faith.

This series will certainly not be the definitive word on faith. My own personal road to believing God has been enhanced by many other ambassadors of God, just as yours will be. I want to share with you some truths that radically changed my personal faith-walk, in hopes that you likewise will be encouraged.

First, I want to ask you to thoroughly commit to this journey of faith. I am asking God to do something dramatic in your life and not just down the road. I am believing God to perform a tremendous work in each life as a waving firstfruit of a harvest to come. In fact, allow me to get a little gutsier with what I'm asking my very able God. I am literally praying that God will perform a miracle of His choosing in every life during our journey. I am praying for this nine weeks to be a microcosmic experience of a lifetime practice of faith. Glory!

The more seriously you take the practices set before you, the more your eyes will be inclined to see beyond the obvious and into the supernatural activity of God. Like most things, the more you put into it, the more you'll get out of it. I ask you to consider two lifelines of participation in our nine weeks together: Watch or listen to all 10 teaching sessions (one per week) and complete the 5 days of homework in between. Each session will have a listening guide to enhance what you are learning by inviting you to fill in blanks and outlines. I hope you'll have your Bible handy as well, but if you can't get your hands on one, you have access to one in your online Bible tools. We are already beginning to hear from women in other countries who do not have Bibles at their fingertips. Praise God for their participation!

Session 1 will be followed by week 1's homework assignments for you to complete. Don't let the word *homework* conjure up a negative connotation. Our homework will not be the kind we used to complain we'd never use in real life. Nothing could be more useful, practical, and thrilling than learning how to believe God in daily living. Please keep in mind that the sessions are vital to the homework experience and vice versa. I deeply hope you'll commit to both! You have five days of homework instead of seven so that you'll always have a little catch-up time after a busy week. Pray for God to enable you to set aside the time and to greatly empower you through each part of the process.

Try to acquire these materials by the end of week 1:

- A set of three-by-five-inch cards (You may also make your own from durable paper or poster board.) These cards are for Scriptures I'll ask you to have with you constantly for meditation—and even memorization, if you are willing. To start believing God, we've got to believe God's Word! Getting specific faith-truths deeply ingrained in our belief systems will be essential. We will also learn the tremendous importance of storing up words for our faith emergencies!
- A very durable eight-inch blue ribbon, thick yarn, or thin braided cord (to be explained in session 1)

Expect your five days of homework each week to include the following elements.

- "Today's Treasure," a focal Scripture for the day
- A Scripture study I've written for you
- A section called "It's Your Turn," which will involve your own study of Scripture
- "Faith Journal," a section in which you can document what God is saying to you personally
- "GodStop," a feature provided for you to record places you see God at work

Hebrews 13:5 tells us that God will never leave us or forsake us. Psalm 139:7-10 tells us that we as God's children cannot flee from His presence or loose ourselves from His hand. John 5:17 tells us that God is always at work and that Christ is ever working with Him. Philippians 1:6 tells us that God's work in each of our lives is good and under constant construction until its completion. Finally, John 14:21 tells us that if we will seek to love and obey God, God will actually disclose Himself and some of His activity to us.

Beloved, God is constantly at work in us! Although He reserves the right to perform any measure of His work beyond our awareness, you and I can see much more of God's activity than we actually do! Scripture tells us that the whole earth is full of God's glory (see Isa. 6:3) and that the heavens constantly declare it (see Ps. 19:1). In essence, God's glory is any way in which He makes Himself recognizable. When I see a brilliant sunset I know no artist could paint, I recognize God through His masterpiece. Likewise, when something happens in my day that I know is more than a coincidence, I am learning to recognize God in it. Part of our faith-walk experience will be learning to recognize God in our midst by noticing visible prints of His invisible hands. We don't want to miss God when He makes Himself observable! I am convinced that the more we learn to recognize and appreciate His interventions and revelations, the more we are likely to receive them!

In this nine-week journey we will call these encounters *GodStops*. The *stop* in GodStop comes from the acronym God gave me: *Savoring the Observable Presence*. When God makes Himself observable, we want to stop and take notice. I want to learn to say to myself, *That's God! Stop and savor the moment!* A Godstop is any means by which God seems to go out of His way during your day to make Himself known to you.

Need examples? Any answered prayer is a GodStop. Any occurrence that you know is more than a coincidence is a GodStop. I even consider a GodStop a time when God suddenly catches me in a sin of action or attitude that I didn't know anyone noticed. One way I know I am cherished is because God loves whom He disciplines (see Heb. 12:6)! A sudden disciplinary action is a GodStop reminding me that He is ever present and loves me too much to let me get away with something that is displeasing to Him. A GodStop can be four successive green lights when I am late to work because my quiet time went too long. A GodStop can likewise be a red light or a traffic jam that I later realize kept me from a collision ahead. God's children are not driven by coincidence. We are people of providence.

A GodStop is any way God discloses Himself to you. The daily section will be your opportunity to jot down ways you've seen Him at work. The GodStop section is meant for bedtime, based on Psalm 63:6: "On my bed I remember you." Nothing will enhance abundant life more than beginning our day expecting God and ending our day remembering God. Though He is active in your life every day, don't be discouraged if you don't observe evidence of His presence every day. Some days are so hectic that we don't look up enough to notice that the world is still turning—let alone notice the One who is turning it! Our GodStop practice is intended to help us grow more aware of God in our midst and learn to take notice. One of the greatest builders of our faith tomorrow is remembering ways He worked today.

We'll have more to learn and practice as we go, but by now you know all you need to know to get started. I have never been more excited! I am expecting God to be huge. Come join me! When you're ready, grab a pen, a Bible if you have one, get out your viewer guide, and pop in the DVD for session 1. I'll be the one with the mouth. God will be the One with the presence.

Lord God, my sibling and I commit ourselves to Your good purposes and avail ourselves to Your precious promises over the next nine weeks. In the mighty name of Jesus Christ our Savior, make our entire journey one glorious GodStop!

Viewer Guide

Believing God for Your Promised Land

The concept of a ___promised LAnd___ is a primary example.

In fact, God not only ___invites___ us to apply the concepts spiritually but also ___insists___ (Heb. 3).

New Testament Applications of the Old Testament Promised Land

1. God originally promised a large segment of prime property (later termed the promised land) to ___Abraham___ and his ___descendants___. New Testament believers are the ___spiritual seed___ of Abraham.

2. While ___heaven___ is the ultimate land of God's promise, the concept of a promised land has profound applications in our earthly lives, just as it did in the lives of the Israelites. In essence, my "promised land" is the place where my ___theology___ merges with my ___reality___.

3. The most concentrated New Testament spiritual equivalent of the promised-land concept is perhaps best captured in ___John 15:1-11___.

    a. Our promised land is a place of ___possession___ In John 15 we are called to possess: ___Christs words___, much ___affirmatively answered___ prayer, and the ___joy___ of Jesus. Our promised lands are places of God's ___unapologetic blessings___ to the ___obedient___.

    b. Our promised land is a place of ___abiding___. Where? In Christ's ___love___.

    c. Our promised lands are places where God brings forth a ___great harvest___.

4. Our promised lands will always involve ___conquests___.

5. Our promised lands are places of ___great victory___ over our ___enemy___ (Josh. 3:10).

6. The original word for "amazing things" is ___Pala___ meaning "to ___separate, distinguished wonderful___, do wonderful things; wondrous things, ___Miracles___. Used primarily with God as the subject, denoting the fact that He does things that are beyond the bounds of ___human power___ or ___expectations___." Our promised lands are places where God is willing to work untold wonders, but He desires two critical preparations from us: ___faith___ and ___Sanctification___.

Five-Statement Pledge of Faith

1. ___God is who He says He is___
2. ___God can do what He says He can do___
3. ___I am who God says I am___
4. ___I can do all things through Christ___
5. ___God's word is alive and active in Me.___

Believing God for Your Promised Land

DAY 1
CAUGHT IN THE ACT OF BELIEVING

Today's Treasure

His incomparably great power for us who believe ... is like the working of his mighty strength.
Ephesians 1:19

If you're unconvinced that nothing works like faith, I'll count on God to prove it to you over the next nine weeks. Faith brings God-ordained dividends, and its absence carries huge costs. Biblically speaking, faith is without equal in its effects on our lives because God is without equal and faith is the normative invitation He answers with proof.

This week we will study the paramount importance of faith and how it is acquired, but before we do, perhaps we'd better define it. In Greek, the original language of the New Testament, the word *pistis* means *assurance, belief, believe, faith, fidelity*. With very few exceptions the words *faith, belief, believing,* and *believe* are translated from the word *pistis*. When I use the phrase *believing God*, you can think of it interchangeably with *having faith in God*. I prefer *believing* for our purposes because it has a far stronger implication of action.

The kind of faith we'll study can turn a noun into an action verb quicker than you can say, "See Spot run." I can still picture my first-grade primer. Spot was neither getting ready to run nor in a past-tense heap of exhaustion beside his water bowl. "See Spot run" meant he could presently be caught in the act of running. What does seeing Spot run have to do with believing God? Verb tenses! Stick with me for a moment, and I'll show you how.

Please read Ephesians 1:11-23, and write a one-sentence synopsis.

_____

The NIV uses two important and distinctive tenses of the verb *believe* in verses 13 and 19. Verse 13 speaks of Christians having believed. This faith-action refers to the exercise of belief that leads to salvation. Every Christian heard the gospel message at some point and chose to believe and receive it. Because we exercised this faith-action, we immediately became Christ's. We were given His Holy Spirit and marked with a seal. This faith-action was exercised in the past with obviously radical results.

Concentrate on verse 19. The tense of the Greek verb *believe* in this verse is vital. It is a present active participle. One of my Greek instructors explained it: "Beth, when you see a present active participle Greek verb, you can think of the word *continually* preceding the verb." In other words, the promise given in verses 19-20 is not applied to those "having believed" as in verse 13 where they had believed to become Christians. Rather, it is applied to those who are presently, actively, and, yes, continually believing God.

Our glorious faith walk began with an act of faith that brought us into relationship with Jesus Christ as our Savior, but it doesn't end there! Having believed in Him, we are called to continue believing all He came to do and say! Tragically, some who have believed in Christ have believed little of Him since. He who began a work in us wants to accomplish far more! God is calling us to leave the passive life bred by a past-tense view of faith and to participate in present-active-participle believing! In the next few days we're going to study what is at stake, but you need turn no further than today's text to see something huge.

What specific promise applies to those who continue believing, as stated in verses 19-20?

_____

Write that truth in permanent marker on the wallpaper of your mind. God exerts incomparable power in the lives of those who continue believing Him. Nothing on earth compares to the strength God willingly interjects into lives caught in the act of believing. Under the inspiration of the Holy Spirit, Paul likens it to the stunning power God exerted when He raised His Son from the dead!

Can you think of any need you might have that would require more strength than God exercised to raise the dead? Me either. God can raise marriages from the dead, and He can restore life and purpose to those who have given up. He can forgive and purify the vilest sinner. You have no need that exceeds His power. Faith is God's favorite invitation to RSVP with proof.

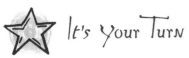 It's Your Turn

1. We've talked about belief and continuing to believe. God gave us His Word first and foremost to call us into relationship with its Author and our Savior. What additional reasons has God given us in 2 Timothy 3:16-17? *It is useful for teaching, rebuking, correcting & training in righteousness so that we may all be equipped for every good work*

The doctrines of our faith and God's commandments are vital to our relationship with God. The Bible records the history of God's people and invites us to learn from their good and bad examples. However, we will focus on the fact that Scripture is stacked with truths and promises we are invited to personally apply and believe God to fulfill in our lives. The Bible bulges with opportunities to be caught in the act of believing God. For our purposes we've chosen to simplify and categorize them into a five-statement pledge of faith. This pledge helps us wrap our arms around the concept and clarify what we are believing God about. We learned and practiced the pledge in session 1. I want you to be able to say this pledge practically standing on your head and in your sleep.

Please write all five statements on the lines below.

1. _____

2. _____

3. _____

4. _____

5. _____

Computer Help

We will provide some word studies for those who do not have access to the Internet. If you do have access, please use it to go further in your personal study. Online Bibles and study tools are available from many Internet sites. The site *ww.lifeway.com/Bible* provides links to several versions of the Bible as well as a Bible Search Tool.

As you use the KJV with *Strong's* in the online Bible library, notice that some words are underlined or appear in a different color. These words are linked; click on them to view the Greek or Hebrew definitions. Some are not underlined or in color because a word in one language may be translated as a phrase in another. If the word you want to know more about is not linked (underlined or in color), click on the words before or after it until you find the Greek or Hebrew word you seek.

Now, if possible, say the five-statement pledge aloud and add your hand motions. You may feel silly at first, but I promise these hand motions will become powerful reminders of an incomparable invitation to faith. And admit it! It's fun!

2. Look up each occurrence of the word *faith* in the Book of Ephesians. Record on the lines below what each tells you about the concept of believing God.

Ephesians 1:15 _____

Ephesians 2:8 _Faith comes from God_____

Ephesians 3:12 _Through my faith (belief) in His, I can approach Him w/confidence_

Ephesians 3:17 _Christ dwells in my heart because of my faith (belief) in Him_

Ephesians 4:5 _____

Ephesians 4:13 _____

Ephesians 6:16 _____

Ephesians 6:23 _____

faith Journal

Lord, the biggest challenges I have before me right now are …

_____

_____

_____

_____

The deepest desires about those challenges are …

_____

_____

_____

_____

From what I understand so far from my relationship with You and from Your Word, Your will seems clear to me about the following challenges.

_____

_____

_____

_____

But it seems less clear to me in these challenges.

_____

_____

_____

Please, Lord, give me insight into Your will so that I will know how best to pray and what to ask.

GodStops

B E D T I M E   M E D I T A T I O N

_____

_____

_____

_____

_____

_____

_____

_____

_____

PLEASURE AND REWARD

Today's Treasure

Without faith it is impossible to please God, because anyone who comes to him must believe that he exists and that he rewards those who earnestly seek him.
Hebrews 11:6

Begin by stating your five-statement pledge of faith. Now soak in the words of Today's Treasure. Read it several times, emphasizing a different phrase each time. Over the weeks to come, we will treat this Scripture like a diamond, turning and tilting it at different angles in the light of divine insight so that we can behold its numerous dimensions. Today we are going to hold this diamond to the light with our eyes cast on the angle presented in yesterday's lesson. We want to consider what's at stake as we turn the noun of our faith into a present-active-participle verb. This week, days 1–3 center on why we should commit to lives of active faith, and days 4–5 will tell us how. In yesterday's lesson we discussed a wonderful motivation for a life of active faith, based on Ephesians 1:19.

According to Ephesians 1:19, what does God choose to exert in the lives of those who continually accept the challenge to believe Him?

_____

Hebrews 11:6 includes two additional motivations for believing God. The most obvious is also the highest priority. Purely and simply, faith pleases God.

please
GREEK STRONG'S NUMBER: 2100
Transliteration: euaresteo
Phonetic Pronunciation: yoo-ar-es-teh'-o
Please, Pleasing, Well-Pleasing (Verb), Pleasure (Verb), Well-Pleasing 1) to be well pleasing 2) to be well pleased with a thing

Hebrews 11:6 uses the Greek word *euaresteo.* Read its *Strong's* definition in the margin. Remember that *Strong's* is based on the KJV, but no matter which English translation you use, the original Greek word is the same.

Why were we created, according to Revelation 4:11? "Thou art worthy, O Lord, to receive glory and honour and power: for thou hast created all things, and for thy pleasure they are and were created" (KJV).

_____

Viewing Hebrews 11:6 and Revelation 4:11 side by side can suggest both a means and an end. No greater or higher goal for our lives exists than to please God. Indeed, it is why we were created. Thankfully, we need not feel cheated or afraid. Romans 12:2 tells us God's will is good, pleasing, and perfect. It is never degrading, but it is always fulfilling. Through the unfolding of His pleasing will for each of our lives,

- God is glorified;
- the body of Christ is edified;
- our souls are satisfied;
- the world is further evangelized.

If the chief purpose of our lives is to please God, Hebrews 11:6 suggests the primary means to such a valuable end is faith. We can't experience the fulfillment and enjoyment of God's perfect will for our lives without present-active-participle believing God. Scan Hebrews 11. In weeks 4 and 5 we will consider the faith challenges of 10 different figures in this passage that is often called the "Hall of Faith." For now, realize that the very reasons their names appear in the chapter are that the end result of their lives was the pleasure of God and the means was clearly "by faith."

Our call to prioritize God and our faith in Him through Jesus Christ is reciprocated in stunning ways certainly not owed to us.

How will God respond to those who believe Him and seek Him (Heb. 11:6)?

He is a _____ of those who seek Him.

Every time this concept falls on me afresh, I am amazed and dazzled. God has already promised that when we seek Him, we will find Him. Is that not enough? Do we need rewards as well? And yet He promises!

Do you see God's heart? Yes, He requires much if we're going to fulfill a divinely ordained destiny. I won't kid you, but what He is prepared to do in behalf of those who are obedient staggers the imagination.

Hear this: anytime you put forth the time and attention a God-seeking Bible study like this requires and you exercise the faith to apply what you learn, you will be rewarded. I don't believe you'll make it through this study without seeing all sorts of rewards. God is the giver of all good gifts. He wants to shower blessings on you! God wants us to be men and women He can bless.

God's pleasure is the end. Our faith is the means. You and I are invited to believe God. The eye-opening news may be that we can also believe Him for reward, as long as the desire for reward doesn't exceed our desire for Him personally. Sooner or later, Dear One, your God-seeking faith will be rewarded. You will never outspend God.

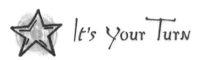 It's Your Turn

seek
GREEK STRONG'S NUMBER: 1567
Transliteration: ekzeteo
Phonetic Pronunciation: ek-zay-teh'-o
Part of Speech: v
1) to seek out, search for 2) to seek out, i.e. investigate, scrutinise 3) to seek out for one's self, beg, crave 4) to demand back, require

1. I think you'll love the definition for the Greek word translated "that diligently seek" in Hebrews 11:6. Read the *Strong's* definition in the margin.

2. The phrase "that diligently seek" is in the verb tense we're highlighting and encouraging in our series. It is a present active participle. Based on my Greek instructor's advice in yesterday's lesson, what does the verb tense tell us about the kind of seeking God most rewards?

_____

_____

_____

_____

Remember not to get discouraged because you don't have or don't presently practice everything God desires of you. Pray for what you lack! When we pray God's will, we will receive what we ask! Pray for a heart and a mind to diligently seek Him. Then immediately begin walking in faith as one who already has what she has asked. Start seeking God through His Word and spending time in prayer, at the same time asking Him for a hunger and thirst to seek Him diligently. He will develop in you what you are seeking!

 faith journal

Complete any of the sentences below that pertain to you.

Lord, I want to please You, but...

_____

_____

_____

The biggest obstacles I encounter in diligently seeking You are ...

_____

_____

_____

_____

(Pray through each obstacle; ask God for insight and empowerment to move or climb over those obstacles.)

God, some of the rewards I've already received through seeking You are ...

_____

_____

_____

Lord, I need to know that Your love for me is steadfast and unconditional even during seasons when my life is not pleasing to You.
(Read Isaiah 54:10. Write a prayer-response to God in the following space restating and receiving what He is saying to you.)

_____

_____

_____

_____

_____

_____

_____

_____

_____

_____

DAY 3
ACCORDING TO OUR FAITH

Sometimes our problem with God is that we don't like the rules. I can remember trying to hang on to both God and my idols. As my grandmother would say, I wanted to have my cake and eat it too. Have you tried that approach? I felt as if God spoke to my heart and said, "Child, My precepts are from everlasting to everlasting. You're not going to be the one for whom the rules change. Repent of your arrogance and lay those idols down."

Today we'll talk about a precept we often wish were different, but we are not going to be the ones for whom the rules change. God is all-wise, and His primary purpose in creating humans was to engage them in active relationship. He's in the business of making present-active-participle verbs out of our phlegmatic nouns. The requirement of faith before we see certain acts of God is one way He enforces engagement.

Read the following Scriptures and record what Christ says about faith. I'll use Scriptures from the same Gospel, but rest assured we could find the principle restated in all four Gospels, then underscored powerfully from the Book of Acts through Revelation.

Matthew 9:20-22 _____

_____

Matthew 9:27-30 _____

_____

Matthew 15:28 _____

_____

Matthew 17:14-21 _____

_____

Today's Treasure

He touched their eyes and said, "According to your faith will it be done to you." Matthew 9:29

During week 3 we will discuss whether miracles have ceased in our day and whether God still heals often enough for us to even bother asking. Today, however, I want you to focus on the required means of faith intimated above rather than the specific kind of result. The faith-precept we're discussing today came straight from the mouth of Christ. Not a single Gospel writer missed it. Nor do we have any biblical grounds to believe that the teaching has changed.

What is this teaching? According to your faith it will be done to you. If you're the way I've often been, you want to have your cake and eat it too. We want to continue in our God-testing unbelief and still see Him move mountains. Sure, it occasionally happens in our individual lives. God is merciful that way.

Why do you think God is sometimes willing to reveal Himself dramatically even when we're not actively believing Him?

_____

_____

_____

_____

Our God is in heaven;
he does whatever
pleases him.
Psalm 115:3

Though God may have countless reasons, the most probable cause is to encourage belief. He graciously reminds us that He can … and still does. If we persist in stubborn unbelief after such merciful revelation, we can probably expect to see less and less activity of God. Mind you, God can do anything He wants under any conditions (see Ps. 115:3).

The story of the widow's son whom Christ raised from the dead is one of my favorite occasions in Scripture when faith was a nonissue (see Luke 7:11-17). Yes, God does what He wants, but He primarily wants our faith (see Heb. 11:6). He certainly makes exceptions, but His primary rule is: according to your faith it will be done to you. That means the more we believe God, the more we are likely to see and experience His intervening power.

You may really be bristling right now. If so, I understand. Perhaps you really believed God in the past for something, but it didn't happen. Later we're going to talk about our disappointments, some of the reasons we didn't get what we asked, and the overriding sovereign wisdom of God. For now let's talk about one of my old reasons for bristling and see if you share it.

My resistance to the faith principle—according to your faith it will be done to you—was primarily spiritual laziness. Believing God can really be work at times! When external evidences scream to the contrary, we have to exert volitional muscle. Deciding to believe God's Word over our circumstances can be a tremendous exercise of the will at times. I'll just go ahead and say it: the great adventure of faith is not for the languid, but if He can raise the dead, He can surely enliven the lazy! We have been called to a present-active-participle walk of faith, not a park 'n' ride.

The walk of faith assumes a walk with God. Faith cannot walk alone. Faith on its own changes nothing. In fact, it cannot even exist independently. Faith's very essence is dependency. For faith to have life, it must find a powerful object in which to be placed or a powerful Person by whom to walk. In your earlier Scripture readings, faith on its own did nothing to heal. The beneficiaries' faith in Christ healed them. Two thousand years later, the God-ordained precepts have not changed. God wants to stretch forth His mighty hand in our lives in manifold ways, but as a rule, it is present-active-participle faith in Christ that most attracts Him. God has much He wants to do and say in our generation. Faith is the primary means by which we place our hand in the outstretched hand of God and join Him.

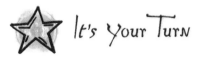 It's Your Turn

1. List the ways Acts 3:11-16 underscores the principles we've considered today.

_____

_____

_____

2. So far, we've discussed four motivations for present-active-participle believing God (one in day 1, two from the same Scripture in day 2, and another today). Write the motivations beside the Scriptures that teach them.

- Ephesians 1:19 _____

- Hebrews 11:6a _____

- Hebrews 11:6b _____

- Matthew 9:29 _____

We have one more motivation to learn in day 4. Then in day 5 we will focus all our attention on how to have faith.

faith Journal

God, my primary hang-up with the faith principle we learned today is that …

_____

_____

_____

_____

Please, Lord, grant me insight or help me simply hang up my hang-up and trust that I'll understand it all when I see You.

Lord, in all honesty I'm probably seeing little because I'm believing little of You in the area of …

_____

_____

_____

Thank You, Lord, that even this week You're going to teach me how to exercise a much greater faith. (Conclude by telling God how much you need Him and why.)

_____

_____

_____

GodStops

B E D T I M E   M E D I T A T I O N

_____

_____

_____

_____

_____

_____

DAY 4
CREDITED AS RIGHTEOUSNESS

Today's Treasure

What does the Scripture say? "Abraham believed God, and it was credited to him as righteousness." Romans 4:3

This lesson is one I begin with tears stinging my eyes. Oh, how I pray God will empower me by His Holy Spirit to do some semblance of justice to the fifth motivation for present-active-participle faith. The truth I'm sharing with you today has been a lifeline for me. Today's commentary will be longer than usual because I'll add a personal testimony. Before we read our text, let's review four motivations for a life of believing God.

- Incomparable power (see Eph. 1:19)
- The pleasure of God (see Heb. 11:6a)
- Reward (see Heb. 11:6b)
- God will often act according to our faith (see Matt. 9:29).

Romans 4 is the home of our next precept of faith. Because it is so critical to our series, I am going to ask you to do something unique to other Bible studies I've written. I'm going to ask you to read it in its entirety, but over the course of the next eight weeks, I am asking you to read it 19 more times. It will not be part of your daily assignment. Rather, I am asking that you read it intermittently throughout the series on your own until it completely invades your belief system.

Week 4 will center on a very important part of Romans 4, so I'm hoping by then you've read it at least five or six more times. Today put a sticky note or a card on the page in your Bible where you find Romans 4, and write the date on it every time you read it. Starting with today's date, I'm asking for 20 date entries before our study ends. When possible, read it aloud. Read it to your spouse. Read it to your dogs, for crying out loud, but read it until it lives in you!

Now I'll hush and let you read. Record the principles that hit you most profoundly.

_____

_____

_____

_____

_____

_____

Right at this moment I wish all of us had a *New International Version*, but all of the major translations say the same thing in verse 12 with various wording. The NIV speaks of those of us who "walk in the footsteps of the faith." I so desperately want to walk in the footsteps of the faith, still warm from the feet of our spiritual forefathers, don't you? I crave to leave a legacy of faith to my children and not just a list of works. I want us to center on the New Testament references and applications to Abraham's faith.

Meditate on the key words in the chapter: " 'Abraham believed God, and it was credited to him as righteousness' " (v. 3). God is obviously very intent on our receiving the concept because He not only stated it originally in Genesis 15:6, but He also said it repeatedly in Romans, then again in the Books of Galatians and James. Unlike me, God is never one to waste words. Any repetitions are to be considered paramount.

What evidence in Romans 4 shows that belief credited as righteousness applies to us?

_____

No better time to make an index card! Please write the words of Romans 4:23-24 from your favorite version. I can hardly stay in my chair to type as I read the glorious words "not for him alone, but also for us"! Beloved, like Abraham's, our faith is what God credits as righteousness! You may ask, "Why is that such a big deal?" I can't answer for everyone else, but I'd be delighted to tell you why it's such a big deal to me: because I have such unrighteousness in my past!

I grew up believing and was still convinced into adulthood that a person's goodness is what pleased God most. By the time I was in early adulthood, I already had so many acts of unrighteousness credited to my account that I thought I'd have to live to be one hundred without a single mistake to tip the scale toward God's approval. Thank goodness not all of you can relate, but some of us have so much defeat in our past that we feel we lost the race before we knew it started. Imagine two teams coming out to the basketball court to play a game. One team lost its previous game by 45 points. The other team won, so it enters the game with no strikes against it. Now picture the new game beginning with the scoreboard reading "0 to 45." Many of us have felt so defeated by our last round that we feel as if we'll never win. Therefore, we play like losers. Beloved, every person God created needs to feel that some way exists to win. That's what Romans 4:23-24 is all about.

My fingers are hitting the keyboard with force as if to raise the volume. God does not credit our righteous acts as righteousness. Indeed, what does Isaiah 64:6 say?

_____

As odd as the concept may seem, not our righteous acts but our faith is credited to our account as righteousness. You may ask, "Beth, are you suggesting we can act as sinful as we want, but if we believe God, we are counted righteous anyway?" Actually, believing God while continuing in wanton sin is ultimately impossible. I hope to prove that those who practice present-active-participle faith will eventually be freed from cycles of sin to live righteous lives the self-righteous could never hope to achieve. How do I know? Because I've lived a measure of this one.

For much of my life I was a habitual sinner, cycling in and out of defeat. I wanted to be good more than anything in the world. I hated myself and the choices I continued to make, but I was powerless to stop. I became convinced that taking away alternatives would be the answer. I got married, moved away from many temptations, soaked myself in church work, and set about to be good. I don't regret those choices, but they weren't enough. I didn't understand that God wanted to heal my heart and change me from the inside—not just my behavior. In my early 30s I fell apart and entered a season of unparalleled despair and uncharacteristic depression. According to God's calendar, it was time to deal with my stuff. And deal we did.

To the praise, glory, and honor of my wonderful God, I have been free from the cycle of defeat for years. Do you know how? I chose to believe God. He said I was forgiven. That I was beautiful to Him. That He had a purpose for my life. That I was a new woman, a virgin, no less. That I no longer had to carry old baggage or turn to old comforts. That Christ Jesus took on my unrighteousness so I could be the righteousness of God in Him (see 2 Cor. 5:21). That His all-surpassing power was within my jar of clay (see 2 Cor. 4:7).

And one day at a time I chose to believe Him.

Some days I cried like a baby because I'd feel the old, destructive habits starting to rise. So often I said to myself out loud, "You are not that woman anymore. You get to make a different choice." And I would. Present-active-participle believing God. That's how God broke the cycle. We have no hope of authentic righteousness—imputed or imparted—without it.

Sweet One, when you feel as if you're surrounded by those with a better "score" than yours, believe God! They'll have nothing on you.

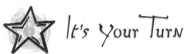 *It's Your Turn*

1. Read Romans 4:24. Notice the word *believe*. The Greek word is *pisteuo*. *Pisteuo* comes from the word *pistis*, the primary word for *faith* and *belief* in the Greek New Testament.

Strong's identifies this word as a verb. My *Complete Word Study New Testament* helps me by placing the letters *pap* above the word. Guess what *pap* stands for. You've got it: present active participle. I could shout hallelujah! Based on all we've learned so far, what does the verb tense suggest in context with this specific Scripture?

_____

2. Read Romans 4:13-14. The NIV translates verse 14, "If those who live by law are heirs, faith has no value and the promise is worthless." According to this translation, what would make faith of no value and the promise worthless?

_____

To the best of your ability, briefly explain why.

_____

_____

3. Read the original Greek word and meaning for *made void* in the margin. It is the same word translated "has no value" in the NIV.

Now read 1 Peter 1:7. What has greater worth or value than gold?

_____

Righteous acts motivated by legalism: no value. Faith: more valuable than gold.

4. Based on today's lesson and the research you've just accomplished, do your best to summarize Romans 4 from your point of view into a one-sentence statement.

_____

_____

If you feel the way I do right now, I have some things I want to say to God. Share your heart with Him in the space below, whether you feel confused, disappointed, hopeful, or elated. Just be real with Him and respond to Him about today's lesson.

_____

_____

_____

faith
GREEK STRONG'S NUMBER: 4100
Transliteration: pisteuo
Phonetic Pronunciation: pist-yoo'-o
Part of Speech: v
1) to think to be true, to be persuaded of, to credit, place confidence in 1a) of the thing believed 1a1) to credit, have confidence 1b) in a moral or religious reference 1b1) used in the NT of the conviction and trust to which a man is impelled by a certain inner and higher prerogative and law of soul 1b2) to trust in Jesus or God as able to aid either in obtaining or in doing something: saving faith 1bc) mere acknowledgment of some fact or event: intellectual faith

void
GREEK STRONG'S NUMBER: 2758
Transliteration: kenoo
Phonetic Pronunciation: ken-o'-o
Part of Speech: v
1) to empty, make empty 1a) of Christ, he laid aside equality with or the form of God 2) to make void 2a) deprive of force, render vain, useless, of no effect 3) to make void 3b) cause a thing to be seen to be empty, hollow, false

faith Journal

_____

_____

_____

_____

_____

_____

GodStops

BEDTIME MEDITATION

_____

_____

_____

_____

_____

DAY 5
HOW TO BELIEVE GOD

Today's Treasure

Faith cometh by hearing, and hearing by the word of God.
Romans 10:17, KJV

Perhaps this lesson is the one you've been waiting for all week: finally, the how of faith! In days 1–4 we concentrated on why any rational, reasoning person should consider surrendering to a life of present-active-participle faith in God. Let's quickly refresh our memories on the motivations the following Scriptures offer.

- Ephesians 1:19 _____

- Hebrews 11:6a _____

- Hebrews 11:6b _____

- Matthew 9:29 _____

And we added a fifth yesterday:
- Romans 4:22-24: Believing God is credited to us as righteousness.

I don't know about you, but I'm pretty convinced at this point that I want to live my life believing God. Too much is at stake, and too much adventure stands to be missed. If faith pleases God and invites such incomparable divine intervention in my life, I want to exercise it lavishly, don't you? But how do we do it? We're going to discover that the better question is, How do we get it? You see, we can't just manufacture faith from what Scripture calls our "natural man" (1 Cor. 2:14, KJV). Like much of what God asks from us, we have to receive it from Him to offer it back. Even our initial faith to believe Christ for salvation comes through the work and conviction of the Holy Spirit. Through each of the following passages, we're about to discover how we can receive more faith so that we can exercise more faith. Today you won't have a separate "It's Your Turn" section because this lesson lends itself more appropriately to our taking turns.

Read in the margin Galatians 5:22-23. Underline the nine qualities of the fruit of the Holy Spirit.

The fruit of the Spirit is love, joy, peace, longsuffering, gentleness, goodness, faith, meekness, temperance: against such there is no law.
Galatians 5:22-23, KJV

Based on what you just read,

1. **Faith is a quality of the fruit of the Spirit.** As New Testament believers, the Holy Spirit comes to dwell in us when we receive Christ as our personal Savior, and He brings His personality with Him. When we are yielded to the Holy Spirit's authority, His personality fills us and eclipses our own. When we're not yielded, we grieve the Holy Spirit and operate from our carnal nature. Thank goodness, He still does not leave us, but our faith consequently shrinks. You see, the more we are filled with the Spirit, the more faith we can possess. Because the Holy Spirit is one with the Father and the Son, He always believes God. When He fills us, our fleshly faithlessness will yield to His belief system, and we get to possess and exercise it as our own.

The original word translated *faith* in Galatians 5:22 is one that has now become familiar to us: *pistis.* Most of the other major translations render the word *faithfulness,* but the original word is the exact one translated in a multitude of other passages simply as *faith.* I am no scholar, but I think the KJV may have done more justice to the translation. Why am I splitting hairs? Because I tend to define faith and faithfulness as two different concepts, based on their varying contexts in my own religious upbringing.

Before I began my research for this study, I conceptualized faith as believing God, while I tended to imagine faithfulness as obediently serving God and keeping His commands. Though faith certainly encompasses serving and obeying God, I am opening my spiritual eyes to the fact that faith is the root of all faithfulness to God. In fact, we might say that ultimately, faithfulness—serving and obeying God—is the outward expression of an inward fullness of faith. With a little different twist on the meaning, we can apply the first words of our first lesson: *faith works.* James, the brother of Christ, wrote an incomparable synopsis of the relationship between faith and works based on the life of Abraham: "You see that his faith and his actions were working together, and his faith was made complete by what he did" (Jas. 2:22).

We've discovered that we receive the capacity to exercise action-oriented faith when we receive the Holy Spirit.

Now let's look at a second means of receiving faith. Please read Romans 10:17. Describe this means of gaining more faith:

_____

_____

Consequently,

2. Faith comes through hearing the Word of God. Without a doubt, one of the biggest faith-builders we have is a relationship with God through His Word. The more we receptively expose ourselves to God's Word through sermons, teachings, lessons, devotionals, and Bible studies, the more fuel we will add to the fire of our faith.

Romans 10:17 says, "Faith cometh by hearing, and hearing by the word of God" (KJV). Read in the margin *Strong's* Greek term for *word* used in verse 17. Define the word as you understand it.

_____

_____

_____

word
GREEK STRONG'S NUMBER: 4487
Transliteration: rhema
Phonetic Pronunciation: hray'-mah
Part of Speech: n n
1) that which is or has been uttered by the living voice, thing spoken, word 1a) any sound produced by the voice and having definite meaning 1b) speech, discourse 1b1) what one has said 1c) a series of words joined together into a sentence (a declaration of one's mind made in words) 1c1) an utterance 1c2) a saying of any sort as a message, a narrative 1c2a) concerning some occurrence 2) subject matter of speech, thing spoken of 2a) so far forth as it is a matter of narration 2b) so far as it is a matter of command 2c) a matter of dispute, case at law

I was pleasantly surprised to find that the Greek term rendered *word* in Romans 10:17 is *rema* or *rhema*. We would more commonly find the word *logos* in reference to God's Word. What's the difference? *Rema* refers not to the whole Bible but to an individual Scripture. In other words, *logos* can refer to the Word of God in its entirety, while *rhema* can refer to very specific words within the Word. Let me illustrate. In my early 20s I used to think if I carried around my Bible and claimed to believe the whole thing, I was doing well. I could live on the Ten Commandments and John 3:16. Wrong. Now I know that to grow in faith and live victoriously, I need to actually study it for myself and hear the expository teaching of others until many parts of the Word literally abide in me. That's what builds our faith!
Let's consider a third means of gaining faith.

Please read Luke 17:1-6. What request did the apostles make of Christ?

_____

_____

3. We can ask Christ to increase our faith. One way to have more faith is to ask for it! Sometimes Christ may respond as He did in this context. Making reference to the grain of mustard seed, He seemed to intimate, *You have all you need for this challenge. Step out in what you have.* If you're like me, sometimes we don't need more of anything. We just need the courage to exercise what we already have. Other times we authentically require an increase to do God's will, and He will not refuse it if we ask in Jesus' name.

Read in the margin the original word for *increase* from the KJV with *Strong's*. Underline the Greek word.

The moving scene in Mark 9:14-25 suggests another means by which we can increase our faith. You can be sure we'll consider this encounter later in our series, but view it for now in our lesson's context. What request did this father make of Christ?

increase
GREEK STRONG'S NUMBER: 4369
Transliteration: prostithemi
Phonetic Pronunciation:
    pros-tith'-ay-mee
Part of Speech: v
1) to put to 2) to add 2a) i.e. to join to, gather with any company, the number of one's followers or companions 2a1) he was gathered to his fathers, i.e. died

_____

_____

I love the NIV rendering, " 'Help me overcome my unbelief!' " Beloved, we just collided with another unmistakable index-card opportunity. In fact, you might say that the purpose of our entire series is to make this exact request of Christ. Can you imagine how our lives would be transformed if we began petitioning Christ every day to help us overcome any areas of unbelief? Why don't we get started today? You see, we're not unlike the father in the scene. Perhaps we're quick to say, "I believe!" But no sooner do those words come forth from our mouths than we are convicted by the Spirit of truth, realizing how utterly paralyzed we are by unbelief at times. Therefore, a fourth means might be the following.

4. Confess our unbelief to Christ and request His help to overcome it. Jesus Christ will never turn us away when we come to Him with gut-level honesty and request what we lack. Because without faith it is impossible to please God, you and I will constantly have new challenges to believe God. If they were easy, they wouldn't require faith. We will find that we can walk on water in countless areas while drowning in unbelief in another. Let's learn to confess our unbelief and ask Christ to empower us to overcome it.

The NASB rendering of Romans 4:20 offers us a fifth means to gain more faith. Of Abraham the Scripture says, "yet, with respect to the promise of God, he did not waver in unbelief but grew strong in faith, giving glory to God."

5. We can grow in faith. Thank goodness, our faith also develops, maturing and growing as we continue to walk with God. I believe the more we practice faith, the more faith we'll have to practice. I am reminded of the *Amplified Version* of Psalm 37:3. "Trust (lean on, rely on, and be confident) in the Lord and do good; so shall you dwell in the land and feed surely on His faithfulness, and truly you shall be fed." I love the idea of feeding on God's faithfulness. Dear One, those who continually feed on God's faithfulness are far more likely to have a ready supply when the challenge arises because it abides in them. In fact, might we say that the more we feed on God's faithfulness, the fatter of faith we will become? How's that for a diet reversal? I'm thrilled to know we can binge on God without guilt!

We could extend our list of hows even further, but I think we have compiled five very distinct means of possessing and exercising faith.

To let the precepts soak in, please list them in order below:

_____

_____

_____

_____

_____

We are concluding our first week of study together, having considered the vital whys and hows of faith. I'm already growing, Beloved! I hope you are too. With the whys and hows fresh on our minds, let's refresh our memories about the whats.

Categorized into our five-statement pledge of faith, exactly what is God calling us to believe? Write our pledge from memory on the lines below.

Five-Statement Pledge of Faith

1. _____

2. _____

3. _____

4. _____

5. _____

Dear One, are you more prepared to believe God than you were before we started? I certainly am. Bless God, I think we're on the right track!

Faith Journal

Lord, the how that resonates most to me from our lesson today is ...

_____

_____

_____

Because ...

_____

_____

_____

My primary request of You as I complete today's lesson is ...

_____

_____

_____

_____

BEDTIME MEDITATION

Believing God Is Who He Says He Is

We will invite the Holy Spirit to ask us three vital questions today, prompted by those Christ prioritized with His disciples in Matthew 16:13-19. For our immediate purposes we will apply them to God the Father, keeping in mind Christ's own words: that the Father and He are one (John 10:30).

Question 1: Who do _people_ **say God is?**

a. Public opinion spans the spectrum from God is _non-existent_

to God is the _God_ of the _Bible_ .

b. Perhaps the most _dangerously_ _influential_ opinions are those held by

scholars and intellectuals who teach a _kind_ of " _God_ " but not the God of the Bible.

c. All attempts to _define_ _God_ cannot help but _minimize_ _Him_. If in our pursuit

of greater knowledge God seems to have gotten _smaller_ , we have been _deceived._ .

Question 2: Who do _you_ **say God is?**

a. Great wisdom resides in taking an _inventory_ of how we have _developed_

our present perceptions of God. Keep in mind that faith that remains _unchallenged_

ordinarily remains _unchanged_ .

b. Sometimes we may realize that we have created a _god_ in _man's_ own image

who is not _God_ at all.

c. Matthew 16:18-20 could very well intimate that God entrusts greater _Supernatural_

empowerment to those who believe _He_ is who He says _He_ is.

Question 3: Who does _God_ **say that He is?**

God reveals Himself two primary ways:

a. His _Word_ . See Psalm 100:1-3.

b. His _Works_ . See Psalm 145:1-6.

Believing God Is Who He Says He Is

DAY 1
A WALK OF FAITH

Prepare to squirm. And don't think for a second I don't know how you feel. Never lose sight of the fact that long before a message God has given me steps on your toes, it has nearly beaten me to death. In the years prior to this series, God pulled, prodded, and elasticized my faith until it had stretch marks. Take heart! Faith unchallenged is faith stifled. How would we ever grow in our faith and get a fresh belief in our systems if we were unconvinced that we could use some alteration? Let's be willing to have our faith challenged this week with the intent of giving it a little fresh air to grow. Some of our belief systems haven't changed in so long that they have cobwebs. Believers who know what they want to believe and refuse to be challenged may have a stand of faith, but they may not have a walk of faith. Galatians 5:25 says, "Since we live by the Spirit, let us keep in step with the Spirit." You and I don't want to get stagnant. We want to keep moving with our God!

The purpose of week 2 is to analyze how we've developed our present spiritual belief system and measure it against the Word. I've read countless books on faith in the past several years with my Bible wide open. As a result, my faith has been altered in a number of ways. The general results have been twofold: I've loosened my hold on some things I might have liked to believe but can find very little applicable permission from the Word. I've also broadened my belief system in other areas in which I thought far too little of God and what He can do. No matter how familiar the doctrine was to me or how comfortable it felt, if it didn't stand up against a well-established concept in the Word, I began placing a question mark beside it. So that you'll know you have a little company, I've been shocked over the past 15 years to realize that a few things I was certain were well established in Scripture were huge doctrines of man built on single Scriptures. Yes, those Scriptures are still true, but they don't necessarily warrant building entire dogmatic belief systems.

In my personal research I get a little worried when I can't get Scripture to teach Scripture. If I can find no other scriptural backup, I tend to think that I'm better off accepting by faith what I cannot explain by reason and leaving it to God. I do not pretend to understand everything in the Bible, but many precepts are affirmed often enough to warrant deep roots in our belief systems.

I hope you've viewed or heard the video presentation for session 2 prior to beginning this week's homework. Throughout the week we will build on the challenges placed before us in our second session. Allow me to repeat the basic premise: if we are going to present-active-participle believe God, our plumb line for measuring the accuracy of biblical concepts must be the Bible itself, not what we've seen or heard. We must

Today's Treasure

I am God, and there
is no other;
I am God, and there
is none like me.
Isaiah 46:9

Remember
to read
Romans 4
twenty times
during our
study.

also be willing for God to broaden our biblical concepts of who He is and what He can do. Keep in mind that our human tendency is to affirm and reaffirm spiritually and biblically what we already believe rather than to search and consider the whole counsel of the Word. Each of us tends to have a cut-and-paste theology based on various denominational views. Please don't misunderstand me. I attend a wonderful denominational church where I enjoy significant freedom to practice and teach what I believe is biblical. But where I discover that my trained belief system lacks biblical support, I respectfully want to have enough courage to believe what God says over what people say.

All of us have had many teachers of theology, whether official or unofficial, formal or informal. Life experiences are teachers. Conversations overheard are teachers. Television can be a frighteningly powerful teacher of theology. To some extent, even nature is a teacher. Obviously, parents, schoolteachers, Bible and Sunday School teachers, and preachers dramatically influence and shape each of our theologies. I'd like to suggest to you in love and without a hint of disrespect that some of our favorite teachers may have helped us package our faith in neat little boxes and even handed us the wrapping paper and bows as if we need not know another thing. Meanwhile, we may be helping others do the same. We think we've got God in those boxes, but we don't. No matter how many Ph.D.'s a professor has or how trustworthy our parents have been about every other subject or how beautifully, intelligently, or lovingly the box is decorated, God doesn't fit.

In the session 2 video we discussed that if in our pursuit of greater theological knowledge God has gotten smaller, we've been deceived—unintentionally but deceived all the same. I am utterly convinced that God is bigger than we will ever stretch our faith to conceive. However high, wide, long, or deep our faith may grow over the weeks, months, and years to come, leave an ellipsis at every point of your spiritual compass. Anything attainable by human understanding is a mere shadow of the reality. Every time you grasp a new concept about God, try thinking, He's *this … and more.*

With a deep sense of love and commitment to you, I'm going to ask you some hard questions this week. Each of them was placed before me first by the Holy Spirit. Their purpose is to help you define how you've developed your present belief system and whether it could use some alterations. This week we will begin to sift what we say we believe from what we live as if we believe. With the loving intention of making you think, I will at times assume the role of antagonist this week by questioning your faith as mine was questioned. I believe you will discover what I did. Some of your concepts will meet the test of Scripture, while others need to be reconsidered. When all is said and done, you may realize something else as I did: my stand of faith exceeded my walk of faith.

I was saddened by what seemed an example of a strong stand, weak walk just the other day. I know and appreciate a woman who actively questions everything about God from her salvation to His love, but she is thoroughly and passionately convinced that all but one translation of the Bible teach heresy. With all due respect, that's a stand. Not a walk. Authentic biblical stands are important, but our purpose through these nine weeks is to see our nouns of belief become present-active-participle verbs of believing.

Today's faith journaling is important. Please don't skip it. Most of our belief systems are deeply rooted. Long-held but biblically unsupported implants will not budge without our willingness to allow God to uproot and replace them. I hope you'll take heart in this assurance: any part of our belief systems the Holy Spirit desires to uproot will be replaced with something better and far more adventurous. Dear One, anything not of the Lord is always the lesser.

 It's Your Turn

Second Corinthians 5:7 from the NIV says "We live by faith, not by sight." The KJV words the verse differently, "We walk by faith, not by sight."

1. Based on your understanding of *Strong's* definitions of *walk* and *sight* as given in the margin, paraphrase 2 Corinthians 5:7 on these lines.

_____

_____

2. Today's Treasure is drawn from a powerful passage of Scripture. Read Isaiah 45:18-25 which precedes it. Record various ways God sets Himself apart from all others.

_____

_____

3. Prepare for your journaling by recalling a question placed before us in the session 2 video: "Who do you say I am?" Based on the reading you've just accomplished, reflect prayerfully and open-mindedly on the following question: How similar is the God He says He is to the God you say He is? You don't need to write your response now. Just think about it before you journal.

walk

GREEK STRONG'S NUMBER: 4043
Transliteration: peripateo
Phonetic Pronunciation:
per-ee-pat-eh'-o
Part of Speech: v
1) to walk 1a) to make one's way, progress; to make due use of opportunities 1b) Hebrew for, to live 1b1) to regulate one's life 1b2) to conduct one's self 1b3) to pass one's life

sight

GREEK STRONG'S NUMBER: 1491
Transliteration: eidos
Phonetic Pronunciation: i'-dos
Part of Speech: n n
1) the external or outward appearance, form figure, shape
2) form, kind

Φ faith Journal

After meditating on the challenges placed before you in session 2 and today's lesson, please write a letter to God inviting Him to prod and stretch your faith and alter your belief system where necessary—or express to Him your reluctance.

_____

_____

_____

_____

_____

_____

_____

_____

_____

_____

_____

DAY 2
A TEST OF FAITH

Today's Treasure

Examine yourselves to
see whether you are in
the faith; test yourselves.
2 Corinthians 13:5

Today's lesson constitutes a creative teaching method God has continued to impress on me for this series. I've almost chickened out a dozen times, but the Holy Spirit's leadership to follow through has been unrelenting. We Christians often talk about having our faith tested. I have good news and bad news. The bad news is: today you and I are going to have our faith tested in a very literal way. We're going to take a faith test. That's right. A written exam. No, I've never taken one in this form. I've never even heard of one until this format began forming in my mind.

The good news? No one is grading it. The sense I'm getting from God is that not even He is grading it. The test is meant entirely for our self-examination and reflection. You don't have to tally a score or consider the outcome to be a reflection of your faith. The test is simply a tool by which we can press toward our week 2 goal: to analyze our spiritual belief system, consider how we developed it, measure it against Scripture, and contemplate whether we'd like to alter it.

Not an ounce of condemnation or desire to pressure you is in my heart. I believe God calls teachers to take deep and wide concepts that seem too big to grasp and organize them into manageable terms and applications. Depending on how closely I'm listening, sometimes I get it right, and other times I don't. *Breaking Free: Making Liberty in Christ a Reality in Life* is my own many-year journey to freedom that God organized into clearer principles to teach others more concisely. During my own process, I could not see that God was performing a very methodical treatment on my heart, soul, and mind, but the Holy Spirit later revealed it to me in succinct outline form.

A similar thing happened for this series. God called me to share some of the things I've learned from Him about faith through the years from a more manageable nine-week series. At one time or another, God placed each of these questions before me. I've simply gathered them into one test for the most intense benefit. Allow me to present you with a few ground rules. Please be completely honest. Don't mark the answers that you think you are supposed to or that you believe most people would mark. Your answers aren't meant to be right or wrong. They are meant to be honest. Don't overanalyze. The first gut-level honest answer that comes to you is probably the most accurate. Mark only one answer. Do not under any circumstances feel condemned by any question. Keep the positive purpose of the test before you. God could very well use this tool to liberate you from an area of bondage to unbelief.

Ask God to help you test your condition of faith to remove any obstacles of unbelief that stand in the way of more abundant, adventurous, and effective life. Then proceed to the test. Circle the letter of the answer that most closely matches your response.

A Test of faith

1. I believe ___ of Scripture is actually God's Word.   a. all   b. most   c. some   d. little

2. I believe ___.
   a. there is only one true God, the God of the Bible
   b. the God of Hebrews and Christians is also the God of Buddhists, Hindus, Muslims, world religions
   c. many gods and many ways provide a peaceful or happy life after death
   d. little about a spiritual world involving God or gods

3. I believe ___.
   a. Jesus Christ is the divine Son of God
   b. Jesus Christ was a great prophet
   c. Jesus Christ was a great teacher
   d. Jesus Christ may be a mythical figure

4. I believe the four Gospels reveal a(n) ___ portrayal of Christ.
   a. absolutely accurate   b. mostly accurate   c. partly accurate   d. questionable

5. I believe the New Testament portrayal of Christ's signs, wonders, and works is ___.
   a. absolutely accurate   b. mostly accurate   c. partly accurate   d. questionable

6. I'm ___ convinced of God's love for me.
   a. always   b. usually   c. sometimes   d. rarely

7. I believe the Jesus Christ of the Gospels is ___ today.
   a. just as powerful and active
   b. very powerful and active
   c. more watchful than active
   d. more distant and less likely to intervene

8. I have seen ___ firsthand evidences of a miracle of God.
   a. many   b. some   c. a few   d. no

9. I tend to ___ testimonies of modern-day miracles.
   a. at least favorably consider   b. give a second thought to   c. discount   d. automatically disbelieve

10. I feel God ___ hears my prayers.   a. always   b. usually   c. occasionally   d. rarely

11. I ___ sense the activity of God in several other people I observe.
    a. constantly   b. often   c. occasionally   d. rarely

12. I ___ believe God is active in my life.   a. constantly   b. often   c. occasionally   d. rarely

13. I believe God speaks through His Word, His Holy Spirit, human vessels, and circumstances to ___.
    a. anyone who is willing to listen
    b. most people who are willing to listen
    c. only those who are most obedient
    d. those in important spiritual positions

14. I ___ that I am forgiven for my past confessed sins.
    a. am thoroughly convinced   b. am ordinarily confident   c. am hopeful   d. have difficulty accepting

15. I ___ that God has a specific, fruitful plan for every believer in Christ, including me.
    a. am thoroughly convinced   b. am ordinarily confident   c. am hopeful   d. have difficulty accepting

16. I feel that God has ___ in the past when I've exercised faith in Him.
    a. actively, affirmatively responded to me
    b. faithfully revealed Himself to me, even if I didn't get what I asked
    c. rarely seemed responsive to me
    d. failed me

17. I am ___ to take my faith to a new level in Christ.
    a. very willing and ready   b. anxious but a little scared   c. scared half to death   d. presently unwilling

18. I ___ pray generic prayers because I don't want to be disappointed by God.
    a. rarely   b. occasionally   c. often   d. most commonly

19. I believe that God is willing, able, and pleased to redeem ___ in any life (including mine) and work it/them for His glory and the person's good.
    a. absolutely anything   b. many things   c. certain things   d. few things

20. When fear comes on me like a tidal wave, I tend most quickly to ___.
    a. recall Scripture and turn it into prayer   b. pray   c. call a friend to pray for me   d. panic

That wasn't too terribly painful, was it? Were you as honest as you could possibly be? My guess is that very few of us circled all *a*'s or *d*'s. Few of us always or never exercise faith. Occasionally, however, I wonder how I'm doing. Do you wonder the same about yourself? Though a test like this could never give us a perfectly accurate estimation, it offers food for thought. Let's consider any indications the test might propose. Remember, our purpose is not to grade ourselves but to examine our faith. Our answers can tell us a lot about our profoundly influential perceptions of God and ourselves. We're not going to get scientific or terribly statistical with the results, but if you'd like a mere suggestion to what degree you may presently be exercising faith, consider the following.

- If you circled mostly *a*'s and *b*'s, you are probably exercising active and abundant faith. I'd imagine your journey with Christ has been pretty adventurous.
- If you circled mostly *b*'s and *c*'s, you are probably exercising a moderate amount of faith. Perhaps you are young in the faith and on your way to developing lavish belief. Or you may have recently had a setback that caused you to be distrustful. Keep in mind that virtually anyone is capable of going from predominately *a* answers to *d* answers almost overnight due to a sudden change in circumstances and the ability to sense God's activity. Happily, the opposite is also true. We are never wise to judge others for a weakness of faith (see Rom. 14:1), because we have no idea what challenges we have ahead.
- If you circled mostly *c*'s and *d*'s, you may battle significant uncertainty and fear. On the other hand, you may also be repulsed by the inferences because any teaching on faith seems a heretical name-it-and-claim-it theology. That's OK! We will address the matter of balance as we continue.

Wherever you found yourself in this exercise, what factors do you feel may have you there? Perhaps you recently witnessed a true miracle, so your faith is soaring, or you may recently have experienced something that left you with doubts and disappointment about God. Explain.

_____

_____

For better or for worse, I am a thinker. I've really enjoyed the thought processes stirred by our faith test. Thank you for being such a good sport. I'm crazy about you.

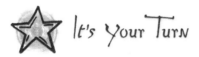 It's Your Turn

1. Would you believe the Word of God directly substantiates an *a* answer to all 20 questions? I won't ask you to look up a Scripture for every question because we will eventually address them all. Look up the following Scriptures and identify by number any question(s) to which the Scripture applies. One verse could apply to several different questions. I'll answer the first one for you so you will understand what I'm asking.

Scripture	Question(s)	Scripture	Question(s)
Romans 8:28	19	1 John 1:1	_____
Hebrews 13:8	_____	Mark 9:21-23	_____
2 Timothy 3:16	_____	Jeremiah 33:3	_____

2. How does Acts 4:23-31 give us an example of answer *a* in question 20? Compare Psalm 2:1-2 to discover the answer.

_____

_____

faith Journal

Share any thoughts with God that today's lesson has stirred in you.

_____

_____

_____

_____

_____

_____

_____

_____

GodStops

BEDTIME MEDITATION

_____

_____

_____

_____

_____

_____

_____

_____

MAKER OF HEAVEN AND EARTH

By faith we understand that the universe was formed at God's command, so that what is seen was not made out of what was visible.

Hebrews 11:3

The overriding purpose of week 2 is to analyze whether we believe that God is who He says He is and how we developed our present belief systems. In our three remaining days we'll consider why we should believe that God is who He says He is. I'd like to set the record straight: the last thing I'm trying to encourage a thinking person to do is to surrender to a life of nothing but stark, blind faith. The reason I don't believe that aliens live on Mars is that we've never seen evidence to suggest they do. If we had evidence, I'd be far more inclined to believe, even if I never saw them with my own eyes. More importantly, I wouldn't encourage anyone to believe in a God of heaven if we had no evidence to support that He exists as the Bible says He does. Beloved, the reason I teach belief in God is that, again and again, I have found Him to be astoundingly believable.

For the rest of this week we'll explore God's high-volume believability reflected in Hebrews 11:3. You'll recognize this verse as Today's Treasure. Carefully look at the verse.

By what means can we "understand that the universe was formed at God's command"?

By _____

Do you realize what this marvelous verse implies? God will not allow every shred of doubt over His creatorship to be removed. I've heard many people ask about a host of theological debates, "Why doesn't God just prove Himself and His claims?" Dear One, Hebrews 11:6 answers that question for us. What is the basic answer?

_____

Because God created us to find great pleasure in us and our faith is what pleases Him most, He relentlessly forces the faith issue. As the old preacher says, no atheists will be in eternity, no matter what side they end up on. Until then, God isn't about to give away all the answers. Hebrews 11:1 says, "Faith is being sure of what we hope for and certain of what we do not see." Our faith is God's favorite revelation to a lost world that He exists.

I grow increasingly convinced that God allows us to take our best shot at being God, even to the point of making believers squirm and wonder if we could be right. Many intellectuals might even proclaim that God has been overruled (or worse yet, is dead) and celebrate their heady victory. Believers who refuse to waver over man's new evidences wonder how God could let a thing like that happen. For starters, God is secure:

"I am the Lord,
   and there is no other…
I, the Lord, speak the truth;
   I declare what is right" (Isa. 45:18-19).

He knows who He is, and He knows what He's going to do—in the course of time. God knows we who are defiant will end up making fools of ourselves. Over time, God invariably embarrasses us in our best attempts to be Him. While the waves of godless intellectualism rise and fall and the trends set the tides, you and I are better off watching from the nearest solid Rock. To be sure, believers should seek to be well educated about current events and intellectual trends, but we need not feel quite so responsible to defend God. I have a tremendous respect for theological apologists, and their arguments strengthen my faith, but most of us are not called to prove unbelievers intellectually wrong. God will tend to that—all in a matter of time. Until then you need not picture God trembling in front of a mirror asking Himself, *Who am I?*

The Bible opens with the words "In the beginning God created the heavens and the earth." In the remarkable and reader-friendly book *The Source*, authors John Clayton and Nils Jansma make one of many cases for creationism by the gross improbability of planet Earth's possessing all of the necessary conditions to support life by chance. They explain how probabilities are figured, using the example of a deck of cards. The chances of drawing a specified card from a shuffled deck are obviously 1 in 52. If the card is reinserted into the deck and the deck is reshuffled, the chances of randomly choosing the same card becomes $\frac{1}{52}$ x $\frac{1}{52}$, or 1 in 2,704. Applying the same kind of math probability, Clayton and Jansma offer the following "Estimated Odds of Selected Variables Vital to an Earth-like Planet Occurring by Chance."[1]

Being in the right kind of galaxy	1 in 100
Being in the right place in the galaxy	1 in 150
Having the right kind of star	1 in 1,000
Being the right distance from the star	1 in 10
Having the proper planetary mass	1 in 10
Having the proper planetary spin	1 in 10
Having the proper planetary tilt	1 in 10
Having comet-sweeping planets	1 in 40
Not being near a black hole	1 in 250
Having a large solitary moon	1 in 10
Possessing a magnetic field capable of shielding	1 in 10
Total odds	1 in 150,000,000,000,000,000

I like the way Clayton brings his point home: "If I offered you a billion dollars (tax free) to jump out of an airplane at 10,000 feet without a parachute, with the proviso that you had to live to collect it, would you accept the offer? Not if you were in your right mind. Obviously, the odds of survival are much too small for any rational person to accept. Yet the odds of there being an 'accidental' planet hospitable for life using only the few parameters we have considered are 15 billion times less likely than surviving a free-fall from an airplane."[2]

Incidentally, John Clayton is a scientist and a former second-generation atheist who "came to believe in God while attempting to prove that the Bible contradicts known scientific facts. Instead of disproving the Bible, he found it to be absolutely reliable."[3]

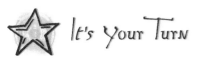 It's Your Turn

1. Read Isaiah 40:21-31. Where does God sit, according to verse 22? _____

The word *circle* could imply several different things, but I like to think it implies that the earth was round when people were still afraid they would fall off the edge.

I also like the idea that one definition and use of the Hebrew word is *compass*. To me, the circle of the earth associated with the points of a compass suggests a global shape. Though the Bible is hardly intended to be a science book, who can estimate how many scientific clues God has hidden in His Word like treasures to be discovered by true seekers? I'm glad people like Clayton and Jansma went to the trouble.

If you have access to the Internet, log on to *www.lifeway.com/Bible*. Review Isaiah 40:21-31. Choose two underlined words for which you'd like to discover the original meanings and click on the words.

Remember, after viewing the first one, click on the Back button on your Web browser to return to the previous screen showing the Scripture and select your next underlined word. Record the words, their meanings, and any insight or thoughts they bring to mind. If you don't find anything interesting or thought-provoking with the first two, keep looking!

• _____:

_____

_____

Insights or thoughts:

_____

_____

• _____:

_____

_____

Insights or thoughts:

_____

_____

2. Read verse 27. Have you ever had a complaint like those? If so, when?

_____

Paraphrase God's general response to the complaint written in verses 28-31.

_____

faith Journal

Express to God the elements of creation that most eloquently express His existence to you personally.

_____

_____

_____

_____

_____

GodStops

BEDTIME MEDITATION

_____

_____

_____

_____

_____

_____

_____

_____

_____

_____

SOMETHING FROM NOTHING

Today I'd like to continue in the same stream of thought that captured our imaginations yesterday. Without a doubt, the foremost fundamental of faith is believing that God is who He says He is. It is foundational to all other areas of faith. Take a moment to rehearse your five-statement pledge of faith. As we use our right hands to count off each categorical statement, our thumb is the digit that represents believing that God is who He says He is. A good reason exists for demonstrating the first statement with the thumb. Not only is it the first and most distinctive digit, it is also the one with the freedom and range of movement to hold the other fingers securely.

Find something small enough to hold in your palm, like your car keys. Anything you can cover with your whole hand will work. Now grip the object as tightly as you can, holding it as securely as possible. How did you position your thumb?

_____

You very likely didn't keep your thumb extended when you made a tight fist. You probably wound your thumb around your fingers to secure them. Try gripping the object again without involving your thumb. Big difference, isn't there? The same principle is true about the practice of our faith. The other four statements are frightfully insecure without the first. If I don't believe that God is who He says He is, what would convince me that He can do what He says He can do? Or that I'm who He says I am if, after all, God is not even who He says He is? Why would I give a second thought to believing that I can do all things through Christ? Or believing that His Word is alive and powerful? Only our thumb principle can secure the rest.

To me, David, the shepherd-king psalmist, was an artist. He painted pictures with words. David painted one of my favorite pictures in Psalm 139:7-10. Read these verses, please. Now picture a child of God fleeing from Him to the far side of the sea. Imagine God's strong arm stretching forth from the heavens and His right hand gripping the prodigal child with such passion and affection that the veins in His hand and wrist bulge. Faith is complete engagement with God: holding on to God and His promises because we know He's holding on to us. Beloved, God is who He says He is.

So who does God say He is? The Author of the Word of God packed Scripture with divine names, titles, and positions so that we could understand that He is everything we could ever need or want. Not coincidentally, the very first identity He prioritized is God our Creator. He knew that all reasoning persons would ultimately wonder how they came to exist. In the beginning God created.

Read in the margin the original meaning of the word _created_ used in Genesis 1:1.

Bara is an extremely important Hebrew word. The essence of the word is beautifully expressed in Hebrews 11:3, yesterday's Treasure. Carefully read the verse. What does it tell us about the way God created?

_____

_____

Today's Treasure

In the beginning God created the Heavens and the earth.
Genesis 1:1

created
HEBREW STRONG'S NUMBER: 1254
Transliteration: bara'
Phonetic Pronunciation: baw-raw'
Part of Speech: v
1) to create, shape, form 1a) (Qal) to shape, fashion, create (always with God as subject) 1a1) of heaven and earth 1a2) of individual man 1a3) of new conditions and circumstances 1a4) of transformations 1b) (Niphal) to be created 1b1) of heaven and earth 1b2) of birth 1b3) of something new 1b4) of miracles 1c) (Piel) 1c1) to cut down 1c2) to cut out 2) to be fat 2a) (Hiphil) to make yourselves fat

Two different Hebrew words are used in the Genesis account for the means by which God caused things to exist: *bara* and *yatsar*. The Hebrew word *bara* represents an act only God can accomplish. It is the solely divine act by which God creates something from nothing. The Hebrew word *yatsar*, often translated *formed*, can represent a thing formed from previously existing materials. Interestingly, both *bara* and *yatsar* are used in reference to the process by which God brought forth man.

Read Genesis 1:27 (*created*) and Genesis 2:7 (*formed*). Write in the blank beside each reference below the two Hebrew words used to describe God's methods of bringing humans into existence.

Genesis 1:27 _____   Genesis 2:7 _____

formed
HEBREW STRONG'S NUMBER: 3335
Transliteration: yatsar
Phonetic Pronunciation: yaw-tsar'
1) to form, fashion, frame
1a) (Qal) to form, fashion
1a1) of human activity 1a2) of divine activity 1a2a) of creation 1a2a1) of original creation 1a2a2) of individuals at conception 1a2a3) of Israel as a people 1a2b) to frame, pre-ordain, plan (fig. of divine) purpose of a situation) 1b) (Niphal) to be formed, be created 1c) (Pual) to be predetermined, be pre-ordained 1d) (Hophal) to be formed

You already know the definition of *bara*. Read in the margin *Strong's* definition for *yatsar*.

Have we discovered a discrepancy so early in the Bible? Hardly! We've discovered a dimension of perfect wonder in the way God created us. I agree with the many scholars who believe that the work of *bara* was most likely the creation of our immaterial essence, or what I like to call our spirit-man. The part of us that most reflects God's image. What does Christ tell us about God in John 4:24?

_____

_____

The same verse also tells us that He is worshiped only in spirit and in truth. I believe the verse means that humans are enabled to worship God only because we have been equipped with a spirit-man from the beginning of creation. The creation of man in God's image was gloriously *bara*. He drew from nothing else He created to give us a spirit. In contrast, the word *yatsar* is used in Genesis 2:7. It is repeated in verse 8, as well. This word is a perfect fit, because you can see that our physical bodies were formed from already-existing materials.

As humbling as it may be, what property did God choose to form our physical bodies?

_____

You might wonder why God couldn't have created our bodies through *bara*, calling them into existence from absolutely nothing. Certainly He could have, but He chose not to. All God had to do to perform *bara* is speak. He simply commanded, and it occurred. I believe God wanted to do more than speak us into existence. I think He wanted to get His hands involved. Remember, our entire purpose for existence is engagement. We were even put together in an act of engagement. God formed our bodies with His very own hands. You might even say that God was willing to get His hands dusty. After He formed man's body, I picture God leaning over this lifeless but perfectly formed physical frame and breathing man's spirit, the *bara* work, right into him.

If my theory is right, I want you to notice that the two human beings were created male and female during the *bara* process of being created in the image of God. My point? I don't think our bodies are the only things that make us male and female. They positively identify us as such, but I love thinking that we are also male and female in our immaterial essence. We will still be man and woman in heaven when we've been freed from these frail and temporary physical bodies. My precious mother's physical body was completely maimed by multiple surgeries to fight cancer. Many other women have endured similar surgeries that threaten to make them feel less feminine. Sisters, you and I are all woman. And if you are married, that man of yours is all man. Nothing can happen to our physical bodies to make us less.

God looked on His creation, and frankly, He thought He had done a masterful job. Man, His delight. In all our imperfections, we are the perfect blend of His finest works.

1. You've already accomplished several word studies today, but I'd like for you to look at one more word using the KJV with *Strong's*. Please look up Psalm 51:10 and then read in the margin the original word used for "create in me a clean heart." What does this particular word usage suggest to you?

_____

_____

_____

create
HEBREW STRONG'S NUMBER: 1254
Transliteration: bara'
Phonetic Pronunciation: baw-raw'
Part of Speech: v
1) to create, shape, form
1a) (Qal) to shape, fashion, create (always with God as subject)
1a1) of heaven and earth
1a2) of individual man 1a3) of new conditions and circumstances
1a4) of transformations
1b) (Niphal) to be created
1b1) of heaven and earth
1b2) of birth 1b3) of something new 1b4) of miracles 1c) (Piel)
1c1) to cut down 1c2) to cut out
2) to be fat 2a) (Hiphil) to make yourselves fat

The word used here is obviously applied spiritually. Don't miss the inference. Dear One, we can do nothing to make our own hearts clean and pure. God creates clean hearts from nothing (*bara*). God does not form (*yatsar*) clean hearts in us with the existing materials of our righteous acts and self-disciplines. If we had all those things, our human natures would more likely form them into the stuff of self-righteousness and pride rather than purity of heart. God creates pure hearts from nothing in response to our sincerest repentance and desire to be pure before Him. Glory to His name!

2. We've come far enough in our study to be more prepared to ask ourselves two very important questions. I beg you to be completely honest. Your answers are between you and God. Throughout our nine weeks, each of us will internally calculate the risks involved in believing or not believing God. Faith can seem like risky business. We take certain risks if we choose active faith and immeasurable risks if we don't. Sometimes our best means of making a decision with pros and cons on both sides is to methodically weigh them against one another. In the columns below try to articulate the risks for your life right now.

What are you risking if you decide to surrender to a life of present-active-participle believing God? (Don't feel guilty about a single answer. Just express your fears and any reluctance.)

What are you risking if you don't?

_____   _____

_____   _____

_____   _____

_____   _____

As we continue, let both sides of the faith issue remain an open dialogue between you and God. You can be completely open with Him. He knows that each of us is calculating risk. The most powerful thing we can do is involve Him in the process.

 *faith Journal*

Based on our discoveries in Psalm 51:10, do you realize that we can experience a divine act of bara *this very moment? Whether I have really blown it or simply rubbed shoulders with the world too much, I love few things more than receiving a brand-new clean and pure heart from God. If you feel the same way, use your faith-journaling section today for a prayer of earnest desire that God would create in you a clean heart.*

_____

_____

_____

_____

_____

_____

GodStops

BEDTIME MEDITATION

_____

_____

_____

_____

_____

_____

_____

CREATION'S UNFATHOMABLE COMPLEXITIES

In our week's overriding emphasis on believing that God is who He says He is, we couldn't begin to consider all the names and titles attributed to God in Scripture. Instead, we are focusing on the first one prioritized by biblical order: Creator God. We could easily have feasted for nine weeks on God's creatorship alone, but our present purposes limit us to bite-size pieces to whet our faith. We will spend our final day of week 2 drawing from our previous day's study on creation. Therefore, to refresh our memories, might we say that today's lesson is *bara* or *yatsar*?

Please begin today's lesson by reading Psalm 139:13-18. No matter how familiar the words may be to you, please drink them in slowly like a cup of fine tea, savoring every sip. If this psalm for worship applied only to David, I doubt that God would have bothered ensuring its inclusion in Holy Writ. The Bible is full of Scripture supporting God's intricate advance planning and personal involvement in bringing each of us into existence. The words in this wonderful psalm apply to you, Dear One.

Though he lived several thousand years before Charles Darwin, a simple shepherd's inspired appreciation for the wonders of human existence far surpassed the acclaimed scientist who convinced much of the world that he had the answers. Evolution is the idea that all living things evolved from nonliving chemicals to simple organisms that then changed through the ages to produce millions of species.

Some of those organisms didn't turn out to be nearly as simple as Darwin imagined. At the time when he and others like him tried to fit life under their mental microscopes, a basic cell was believed to be an unimpressive daub of protoplasm. The assumption made a simple and rapid evolution from basic chemicals far more plausible. Time proved complexities beyond comprehension. I'll call on the expertise of authors Clayton and Jansma once more:

> We now know that a single cell with a nucleus is the microscopic equivalent of an entire high-tech, industrialized city. It is surrounded by a wall armed with a tight security system, selectively allowing raw materials to enter and manufactured products to leave. The city contains a factory in production around the clock, tied to a trillion other similar factories by a mysterious communications network that dictates repair schedules and keeps track of all inventory.
>
> A special library within each city is filled with detailed blueprints for every piece of machinery and maintenance equipment it uses. In living organisms, this information includes every minute characteristic of the organism, …
>
> Directions for all of this activity are encoded in DNA, the genetic material of each cell, that is wound into the shape of a double helix within the microscopically small nucleus.[4]

I learned that about 2 meters of DNA can be found in every human cell, each packaged with 46 chromosomes in an infinitesimal nucleus. While Darwin sat at his desk and reduced all of creation to simple blobs of protoplasm, the outstretched DNA in his body could have reached back and forth to the sun about 50 times. Charles Darwin was fearfully and wonderfully made. He just never knew it.

So are you, Dear One.

Today's Treasure

You created my inmost being;
You knit me together in my mother's womb.
I praise you because I am fearfully and wonderfully made.
Psalm 139:13-14

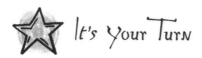 *It's Your Turn*

marvelous
HEBREW STRONG'S NUMBER: 6381
Transliteration: pala'
Phonetic Pronunciation: paw-law'
Part of Speech: v
Vines Words: Marvelous (To Be)
English Words used in KJV:
(wondrous / marvellous...) work;
wonders; marvellous; wonderful;
things; hard; wondrous;
wondrously; marvellously;
performing
1) to be marvellous, be
wonderful, be surpassing, be
extraordinary, separate by distinguishing action
1a) (Niphal) 1a1) to be beyond
one's power, be difficult to do
1a2) to be difficult to understand
1a3) to be wonderful, be
extraordinary
1a3a) marvellous (participle)
1b) (Piel) to separate (an
offering) 1c) (Hiphil) 1c1) to do
extraordinary or hard or difficult
thing 1c2) to make wonderful,
do wondrously 1d) (Hithpael) to
show oneself wonderful or
marvellous

1. Read in the margin Psalm 139:14 and the original word that is translated *wonderful* in the NIV (see Today's Treasure) and *marvelous* in the KJV. What is the Hebrew word, and what are some of its English synonyms?

_____

(I hope this Hebrew word rings a bell! Remember our first session? To jog your memory, this same Hebrew word appears in Joshua 3:5.)

2. If you were not adopted in infancy and know or knew your birth mother, what is or was her name? _____ How old was she when she became pregnant with you? _____ Did she ever share any details with you about her pregnancy and your delivery? If so, share as many as you can.

_____

_____

Perhaps you are adopted, and although you know the mother who raised you, you don't know your biological mother. God certainly did and still does. God knew her intimately enough to choose her womb for the place where He would fearfully and wonderfully fashion you. God hid you in a blanket of soft tissue and bid your heart to beat. For many days He alone knew you existed. You were His secret. God's own skillful hands knit you together, His watchful eyes gazed on you, and His wise counsel ordained each of your days before you squinted from the light of your first. Long before technology ordered the first sonogram, God watched you suck your thumb in your mother's womb. Amazing, isn't it? Give some facts about your birth. What day and year? What time? How much did you weigh? Did you have any hair? If so, what color was it?

_____

_____

searched
HEBREW STRONG'S NUMBER: 2713
Transliteration: chaqar
Phonetic Pronunciation: khaw-kar'
Part of Speech: v
1) to search, search for, search
out, examine, investigate
1a) (Qal) 1a1) to search (for)
1a2) to search through, explore
1a3) to examine thoroughly
1b) (Niphal) 1b1) to be searched
out, be found out, be ascertained,
be examined 1c) (Piel) to search
out, seek out

3. Obviously, God's intimate knowledge of you was not limited to the time He fashioned you and then gazed on you with familiar affection in your mother's womb. Consider again Psalm 139:1-5 and describe how closely God watches you.

_____

_____

Read in the margin the original word and definitions for *searched* used in Psalm 139:1, and then write any insights you receive.

_____

_____

4. The NIV translates Psalm 139:16 to say,

> All the days ordained for me
> were written in your book
> before one of them came to be.

What comfort to know that not only did God fashion us in our mothers' wombs, but He also knows the exact moments our hearts will cease to beat. God's desire to have us with Him will finally eclipse His desire to have us on earth, and He will take us to glory. How does Philippians 3:20-21 compare the bodies we have now to the bodies we'll have then?

_____

_____

Dear One, if the simplest cell in this comparatively lowly body is so fearfully and wonderfully made, can you even imagine the intricacies and the abilities our eternal bodies will possess? Oh, that we would join the psalmist, who said, "I will praise thee … marvellous are thy works; and that my soul knoweth right well" (Ps. 139:14, KJV).

faith journal

For whatever reason, believing that you or someone you love is fearfully and wonderfully made may in itself require great faith. Possibly, another part of this psalm pricks a tender place or wound in your heart. Use the space below to dialogue with God about any questions or feelings today's lesson stirs in you.

_____

_____

GodStops

B E D T I M E   M E D I T A T I O N

_____

_____

_____

_____

_____

¹John Clayton and Nils Jansma, *The Source* (West Monroe, LA: Howard Publishing, 2001), 28.
²Ibid., 29.
³Ibid., book jacket.
⁴Ibid., 42–43.

Believing God Can Do What He Says He Can Do

PS 77:12-14

1. God is who ___He___ says He is.

2. God can do what ___He___ says He can do.

"You are the God who ___performs Miracles___."

Part 1: Miracles and Our Current Religious Culture

miracles have ceased   *It's all about miracles*

a. Consider the extreme teachings on miracles: ___Cessationism___ versus ___Sensationalism___.

Cessationism

  • In the Gospels Christ called those without faith to believe in miracles an ___unbelieving___

Sensationalism

and ___perverse___ generation (see Luke 9:41)

  • and those who focused on miracles alone a ___wicked___ and ___adulterous___ generation.

b. Perhaps the most serious offense of sensationalism is that it is ___self___-centered rather than ___God___-centered

and prioritizes what God ___can do___ over who He ___is___.

Isa 44:6
J Rev 1:8   c. The profoundly serious disservice of cessationism is that it ___cheats___ the believer and undercuts

Rom 4:18   ___hope___. "'___Everything___ is possible for him who ___believes___'" (Mark 9:23).

I Cor 13:13

Judges d. Though our present session will answer somewhat to both extremes, more of us participating are probably
6:12-13

caught in the prevalent ___cycle___ of ___unbelief___. In other words, we believe ___little___

because we've seen ___little___, and we've seen ___little___ because we believe ___little___ (A Viscious cycle)

Part 2: Discerning Which Promises Are Ours to Claim

PS 74:9   a. God's covenant promises are directed to the people of ___Israel___, the body of ___Christ___, and
Hab 3:2

His ___children___ in general.

b. With the right ___heart___ we (can) request the fulfillment of any ___promise___ in the entire

Heb 9:19-22   Word of God. We are greatly helped, however, by understanding that God has not ___obligated___
Luke 22:20

Himself to ___fulfill___ every promise from Genesis to Revelation to every believer throughout history.

c. Generally speaking, God's covenantal promises are best understood under their subsequent ___covenants___.

You and I are under the ___new___ covenant. (In His blood)

d. Insight into why God may make certain sovereign ___decisions___ regarding what kind of miracle

Heb
10:13-18   He supplies may be found in one of the primary ___objectives___ of the new covenant.

Heb 8:6   e. The bad news is that ___suffering___ has an undeniable role under the new covenant.

II Cor 3:6   The good news is that our covenant "glories" ___far surpass___ those of the old covenant.
II Cor 4:7

Ephes 3:7   ## Conclusion   (Ephes. 3:20)
Matt 9:
14-24   In the meantime,

John 15:   • keep believing God for a ___Miracle___;

  • give Him every ___opportunity___ through your ___FAITH___ to perform the one you desire;

  • don't ___argue___ with a ___Pharisee___!

W E E K

3

Believing God Can Do What He Says He Can Do

DAY 1
PERMISSION TO BELIEVE

Our focus throughout our third week of study will be God's ability to intervene miraculously in the lives of mortals. I deeply hope you have either viewed or heard session 3. The lecture and this subsequent unit is so important that I want to recapture several foundational points and add a few others. Please consider each one prayerfully.

- Although the Kingdom era in which we live is not necessarily characterized by signs and wonders, God certainly still performs miracles. The Word of God also teaches that signs and wonders will dramatically increase in the latter days.
- Though God makes countless merciful exceptions, He still reserves the right to supernaturally respond most readily to faith. Remember what we've learned: faith fills the gap between our theology and our reality.
- Much of the body of Christ is paralyzed by unbelief. Our unbelief has likely ushered us into a frustrating, disabling cycle: we believe little, so we see little, so we continue to believe little and see little. ✱ *Important truth*
- A popular explanation for the rarity of obvious miracles today is that God no longer performs them, but the unbelief of this generation may be the real obstacle.
- God is not offended by our requests for supernatural intervention. On the contrary, God is pleased when we exercise faith. God is offended when our desire for signs and wonders eclipses our desire for Him or becomes a request for God to prove Himself. God reads every petition we make on the tablets of our hearts.

I am convinced that our primary obstacle in believing God can still do what He says He can do is that we have chosen to believe our own eyes and ears over the Word of God. Let's consider the eyes first. If our eyes have seen few supernatural interventions of God, we often convince ourselves that He is unwilling to perform them. In other words, we haven't seen them, so God doesn't do them. Not as one lording authority or criticizing the church but as your fellow sojourner in Christ, I'd like to ask you to consider with me our arrogance to draw such a conclusion.

I have taught some foolish things in my day and don't doubt that I will accidentally teach some more. May God help me and have mercy on me. Thankfully, however, I don't think I throw around the words always and never nearly as often as I did in the old days. Particularly during my first decade of teaching, I would take a loud and dogmatic stand over something and would sense an unnerving commentary I knew was coming from God: "Child, you don't have a clue what you're talking about." That's where my ears got me into trouble. You see, I taught exactly what I heard. Like a parrot.

Thankfully, God equipped me with some fine teachers. By the time I learned to test what I'd been taught, I found that much I had learned did indeed reflect the whole

Today's Treasure

You are the God who performs miracles; you display your power among the peoples.
Psalm 77:14

counsel of God's Word. I still believe much of what I was taught in those early days of studying solid Bible doctrine, but after years of also seeking God for myself, I've become convinced that He is able and willing to do more than I first imagined. I hold this conviction because He performed the impossible in me. Just as His Word says He can do, God sent forth His Word and delivered me from mental processes I had accepted as part of who I was. I have been radically delivered from bondage. In this blessed dimension my theology became my reality. I may be a bit more demonstrative than some of my teachers who didn't require such drastic measures, but because of them, my feet stay on solid ground even when my hands are lifted high. Authentic biblical freedom feels the wind of the Spirit while standing steadfastly on the rock of Truth.

We will never outgrow our need to be taught by others who are wiser and more knowledgeable. The body of Christ would nearly collapse without the gift of teaching. We must be careful, however, not to fashion our faith secondhand. Christ taught that students reflect their teachers (see Matt. 10:25). Our faith is unlikely to exceed our most studied teachers. That's why we've got to make sure that our primary teacher is the Rabboni Himself, Jesus Christ, and that our student-teachers agree with Him.

Read Acts 17:10-11. How are the Bereans' examples to us?

We need to examine everything we learn to be sure it agrees w/ scripture

J. I. Packer wrote, "All Christians are at once beneficiaries and victims of tradition—beneficiaries, who receive nurturing truth and wisdom from God's faithfulness in past generations; victims, who now take for granted things that need to be questioned, thus treating as divine absolutes patterns of belief and behavior that should be seen as human, provisional, and relative. We are all beneficiaries of good, wise, and sound tradition and victims of poor, unwise, and unsound traditions."[1]

The Word of God is our only plumb line. Maturing in the Word takes time, effort, and spiritual understanding, but keep in mind that the process is as valuable as the end result. We seek God primarily to find Him, not to see Him perform. Yes, God can perform miracles, but I can hardly imagine that any of us will arrive at such a maturity of faith that we will always receive what we ask. Sometimes God may prioritize the faith required to continue trusting Him when we don't get what we ask over the faith required to receive it.

A powerful safeguard in the study of Scripture is to develop our theology primarily on the Bible's most repetitive principles. First and foremost is the priority of Christology. Jesus Christ is preeminent over all things. Just a few among many other recurring themes would be redemption, forgiveness, deliverance, covenant, prophecy, sacrifice, the shedding of blood for the remission of sins, and eternal life. As New Testament believers, we view each of these concepts in relationship to its meaning and fulfillment in Christ.

You will undoubtedly find God's miraculous intervention among the repetitive concepts in the Word. Both Old and New Testament Scriptures are full of miracles. Even though I greatly respect some of those who teach that God performed miracles in only a few periods of history, I believe Scripture suggests the contrary. I do agree that signs and wonders characterized certain eras while others saw few, but miracles are strewn throughout the Word. God is never less than who He was the day He spoke the worlds into orbit. The challenge placed before us is, What would we believe Christ Jesus could do if all we had was a New Testament?

As I shared in session 3, I dearly love the whole body of Christ. I have no desire to be divisive or argumentative. I just want Christians to exercise their biblical right to believe that God still can and often does perform miracles. We desperately need God to show His glory, and I believe He's willing. To use computer terminology, I am convinced He's looking for invitations of faith written in bolder fonts! I cry out with the prophet Habakkuk, who prayed,

> Lord, I have heard of your fame;
>   I stand in awe of your deeds, O Lord.
> Renew them in our day,
>   in our time make them known (Hab. 3:2).

Christ asked a very unsettling question in Luke 18:8: " 'When the Son of Man comes, will he find faith on the earth?' " If the answer to that question is going to be yes, the people of God must start believing their God. Beloved, it's time for a revival of faith.

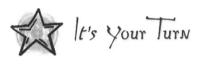 **It's Your Turn**

Write Psalm 77:13-14 on the lines below.

Your ways, O God, are holy.
What god is so great as our God?
You are the God who performs miracles;
You display your power among the people.

Interestingly, when God withheld His wonders, the ancient Hebrew people tended to conclude that something was wrong. I am by no means suggesting that we should assume something is wrong in our relationship with God if we don't see miracles. We will learn that many variables may be at work in whether God responds to our prayers, needs, or desires with an obvious miracle. I just want you to consider that God's wonders were such a part of Israel's history that the people started asking questions when they saw little or no divine intervention.

Read Psalm 74:9-23. Then paraphrase verse 9 in updated language.

Hear the desperation in the NIV:

> We are given no miraculous signs;
>   no prophets are left,
>   and none of us knows how long this will be.

HEBREW STRONG'S NUMBER: 226
Transliteration: 'owth
Phonetic Pronunciation: oth
Part of Speech: n f
English Words used in KJV:
sign(s), token(s), ensign(s),
miracles, mark
1) sign, signal 1a) a distinguishing
mark 1b) banner 1c) remembrance
1d) miraculous sign 1e) omen
1f) warning 2) token, ensign,
standard, miracle, proof

Read in the margin *Strong's* definition of *signs* in verse 9. Write some of the definition's English synonyms.

token(s) miracle(s) proof

What was the psalmist doing in verses 12-23? Mark one.

- ☒ Reminding God of several wonders He had performed on Israel's behalf in the past and asking Him to act again
- ❑ Lamenting that God was obviously unwilling to perform any more miracles on Israel's behalf
- ❑ Calling on the nation of Israel to act valiantly in God's obvious absence

The psalmist asked God to act again! Beloved, ours is the same God who split open the sea by His power, hung the sun and the moon, and established all the boundaries of the earth. How do we know that God can stretch forth His hand and act on behalf of His people? Because He's done it throughout biblical history! Mockers surround us. The enemy seeks to devour us. Church attendance is dropping. Many believers are in bondage. Never before have such "haunts of violence" filled "the dark places of the land" (v. 20).

Destruction and depravity threaten to suffocate our society. The last days draw nearer, and many people remain lost. God has promised that the true testimony of Jesus Christ will invade every people group (see Matt. 24:14). The world is in desperate need of true spiritual awakening. The church is in desperate need of great revival. Believers are in desperate need of a fresh infusion of faith. Beloved, we need some miracles! May God take His hand from the folds of His garment (see Ps. 74:11) and show us His glory.

faith journal

I can think of few biblical subjects that require more depth of insight and understanding than miracles. We certainly won't discover all the answers this week. In fact, we will still have questions as long as we occupy planet Earth, but we can know more than we do. Please read Proverbs 2:1-5. Use the lines below to personalize the concepts taught in these verses, asking God to give you a new depth of understanding about miracles this week and throughout this series. In other words, use this opportunity to call out to God for insight!

*Father,
I cry out for insight & understanding
I search for it as hidden
treasure. And as I do this I will
understand the fear of the Lord
and you will give me knowledge &
understanding.*

B E D T I M E   M E D I T A T I O N

_____

_____

_____

_____

_____

_____

_____

_____

_____

D A Y   2

ALL SHAPES AND SIZES

The purpose of yesterday's lesson was to encourage belief that ours is a God of wonders who is still very capable of performing miracles even if we don't live in a biblical era characterized by them. In session 3 we discussed that as people of the new covenant (see 2 Cor. 3:6) occupying earth on this side of the cross, our primary barometer is the New Testament. Do not misunderstand. The Old Testament is God's Word to us as well. I love it so much that I can hardly stay out of it. But the degree to which you and I can confidently apply every promise and principle extended to Israel is most appropriately measured by the New.

Throughout history God presented Himself to His chosen people in many ways and by many titles. Yesterday we centered on His deliberate presentation to them as the God of wonders. I often throw around the adjective *wonderful*, but I love knowing that when I use it to describe God, it takes on its most literal meaning. He is indeed full of wonders! God applied the word to His own Son in Isaiah 9:6. *"wonderful counselor"*

Read Isaiah 9:6. This verse uses the word *wonderful*. Using *Strong's* information in the margin, what is the original word, and what does it mean?

pele' (peh'-leh) (1) wonderful, marvel (1a) wonder (extraordinary, hard to understand) (1b) wonder (of God's acts of judgment and redemption)

Today's Treasure

"Men of Israel, listen to this: Jesus of Nazareth was a man accredited by God to you by miracles, wonders and signs, which God did among you through him, as you yourselves know."
Acts 2:22

wonderful
HEBREW STRONG'S NUMBER: 6382
Transliteration: pele'
Phonetic Pronunciation: peh'-leh
Part of Speech: n m
1) wonder, marvel 1a) wonder (extraordinary, hard to understand thing) 1b) wonder (of God's acts of judgment and redemption)

This Hebrew word should be getting increasingly familiar to you. It is the same word used in Joshua 3:5 (KJV). Do you see the association? In the most literal sense, wonderful cannot be disassociated from wonders, nor can marvelous be disassociated from marvels. Yes, Jesus is so much more than a miracle worker, but I don't want you to miss the fact that God unashamedly associates Himself and His Son with wonders. Proof lies in the fact that we exist with intelligent, reasoning minds that can ponder the issue!

Today and throughout the remainder of the week, we're going to center our thoughts on the wonders of Christ.

According to Acts 2:22 (p. 51), why did God display signs and wonders in Jesus' day?

So that the people would recognize who He was — the Son of God.

God not only accredited Christ by miracles, wonders, and signs, but He also used these events to introduce Him.

Carefully read Matthew 1:18-24. What part of this scene would have seemed impossible apart from the miraculous intervention of God?

* 1. Joseph believing the angel & taking Mary as his wife.
2. To conceive a child thru the Holy Spirit

sign
HEBREW STRONG'S NUMBER: 226
Transliteration: 'owth
Phonetic Pronunciation: oth
Part of Speech: n f
1) sign, signal 1a) a distinguishing mark 1b) banner 1c) remembrance 1d) miraculous sign 1e) omen 1f) warning 2) token, ensign, standard, miracle, proof

Now read the Old Testament prophecy in Isaiah 7:14. Keep in mind that this prophecy applied to events in Isaiah's day, but it was ultimately and completely fulfilled in Jesus. Read Strong's translation in the margin of the word *sign* used in Isaiah 7:14. When have you seen this word before? _PS. 74:9 "We are given no miraculous signs; no prophets are left, and none of us know how long this will be"_

I hope you remember that we saw the word in It's Your Turn in our previous lesson. Asaph, the inspired writer of Psalm 74:9, was like many other children of God throughout history who feared that God's wonders on behalf of His children might have ceased. Little did Asaph know that the greatest wonders of all were yet to come. The virgin birth was only one of many miracles surrounding the introduction of Jesus to our fallen world. Did wonders cease once Christ was introduced through such signs and miracles? They may have quieted while He grew to maturity, but when the proper time came, Christ burst on the scene with one miracle after another. Today we will interject It's Your Turn in the middle of mine as we research the kinds of miracles Christ performed on earth.

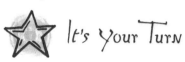 It's Your Turn

Look up each of the following passages and record the kinds of miracles described. Please don't let familiarity cheat you. Absorb these Scriptures with fresh amazement.

Matthew 4:23-24 (23) _Jesus healed every disease & illness._
(24) _demon possessed, paralyzed, those suffering severe pain, those having seizures — (Jesus healed them)_

Matthew 8:16-17,28-32 _8:16-17_ He drove out the spirits w/ a word & healed all the sick

_8:28-32_ Jesus drove demons out of two men & drove the demons into the swine and they went over the cliff and they drown in the lake

Matthew 8:23-27 Jesus was sleeping in a boat & a furious storm came up on the lake. The disciples woke Jesus fearing they would drown and Jesus rebuked the wind & the waves and it was completely calm

Matthew 9:20-22 A woman who had been bleeding for twelve years touched the edge of Jesus cloak and she was healed. Jesus told her that "her faith had healed her.

Matthew 14:22-31 (Look for two miracles in this one.) Jesus walked on water and Jesus told Peter to step out of the boat & Peter walked on water until he took his eyes off Jesus & he began to sink

Matthew 15:32-39 He took seven loaves & a few small fish & prayed. And they provided enough to feed 4000 men plus women & children. Then His disciples gathered the remains which filled seven baskets.

Matthew 17:1-3 Jesus was transfigured before Peter, James & John. Then Moses & Elijah appeared before them talking to Jesus.

Matthew 21:18-22 Jesus spoke to a fig tree and said; "may you never bear fruit again - and it immediately withered

Luke 7:11-15 Jesus brought a young man back from death because His heart went out to his mother

John 2:1-9 He turned the water to wine at the wedding at Cana

John 19:33; 20:19-20 Jesus was dead - God raised Him from the dead & He appeared to His disciples in a locked room

Acts 1:9 Jesus ascended into a cloud before His disciple's eyes

What statement about Christ's miraculous abilities could you make after reading these few examples?

There was nothing that He couldn't do!

Beloved, obviously Christ can trump any authority on any turf. He can stop the wind, flatten the sea, or walk on the waves. He can heal any disease, feed any crowd, change water to wine, raise the dead, conquer the grave, walk through walls, and ascend to heaven from mountaintops. Beloved, when it comes to Jesus, everything is possible. And the possible becomes far more probable for those who—with a present-active-participle faith—believe God (see Mark 9:23).

Christ not only performed all kinds of miracles, but He also performed them for all sorts of reasons. As we noted earlier, Today's Treasure tells us one of the reasons Christ performed so many signs, wonders, and miracles. God wanted to accredit Christ to His observers. The KJV employs the word *approved*.

approved

Greek Strong's Number: 584
Transliteration: *apodeiknumi*
Phonetic Pronunciation: *ap-od-ike'-noo-mee*
Part of Speech: *v*
1) to point away from one's self, to point out, show forth, to expose to view, exhibit 2) to declare, to show, to prove what kind of person anyone is, to prove by arguments, demonstrate

Read *Strong's* translation of the word *approved*. Write some of the definitions below.

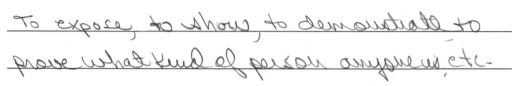

To expose, to show, to demonstrate to prove what kind of person anyone is, etc.

In your own words, based on your understanding of these definitions, what must *accredit* or *approved* mean in Acts 2:22?

To show - to prove by demonstration

Obviously, one of the priority reasons God ordained for Christ to show such authority through miracles was to offer proof that His claims of divine sonship were true. The miracles lent tremendous authenticity, though some chose not to accept it.

Another profound reason for the performance of certain miracles is mentioned in John 2:11 and John 11:40. What is it?

To reveal His glory

As supreme as they are, accreditation and glorification aren't the only reasons Christ performed miracles. I hope you caught various motivations implied in the earlier scriptural examples.

Christ also performed miracles—
- because He saw great faith (contrast Matt. 13:58!);
- because He saw great need;
- because He was moved with compassion;
- because God sovereignly appointed it;
- for reasons beyond our understanding.

In session 3 we considered a possible explanation why God may not choose to intervene with a miracle in an earnestly seeking Christian's life. God often uses difficulty and suffering to complete His good work in us. We can clearly see the role of suffering in the New Testament from the Book of Matthew to the Book of Revelation.

Don't get the feeling that we signed up for suffering when we received Jesus. Beloved, we live in a fallen world where every human being suffers to some extent.

The difference is that our suffering need never be in vain. As we allow God to minister to us in our fiery trials, He is glorified, the church is edified, and we are qualified for greater reward.

On day 5 we'll think about how we might deal with the profound challenge when God denies us a miracle we think we desperately need … particularly when we know that God has the power to perform it. Between now and then, however, those of us who are willing are going to celebrate the fact that Christ still performs miracles.

A number of Bible teachers I highly respect and still choose to study under feel differently than I do about miracles today. They certainly believe that God can perform miracles, but they think we live in an age when He most often does not. I have so much to learn, and in many ways I wouldn't feel worthy to help them put on their shoes. Still, I think they are reasoning backward from the shortage of unquestionable miracles in our day instead of basing their teaching on repeated statements in Scripture.

Christ gave no time qualifier when He said, " 'Everything is possible for him who believes' " (Mark 9:23). On the subject of miracles God left so many explanations unsaid that all of us are at risk of error on how to approach them today. I can't help but think that if I err, let me err on the side of belief. I don't want you to take my word for it any more than I'm suggesting you take that of other student-teachers. Study. Pray. Contemplate the biblical facts. Then, by all means, consider well-respected points of view on both sides of the subject—perhaps exercising a little caution toward the extremes. You can't lose when you earnestly seek God. Even if you don't find the answer, you find the Author.

You should have already completed It's Your Turn, so let's go ahead to our Faith Journal for today.

faith Journal

Pray the words of Psalm 146 in first person as if they are coming from your own heart to God. Think about your circumstances and challenges as you pray these words. Use the lines below to apply any phrases of the psalm to your own praises or petitions to God.

Praise the Lord, O my soul

I will praise the Lord all my life.

I will sing praise to you Lord as long as I live.

_____

_____

_____

_____

_____

_____

_____

_____

DAY 3

WONDERS NEVER CEASE

Today's Treasure

Dear friend, I pray that you may enjoy good health and that all may go well with you, even as your soul is getting along well.
3 John 1:2

I have a delightfully rich heritage of sayings. When my extended family gets together, anyone listening might think we speak a foreign language unless they were from the hills of Arkansas where my parents grew up. Where my family's from, we don't just think. We reckon. We don't just speak. We do declare. We don't just look alike. We're the spittin' image. We're not just on the run. We're a-comin' and a-goin'. And when we're thoroughly amazed, we sit a spell, shake our heads, and say, "Well, wonders never cease."

That's precisely what I've come to say. Both today and tomorrow I want to suggest to you that wonders have never ceased. I don't doubt that they have a different role and objective in our day, but God has never ceased showing off to an adoring audience. If we could take a poll of the entire Christian population and learn ways—if ever—each believer has personally witnessed unquestionable divine intervention, I'm convinced that we'd be stunned.

Believers in Third World countries often report miracles. The most obvious explanation is probably that they are in far greater need. Speaking of great need, the work God has begun in the Middle East is nothing less than staggering. Do you know what appears to be one of the primary ways Christ is revealing Himself to Muslims? Through dreams! The similar testimonies of people who have never conversed with one another are too plenteous to ignore. Many Christians on the field have reported that when the time to witness finally presented itself, many of those who accepted Christ did so because the encounter confirmed their dreams. In most of the dreams I've read about, Christ Himself appeared to them, telling them that He was the Son of God and that they could confidently believe.

Right about now you would be wise to ask whether a biblical precedent exists for such a move of God. You better believe it! Familiar biblical figures who received messages from God in dreams are Jacob; his son Joseph; and the New Testament Joseph, to whom Mary was betrothed. Scripture also recounts times when God spoke to those who did not formerly know Him or have a relationship with Him.

Read each of the following passages and record the basic story line.

Genesis 20:1-7 _Abraham had told King Abimelech that Sarah was his sister but God revealed to the King that Sarah was his wife & told the King to return her to him_

Daniel 2:1-3,24-29 _God revealed to Daniel in a dream the interpretation of the kings dream. Then Daniel was able to tell the King that his dream was about what was to come_

Now read Acts 2:17. Why should we not be surprised if we hear increasing testimonies of God revealing Himself or a message through dreams?

Because His Word says that in the last days the old men will dream dreams.

I personally have never received a message from God through a dream, but I have undoubtedly witnessed miracles. In our previous lesson we talked about a prevalent assumption in the body of Christ that God is not willing to work many miracles in our day, based on the fact that we've seen so few. We are challenged to believe God's Word over what our eyes have seen. The lack of supernatural intervention could very well be a result of our stronghold of unbelief. I'd also like to suggest that far more miracles are occurring in and around the body of Christ than most of us know.

Point of Intersect (point of distrust)

I've heard testimonies from people who had to leave churches they had attended and loved for years because they were desperate to be surrounded by faith-filled people in a time of crisis. What a tragedy! Faith was never meant to be denominational. Every believer is invited and encouraged by God to practice biblical faith. I attend a church that is part of a denomination that has historically been associated with many wonderful pursuits, such as evangelism and mission work. Our strong suit historically has not been superabounding faith, although I believe this is changing. That's why I'm delighted to tell you that I would not have to leave my church to be surrounded by faith-filled people. For 25 years we were privileged to have a pastor who had a gift of faith (see 1 Cor. 12:9). We have witnessed miracles of many kinds.

When believers think of miracles, our thoughts often turn to miracles of healing. When you consider the prevalence of sickness and disease, no wonder some of our most fervent prayers are for physical healing. Although I pray that you and I will learn to think far more broadly than miracles of healing, I am very aware of our desperate hope in this area. The need is overwhelming, and the seasons are rare when I haven't joined other believers in earnest intercession for God to heal someone physically. I am happy to report that I have witnessed more than a few medical miracles. Today and tomorrow I will share a handful of those I've watched most closely. Each of the following cases has been documented by physicians. May these testimonies fuel your faith.

My friend Rick Jones, a pastoral minister at my church, was diagnosed with inoperable pancreatic carcinoma in 1990. This godly family wept together after receiving the report. Then Rick asked a question he believes, in retrospect, that patients are better off not asking: "How long do I have?" The doctor replied, "Ninety days at the most." He assured Rick and his family that he would do anything he could to make him comfortable. Though he had issued the diagnosis, something inside the Christian internist compelled him to reject it relentlessly. After much research the doctor discovered a kind of radical surgery that was showing marginal results in slightly extending the lives of some patients with Rick's diagnosis. The most important factor for even marginal success was the absolute inactivity of cancer in any other location besides the pancreas.

The internist found an experienced surgeon who was willing to perform the radical procedure, but on opening Rick up, they found cancer everywhere. The deflated surgeon told those attending him that nothing else could be done and to close him up. Just moments later when he walked away, a man put a hand on his shoulder and said, "James, you can do this surgery. I gave you the talent. What would you want them to do with you?" He turned to see who was talking to him, and no one was there. He returned to the operating room and announced they would continue the procedure. After removing as much infected tissue as possible, he turned away to take several sips of orange juice. When he turned back to his patient, every visible sign of cancer in Rick's abdomen had disappeared. Does documentation exist? Yes, indeed. Not only is it on paper. It's on videotape. The sight was so dramatic that the doctor looked straight into the camera taping the procedure and said, "What you've seen here is the hand of the Great Physician." Furthermore, after tissue samples were sent to the lab, the surgeon received a message saying they must have received the wrong samples. The patient whose tissue they received had no sign of ever having had cancer. Rick is alive because God appointed him to stick around and proclaim His glory. He is a thriving minister with a darling granddaughter who thinks Pa Pa is practically the center of the universe. If anyone knows better, Rick does.

My friend Belinda Edgerton was diagnosed with breast cancer when she was 32 years old and her youngest child was only 3. Two lumps were discovered within a year of each other, resulting in bilateral surgery and appropriate treatments. High hopes for a cancer-free future were dashed when she saw the doctor 7 years later for back pain. Bone scans revealed cancer in literally every bone from her head to her knees—her skull, every vertebra, every rib, every finger. It was a nightmare. Though the doctor would not tell her she had no hope, he told her that their primary focus needed to be on quality of life. Belinda believed that God plainly told her that she would not die from this disease. She took the treatments and underwent a radical procedure that many believed would do little to slow the ravenous spread of cancer in her body. When people told Belinda they were praying for her healing, she'd thank them and ask them also to pray for her faith. She wanted so much to believe what she felt God had said to her. Today Belinda is cured. Even her formerly reluctant doctor has no other excuse. Her precious three-year-old son is now in college.

My friend Becky Tabor was diagnosed with Stage IIIC ovarian cancer the same year Belinda's bone scan revealed such a dramatic spread of cancer. Belinda was in my Sunday School class, and Becky had been part of a weekday Bible study I taught at another church. I remember feeling absolutely overwhelmed with concern for these two women, who were very close to my age with children much too young to experience such a loss. Becky's children were 10 and 2 years old at the time of her diagnosis. Those of us who knew and loved her were devastated by the thought that Katherine would not remember her mother at all if God did not extend Becky's life. Prayer warriors instantly rose up around her and began beating on the doors of heaven on her behalf. At times we received very discouraging news. The surgeon discovered that the cancer had already seeded into surrounding tissue, and he had to close her with 3 to 5 percent of the cancer spread like a "handful of sand" in her abdomen. Becky is a woman of prayer if I've ever met one. She earnestly sought God and believed He gave her Deuteronomy 7:20 as a promise. I think you'll enjoy reading this verse.

What does Deuteronomy 7:20 describe? *The Amorites were able to chase the Israelites off the battlefield (Deut 1:44) because of their lack of trust in the Lord. What I believe is being said is that the results could have been reversed if they only believed. Therefore if she (Becky) trusted the Lord for victory - she would see it!*

Becky believed that the "hornet" God was going to send into her body was the chemotherapy and that the "survivors" in hiding were the cancer cells that the doctors could not remove. Becky has fought quite a battle since her diagnosis in 1993, but I celebrate with you today that she is presently healthy and very active. Her son is now in college, and the daughter who was only 2 at the time of the diagnosis is 11. Becky testifies to the grace and glory of God every opportunity she gets.

Rick's, Belinda's, and Becky's stories have several important common denominators. Each of them believed that God is still in the business of healing if it is His sovereign desire in a particular case. Each of the three would have testified to God's love and faithfulness even if He had not granted physical healing. Each of them believed that God continued to compel them not to accept the diagnosis. Each of them was surrounded by numbers of others who were also willing to pray big prayers and believe God would physically heal them until He said or proved otherwise. Each of them received the treatment prescribed to them by wise physicians. I most commonly hear those who have been physically healed say that they believe each person should allow doctors to do what they can do and then invite God to do what only He can do. Beloved, believe that God can do anything He says He can do.

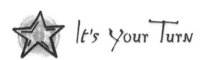 ## It's Your Turn

I know. I know. I feel the same way. I also have godly friends and loved ones who faithfully prayed for physical healing on this earth but didn't receive it. Do you want to hear some refreshing news? So did the Apostle Paul! What did he write to Timothy in 2 Timothy 4:20?

He left Trophimus sick in Miletus.

Read and then contrast the phenomenon described in Acts 19:11.

God did miracles thru Paul. He sent his aprons & hankerchiefs to the sick & they were cured

Some commentators offer the explanation that Paul's supernatural empowerment diminished with age because the accreditation of miracles served its purpose with the establishment of the early church. However, several things don't add up. (We'll discuss some of them tomorrow.) Much earlier when Paul was in Philippi, he testified to the illness that nearly took the life of Epaphroditus. I think Paul experienced what we experience now: the unexplainable sovereignty of God. Can you imagine how frustrated Paul must have been to leave Trophimus sick after he had seen so many others miraculously healed? Surely Paul prayed over him with all his might, and he certainly wasn't short on faith. Don't you imagine that he too was at a loss to explain the difference?

Furthermore, during the very days when God used Paul so powerfully in the lives of others, he testified to many personal sufferings.

In the following two Scriptures, what greater purposes caused God to allow suffering?

2 Corinthians 1:8-11 _So they wouldn't rely on themselves but on God_

2 Corinthians 12:7-10 _A thorn in his flesh was given to Paul to keep him from becoming conceited and to realize that God is sufficient_

Beloved, in all honesty we just do not know why God physically heals some and not others. We can know without a shadow of doubt that the issue is not a lack of divine love or kindness. Many eternal factors are involved that we won't understand until we see Christ face-to-face. Until then we must not lack faith for the healing of many because we don't see the healing of all.

I am convinced that Paul described the best philosophy in Philippians 1:20-27. Please pore over these words, and write a brief synopsis of Paul's philosophy of life and death.

Until we go to glory we need to be doing God's work here on earth - furthering the Kingdom

faith Journal

Pour out your heart to God over someone you love who could use a miracle of healing. Tell God the desires of your heart and ask Him how He would have you pray. Ask Him for the faith to believe that He is God; that He can do what He says He can do; and that if He does not grant the requested miracle, He will grant a greater one.

Lord how should I pray? Because I am too close to the situation, it is difficult to pray because I can't see the whole picture. You know I believe Lisa should come home - But that may not be your plan and your plan is perfect so I surrender to your will knowing that your plan is perfect & it will be in your timing

GodStops

_____

_____

_____

_____

_____

_____

_____

_____

_____

_____

_____

_____

DAY 4
WHEN NOTHING ELSE COULD HELP

No one in my church in Houston, Texas, will ever forget Duane Miller's miracle. I love the fact that Duane says if it had not happened to him, he probably wouldn't have believed it. In 1990 Duane was the senior pastor of First Baptist Church in Brenham, Texas. One Sunday morning he came down with flu-like symptoms and lost his voice. He apologetically made his way through the sermon and assumed that his malady would quickly pass like any other case of laryngitis. It didn't. Duane's condition worsened until he ended up at the Baylor College of Medicine in the hands of knowledgeable but baffled specialists. Five months had passed since Duane croaked his way through his last sermon. He was horrified when the specialist knew nothing to prescribe but an additional six months of absolute silence. Any Holy Spirit-invaded speaker, preacher, or teacher knows that's nearly a fate worse than death. Six months later, Duane's voice showed absolutely no improvement. Devastated, Duane resigned his pastorate and returned deeply wounded in soul and wallet to our home church in Houston.

Before Duane took the pastorate in Brenham, he had taught a class of several hundred people at our church called the Catacombs. On his return the members of the class lovingly embraced Duane and formed a tight knot of support around him.

Today's Treasure

She had suffered a great deal under the care of many doctors and had spent all she had, yet instead of getting better she grew worse.
Mark 5:26

God used this precious class to be the bedrock while life tossed Duane and his wife, Joylene. In addition to his inability to speak above a whisper, he began to have trouble focusing his eyes. At one point the medical facts began adding up to multiple sclerosis, but the tests continued to come back negative. Finally, the doctors told Duane that he'd never get better. On the contrary, they told him that within two years he'd lose his voice completely.

Early the next year the teacher of the Catacombs Class resigned, and the director insisted that God told her Duane was to take the position. Duane was not among the very few people who believed her. Reluctantly, but with the encouragement of our faith-filled pastor, Duane took the position. Class members rigged an ultrasensitive microphone that would pick up the slightest whisper. A mighty fine teacher indeed is the one people would rather strain to hear than miss. Duane knew that using his voice enough to teach a weekly class could very well hasten what appeared inevitable. Others, however, refused to accept that diagnosis. Read Duane's words for yourself from his wonderful book *Out of the Silence*: "Looking back, I see that though I was emotionally demolished, physically decimated, and spiritually devastated, God knit a family around me who just would not give up: my precious mom, who never stopped telling me I was going to be healed, despite my protests; my wonderful in-laws; my daughter Jodi. They all approached the Throne Room at different times and from different perspectives, but each one of them heard the same voice and the same message: Duane's condition will not be permanent; his voice will be restored."[2]

Like many to whom the malady is a 24-hour reality, Duane did not hold the same hope as those who surrounded him: "Both Joylene and I knew God could heal. We also continued to hope that He would yet heal me. But after almost three years of unanswered prayer, I had become a pragmatist. I felt that it was time to learn to deal with life as it was instead of wasting any more time trying to make it what it could not be. It was just too exhausting to maintain a spirit of expectation."[3]

On his knees Duane surrendered to God's will, whether or not it meant healing. His condition went from bad to worse. One Sunday morning at our church he rasped his way through part of a lesson on the Psalms with the help of his sensitized microphone. He read the words of Psalm 103:1-5 and reminded his class never to forget the benefits of God. Not bad advice. Why don't we stop and take a look for ourselves.

What benefits of God are listed in these five verses?

He forgives our sins heals all our diseases who redeems us and crowns us with love & compassion. He satisfies our desires w/good things & rene our you

Duane then began to talk about the second benefit: God heals all my diseases. He writes,

> It pains me that such a precious truth has been dragged through the mire and muck of controversy and theological haranguing, but I also understand why it has happened. Like many other pastors, I have been dismayed and embarrassed at the showmanship that often accompanies a "healing ministry." The circus atmosphere, the proven charlatans, the glorification of the minister: we should rightly recoil when confronted with such distortion.
>
> On the other hand, some conservative evangelicals have developed a systematic theology of dispensations that has left absolutely no room for the miraculous. …
> The argument goes like this: When the Scriptures were completed, that which is

"perfect" came. Therefore, we no longer have any need for miracles, ... because we have all we need contained in the completed Bible.

You know what this theology reminds me of? It's like putting an eternal God in a time box and telling Him to stay there and behave Himself.[4]

Duane taught his class that morning that God is neither a genie in a bottle nor an apathetic bystander. Like me, he doesn't want to be forced to take a stand at one extreme or the other. He just wants to let God be God. Continue reading the testimony of that particular Sunday morning lesson: "Ironically and prophetically, I asked the class, 'What happens when we put God in a box and say He doesn't heal anymore?' I paused for maximum effect. 'He kicks all the walls down.' "As Duane says, right about that moment "God was putting on His boots."[5]

By this time the pain in Duane's throat was excruciating. He continued the lesson with the mention of the next benefit: He redeems my life from the pit. He started to refer to his own ordeal, but the moment the word pit slipped from his mouth, whatever seemed to have choked him for more than three years suddenly released. Before the ears of his loving class and prayer warriors, God performed a miracle!

Every bit of it is recorded on tape. You can hear the class gasp. You can hear praises and hallelujahs. You can hear Duane's obvious shock and emotion, and then you can hear the entire class break into the Doxology. I can hardly hold back the tears! Our God is so awesome! So powerful and mighty! His ways are beyond our ways, but they are always good, always right, always for the kingdom.

If you know the song, would you sing it with me right where you are?

> Praise God, from whom all blessings flow;
> Praise Him, all creatures here below;
> Praise Him above, ye heavenly hosts;
> Praise Father, Son, and Holy Ghost.[6]

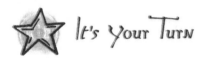 It's Your Turn

1. Read in the margin *Strong's* translation of the original Hebrew word for *heals* or *healeth* in Psalm 103:3. What is the word, and what are some of its meanings and insights?

Rapha' orraphah — To heal, to make healthful

Physician of men

heals or healeth
HEBREW STRONG'S NUMBER: 7495
Transliteration: rapha' or raphah
Phonetic Pronunciation: raw-faw'
Part of Speech: v
1) to heal, make healthful 1a) to heal 1a1) of God 1a2) healer, physician (of men) 1a3) of hurts of nations involving restored favor 1a4) of individual distresses 1b) to be healed 1b1) literal (of persons) 1b2) of water, pottery 1b3) of national hurts 1b4) of personal distress 1c) to heal 1c1) literal 1c2) of national defects or hurts 1d) in order to get healed

One part of the definition that is not mentioned in the margin is found in *The New Strong's Exhaustive Concordance of the Bible*: "to mend (by stitching)."[7] I love the thought of God bringing wholeness and restoration to a life as someone would mend by stitching. A seamstress cannot mend a fabric she does not hold in her hands. Likewise, God cradles us in His careful hands as He stitches our broken pieces back together again, forming a new and far more beautiful garment. The word picture also suggests process to me. God has performed miraculous healing in my life. My cancers were not physical, but they were just as malignant. Almost all the healing works God has accomplished in my life have been processes, stitch-by-stitch so that I would learn to appreciate being continually in His hands.

I know a precious woman of God in Houston who was healed of cancer of the liver. She had multiple tumors on her liver and a cancer so advanced that she was told treatment would be virtually useless. She was to have died within several months. That was 20 years ago. Today she is the picture of vitality and health—completely cancer free. I'm embarrassed to say that I had heard about Dodie's story in the old days when I still automatically doubted any testimony of physical healing. By the time I actually read her story for myself, I had seen such miracles of God that I knew many testimonies could be absolutely authentic. A student at heart, I was most interested in those with undeniable medical documentation like hers. Dodie's testimony also has an additional intriguing element. Dodie says that God did not reveal her healing instantaneously but over the course of months. She took no treatment, having been told that it wouldn't work, though she certainly recommends that others take it. The evidence of her healing came in process.

I have heard the same kind of story from a number of others. Certainly in the Gospels we see instantaneous healing. (One interesting exception is Mark 8:22-26.) What could be the difference between Dodie's case and the biblical examples? I don't know the answer, and God doesn't owe us one—but I wonder whether the way He heals may vary according to His objective. If the primary objective is to show His supremacy (for instance, accreditation), perhaps He might choose to heal instantaneously. If His primary objective is to teach sufficiency in Him or to mature and build faith, I wonder whether He heals through a stitch-by-stitch method. Remember, God is far more interested in our knowing the Healer than He is in the healing. God can be vastly glorified through either objective: showing His supremacy or His sufficiency.

save
GREEK STRONG'S NUMBER: 4982
Transliteration: sozo
Phonetic Pronunciation: sode'-zo
Part of Speech: v
1) to save, keep safe and sound, to rescue from danger or destruction 1a) one (from injury or peril) 1a1) to save a suffering one (from perishing), i.e. one suffering from disease, to make well, heal, restore to health 1a2) to preserve one who is in danger of destruction, to save or rescue 1b) to save in the technical biblical sense 1b1) negatively 1b1a) to deliver from the penalties of the Messianic judgment 1b1b) to save from the evils which obstruct the reception of the Messianic deliverance

sick
GREEK STRONG'S NUMBER: 2577
Transliteration: kamno
Phonetic Pronunciation: kam'-no
Part of Speech: v
1) to grow weary, be weary
2) to be sick

2. Read James 5:14-18. God did not place these verses in the Book of Acts in the midst of the fireworks wonders of the early church. The Holy Spirit placed them not in a book of New Testament history but in a book of undeniable New Testament doctrine. The NIV translates verse 15 like this: "The prayer offered in faith will make the sick person well." The KJV translates verse 15 like this: "The prayer of faith shall save the sick." Read in the margin *Strong's* translation of the original Greek words and the definitions for *save* and *sick*.

Save _____

_____

Sick _____

_____

Record any insights you receive. _____

_____

_____

_____

As you can see, the words *save* and *sick* have broad meanings that can suggest various kinds of restoration.

3. I want you to see one more jewel in the James 5 passages. Look at verse 17. What point was James trying to make when he used Elijah as an example?

That Elijah was a man who believed God and because of this his prayers were powerful & effective

The NIV translates, "Elijah was a man just like us." The KJV translates, "Elias was a man subject to like passions as we are." Read in the margin *Strong's* translation of the word used for *passions*, and write the meaning below.

Suffering, of like feeling or affections

passions
GREEK STRONG'S NUMBER: 3663
Transliteration: homoiopathes
Phonetic Pronunciation:
hom-oy-op-ath-ace'
Part of Speech: adj
1) suffering the like with another, of like feelings or affections

If you will carefully look at the Greek word, you will see that the first part of the word *homoio* suggests being like or similar, while *pathes* suggests pathos or passions. Under the inspiration of the Holy Spirit, James meant to greatly encourage us. He is telling us that we tend to see biblical figures like Moses and Elijah as superhuman, but they were not. They experienced our same feelings and passions. They also had insecurities, fears, disappointments, and all sorts of personality issues. They were like us, but James is telling us we can also be like them. Elijah was flesh and blood who chose to believe God. Because he did, many of his prayers were powerfully answered. Please keep in mind that Moses and Elijah were tremendously used by God, but neither got everything he asked. Dear One, we can't let our fear that God may not affirmatively answer our every prayer keep us from praying! No, we're not likely to get everything we ask. You will be hard pressed to find anyone in Scripture who did. Including Christ. Check out the garden of Gethsemane. What if these men of God hadn't asked anything because they couldn't have everything? Can you imagine the loss? As we pray fervently and faithfully, we will experience many astounding and affirmative answers. Pray on, Beloved!

faith journal

How has God most powerfully revealed His supremacy or His sufficiency to you personally? Answer the question by writing a prayer of thanksgiving to Him.

_____

_____

_____

_____

_____

_____

PS 23   The Lord My Shepherd - Jehovah-raah
PS 7:17 The Most High God - El Elyon
Gen 1   Creator - Elohim
Gen 22:14 The Lord will provide - Jehovah Jireh
EX 17:15 The Lord My Banner - Jehovah nissi
Jud 6:24 The Lord of Peace - Jehovah Shalom
Gen 16:13-14 The God who sees - El Roi

Gen 17:1 The All-Sufficient One - El Shaddai

Gen 15:2 Lord Master - Adonai

          Lord - Yahweh (Jehovah)

EX 15:26 The Lord that Healeth - Jehovah-rapha

EZ 48:35 The Lord is There - Jehovah Shammah

BLESSED ARE THE UNOFFENDED

Today's Treasure

Blessed is he, whosoever shall not be offended in me.
Matthew 11:6, KJV

This lesson has been deeply inspired by Gene Edwards' marvelous work *The Prisoner in the Third Cell*. In fact, the emotion is still tight in my throat from turning the last page. Edwards is a master of biblically and historically based fiction that helps us explore some of the more troublesome concepts in Scripture. Most of his works can be read in a couple of hours, but they won't be forgotten for a lifetime. *The Prisoner in the Third Cell* captures some of the possible heart processes Jesus and his forerunner, John the Immerser, experienced as the latter faced imprisonment and death.

Please read Matthew 11:1-19. Imagine being John. List every potential challenge and opportunity for confusion John may have experienced as a result of his imprisonment and Jesus' ministry.

If Jesus was the redeemer why didn't He do something about the fact that John was sitting in a cell

John's lifelong devotion to God and to his calling is unparalleled in Scripture. He lived his entire life observing the Nazarite consecration vow (see Num. 6:1-4; Luke 1:15). John not only lived without countless simple pleasures but also withheld from himself comforts that many would consider their inalienable rights. John poured out his life like a drink offering for one purpose: to prepare the way of the Lord. In many ways this partnership of sorts started well. John was baptizing the repentant in the Jordan when he looked up and saw Jesus walking straight toward him.

Please read John 1:29-34. What evidence do we have from this text that John the Immerser was certain that Christ was the One for whom he prepared the way?

Because the Lord had told John that the Spirit would come down as a dove from heaven and remain on the man who would baptize w/the Holy Spirit

From a windowless cell, however, things did not look nearly as clear. Imagine John's predicament. If he had been wrong about Jesus, he had either sacrificed all for nothing or missed the real Messiah. And if he had been right? Then Jesus had the power to free him from prison and death. He simply wasn't using it. Have you ever had a time when none of your obvious multiple-choice answers were good options?

John experienced the most excruciating dilemma any devoted child of God ever faces. If I may pickpocket Edwards, surely no pain is like the searing of the heart when " 'your God has not lived up to your expectations.' "[8] Even writing those words makes me want to sob. I have loved my God so much. He has so far exceeded the expectations of this simple-minded former pit-dweller that I can hardly bring up the subject. But I must. Why? Because all of us called to faith will have this knife-sharp experience in some form and at some point. I would not dare avoid this subject and insult some of you who have lost loved ones, even innocent children, to disease or accident, having pleaded with God to deliver them. I'd go so far as to suggest that the deeper we have loved God, the deeper the potential for devastation when He doesn't intervene as we know He can.

With their fervent leader in a putrid cell, John's disciples asked Christ a question on John's behalf that I'd paraphrase, "Are you God or not? If You are, why aren't You acting like it?" God is not shocked, Beloved. He reads our hearts. He knows our confusion, disappointment, and devastation. Our Teacher gives no accidental exams. Read a little of Edwards' story line, picking up at the point after Jesus responded to John's disciples.

"Leave me," said Jesus to His companions. With those words, Jesus wandered off to a sequestered place to be alone. Never before in all his thirty-one years, nor in all his preexistence in eternity, had he ever longed so intensely to answer the cry and the question of someone struggling to understand the mysterious ways of his God.

If ever there was a time for him to give a clear answer, if ever there was a person to whom he should speak clearly, surely the time was now and the person, John. If any man ever lived who had a right to have an explanation given to him, that man was his own flesh and blood, his own cousin. "John, your pain is great. I feel it. Tonight you so desperately need to understand me, to fathom my ways, to peer into the riddle of my sovereignty. Your heart is breaking. But, John, you are not the first to have this need. You are but one in a long train of humankind stretching across all the centuries of man who have called out to me with questions and doubts. You are but one voice among so many who wonder, and who agonize over my ways."[9]

" 'Blessed are you if you are not offended with me.' "[10] Few of us will escape a painful opportunity to be offended with Christ. I have little doubt it is part of the believer's life test. More often than not, the scenario of such a challenge will be similar to John's. At times we'll be tempted to think, *If Christ is who He says He is and can do what He says He can do, and I am His beloved, why isn't He coming through for me? Is it our insignificance? Is He too busy to notice? Or is the situation simply not critical to the overall plan? Are we or is our loved one simply dispensable?* Blessed are we when we could be offended and choose with every shred of tattered faith not to be.

According to Matthew 11:9-11, how did Christ affirm John's profound importance in the kingdom of God? *"I will send my messenger ahead of you, who will prepare your way before you & among those born of women — there has not risen anyone greater than John the Baptist"*

No one was more important to Christ and His mission than John. His mission wasn't dispensable. As hard as this fact is, his mission was simply complete, though he never saw his 34th birthday. He, like many others described toward the end of Hebrews 11, died with the promise in the distance. Do you realize, Dear One, that by the time the assassin's sword hit the block, John saw the promise high and lifted up, seated on a throne, and the train of His robe filled the temple? Imagine that John's faith gave way to sight and that silence gave way to "Well done, my son. Very well done. Now have a seat close by and watch the rest of the story with Me."

Surely a young Jim Elliott and the others who had surrendered their lives to take the name of Christ to Ecuador cried out for deliverance as spears sailed through the air toward them. If they did, those prayers were answered with a no but only so that God could grant a greater yes. In the years that followed, the tribe was evangelized probably more completely and thoroughly over the living-word picture drawn for them: the death of the innocent on behalf of the guilty.

Oswald Chambers. Keith Green. Rich Mullins. The list could go on and on. Their deaths before a fullness of days surely seemed like a no to their loved ones; yet every day the world is somehow enriched by their greater yes.

" 'Blessed are you if you are not offended with me.' "[11] Beloved, our God is a God of wonders. Will we not ask because we are afraid of being offended? Embarrassed? Disappointed? Or will we ask, knowing that He is able but trusting that He is good if He doesn't act? Blessed are we if we are not offended with Jesus.

O God, grant us a faith to be healed and a faith to be delivered but, above all, a faith to trust.

It's Your Turn

1. Read in the margin *Strong's* translation of the Greek word for *offended* in Matthew 11:6 and consider all the meanings. Which of the meanings most readily apply to the predicament of faith we've considered today? Why?

(1b) To cause a person to begin to distrust and desert one whom he ought to trust and obey

---

offended

Greek Strong's Number: 4624
Transliteration: *skandalizo*
Phonetic Pronunciation: *skan-dal-id'-zo* ("scandalize")
Part of Speech: v

1) to put a stumbling block or impediment in the way, upon which another may trip and fall, metaph. to offend 1a) to entice to sin 1b) to cause a person to begin to distrust and desert one whom he ought to trust and obey 1b1) to cause to fall away 1b2) to be offended in one, i.e. to see in another what I disapprove of and what hinders me from acknowledging his authority 1b3) to cause one to judge unfavourably or unjustly of another 1c) since one who stumbles or whose foot gets entangled feels annoyed 1c1) to cause one displeasure at a thing 1c2) to make indignant 1c3) to be displeased, indignant

2. Share a time when you've either been offended by Christ or have been tempted to be offended by Christ. (Thankfully, being offended is not terminal or unforgivable.)

_____

_____

_____

3. Read Daniel 3:16-18. How did Shadrach, Meshach, and Abednego exercise a faith that was harder to offend?

They stepped into the fire knowing that God could save them — but He might have chosen not to

4. The following is a more difficult question, but keep in mind that we don't have a clear-cut right-or-wrong answer. James 1:6 exhorts us to make our petitions to God without wavering with doubt. How is it evident that Shadrach, Meshach, and Abednego were not just covering for themselves or for God just in case He didn't come through?

They stepped out in faith

_____

_____

❦ faith journal

You and I spent days 1–4 focusing on miracles of healing. Today we explored what happens when we know that Christ can do what He says He can do, we follow Him faithfully, we ask Him fervently, and He doesn't do it. In closing, I'd like to prompt your time of journaling by asking you to look at Colossians 1:15-17. These powerful verses describe Jesus Christ. Verse 16 tells us all things were created by Him. Verse 17 tells us that in Him all created things hold together. In other words, not only is Christ responsible for creating the heavens and the earth, but the fact that each still operates and cooperates with its environment is also His doing. Christ also created the human body, perhaps more "fearfully and wonderfully" (Ps. 139:14) than any other work. In our second week of study we considered the intricacies of one simple human cell. When you calculate the thousands of functions simultaneously occurring within the human body, the wonder that any of us are well exceeds the perplexity that any of us are ill. Therefore, it is likely that each one of us has experienced God's miraculous healing any number of times without knowing it. Every day our fragile tents of flesh hold together, we again experience His miraculous healing. All healing flows from His hand: from the healing of a cold to the healing of cancer. And when the day comes that I no longer experience His physical healing on this earth, ah, to live has been

Christ ... and to die will be gain. Please spend your journaling time responding to the supreme authority of Christ over all created things, as stated so beautifully in Colossians 1:15-17.

_____

_____

_____

_____

_____

GodStops

BEDTIME MEDITATION

_____

_____

_____

_____

_____

_____

_____

_____

_____

[1] J. I. Packer, "The Comfort of Conservatism," in Michael Horton, ed., *Power Religion* (Chicago: Moody Press, 1992), 289.
[2] Duane Miller, *Out of the Silence* (Nashville: Thomas Nelson, 1996), 101.
[3] Ibid., 102.
[4] Ibid., 120–21.
[5] Ibid., 123.
[6] Thomas Ken, "Praise God, from Whom All Blessings Flow," *The Baptist Hymnal* (Nashville: Convention Press, 1991), 253.
[7] James Strong, *The Exhaustive Concordance of the Bible* (Nashville: Holman Bible Publishers, 1982), 7495.
[8] Gene Edwards, *The Prisoner in the Third Cell* (Wheaton, IL: Tyndale House Publishers, 1991), 58.
[9] Ibid., 55–56.
[10] Ibid., 63.
[11] Ibid.

Believing You Are Who God Says You Are

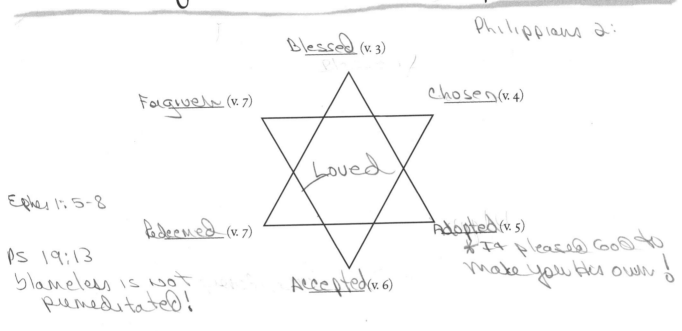

Blessed (v. 3)

Forgiven (v. 7)

Chosen (v. 4)

Loved

Ephes 1: 5-8

Redeemed (v. 7)

Adopted (v. 5)

Philippians 2:

It pleased God to make you His own!

PS 19:13
blameless is not premeditated!

Accepted (v. 6)

What are several priority results of believing we are who God says we are?

1. __Security__ : countless __poor__ decisions are made from nothing more than __insecurity__.

2. __Righteousness credited__ to our __account__. - Romans 4:1-5
   Romans 1:17

3. Glorious __liberation__ from the __burden__ of our own sins. Romans 4:6-8
   PS 32:1-5

   • "Transgression"—*pesa*—generally represents __rebellious__ sin. "Denotes __willful__ deviation

   from the __path__ of righteousness, a __premeditated__ crossing of the __line__ of God's law,

   a __rebellious__ act of rejecting God's __authority__."

   • "Sins"—*hata'ah*—is often used in reference to __sin__ in __general__.
   PS 32:2
   PS. 32:5-6
   Rom 1:5

4. __Obedience__ : Obedience comes from __faith__.
   Luke 22:31-32

4

Believing You Are Who God Says You Are

DAY 1
A BETTER SACRIFICE

Today's Treasure

By *faith Abel offered God a better sacrifice than Cain did.*
Hebrews 11:4

Some months ago I was walking toward the platform to teach the introductory session of a video-driven Bible study. The set was beautiful. The room was filled with a ready and willing audience. As I fought back tears, I caught myself apologizing to God for having to use me. I could cry about it again! Before each taping I do my best to pick at every scar I have until it returns to a wound. Miserable. Surely a mind-set exists between self-aggrandizement and self-torture, but I, along with most people, ordinarily seem unable to find it.

In the few seconds it took to get to the stage, a peculiar sense of God's voice fell on me, speaking a concept rather than words to my heart. I knew He was asking me why I could not fathom that His plan all along had been to reach people through people. In other words, "Child, quit apologizing for something I did. I like this plan. I made it up Myself." We forget God had complete foreknowledge when He created us, don't we? Our infirmities, insecurities, and insufficiencies neither surprised nor repulsed Him. They were all part of the human package. We wonder how divine God could choose us, while God delights when hearts so prone to wander choose Him. What would be His greater source of joy—for perfect people to do perfect things or for pitifully self- and world-centered humans to fight the daily battle to become God-centered? Beloved, our victories bring far more delight to God than our defeats bring disappointment:

> He knows how we are formed,
> he remembers that we are dust (Ps. 103:14).

This week our challenge is to start behaving like people who believe we are who God says we are. Each day we will glance at one of the lives listed in the Hebrews 11 hall of faith. Not one of them was superhuman. Not one of them was better equipped to believe God than we are. Not one of them was genetically predisposed to greatness. Not one of them failed to struggle with the calling. How do I know? Because each was commended for his or her faith. The evidence of faith always indicates the existence of a viable alternative. That which is completely obvious and explainable is not faith.

Enter Abel, the first portrait of a mortal in this hallowed hall of faith.

Read Hebrews 11:4 and the original story in Genesis 4:1-16. What might have made Abel's offering to God more acceptable than Cain's?

His heart, (He came with the correct attitude)

At first glance Cain and Abel's account might seem unfair, but several elements beg to differ. Let's take the most obvious first. Even in today's violent society we rarely read about a young man killing his little brother in cold blood. Something in Cain's heart was vicious.

Second, Cain was rebellious. Genesis 4:7 is our clue: " 'If you do what is right, will you not be accepted?' " Cain still had a chance to make it right. God did not say, *If only you had done what was right, you could have been accepted, but now it's too late.* Don't miss the intimation that Cain knew what was right. He simply didn't do it. Cain's offering represents every time a believer knows what God wants and refuses to give it. We often quickly give Him other things, as if He won't notice. Sometimes we give more in many other areas but doggedly withhold the one thing we know He wants. And sin crouches at our door.

Why was Abel's offering more acceptable? I have a feeling Abel didn't know the answer himself. God had obviously made clear to both Cain and Abel that He wanted a sacrificial offering, and Abel presented it … by faith.

Genesis 3:21 could be the connection. What does it tell us?

A blood sacrifice is needed to cover sin

You see, the concept of the death of something innocent for the covering of sin is as old as the garden. Both Cain and Abel were born with a sin nature just as we were. God desired their fellowship, but access came through faith that looked forward (through symbolic offering) to the substitutionary death of Christ. Cain's ongoing refusal to obey or repent ultimately led to his expulsion from God's presence.

I love the reference to the blood of Abel in Hebrews 12:24. Read this verse and compare it to Genesis 4:10. For what do you think the blood of Abel cried out to God?

For vengeance, the murder of Jesus proclaimed grace instead!

I have a feeling that the blood of Abel cried out to God for justice if not for vengeance. How I praise God that the sprinkled blood of Christ speaks a better word! I don't want God to simply treat me justly. I've made many mistakes and committed countless sins. I need mercy! How about you? The blood sprinkled from Christ's torn body speaks grace to all who accept the perfect offering by faith.

The payment for all sin—past, present, and future—has already been made. God, however, still calls His own to obedience. We've not all nursed murderous thoughts like Cain, but most of us at one time or another have been unwilling to give God the very thing we know He wants from us most. Faith means believing that blessing never fails to follow obedience, no matter the sacrifice.

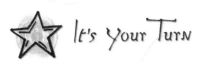 It's Your Turn

1. Read in the margin *Strong's* definition of the words *covenant* and *better*, used in Hebrews 12:24. Write in your own words a summary of the definition.

Covenant An agreement between God & Man

Better An improved (superior) word

covenant
GREEK STRONG'S NUMBER: 1242
Transliteration: diatheke
Phonetic Pronunciation:
   dee-ath-ay'-kay
Part of Speech: n f
1) a disposition, arrangement, of any sort, which one wishes to be valid, the last disposition which one makes of his earthly possessions after death, a testament or will 2) a compact, a covenant, a testament 2a) God's covenant with Noah, etc.

better
GREEK STRONG'S NUMBER: 2909
Transliteration: kreitton
Phonetic Pronunciation: krite'-tohn
Part of Speech: adj
1) more useful, more serviceable, more advantageous 2) more excellent

You might be blessed to know that the verb tense for "speaketh better things" is present-active-participle. This verb tense has become familiar to us. What does this verb tense tell us about how the blood of Christ speaks?

the blood of Christ continues to work

If you put the word *continually* in your answer, you have the concept. Present-active-participle means the blood of Christ continually keeps speaking a better word.

How do you feel about the fact that Christ's blood continues to speak on your behalf?

☒ relieved ☐ elated ☐ skeptical ☐ puzzled
☐ overwhelmed ☒ loved ☒ encouraged ☐ other

2. Second Corinthians 3 also talks about those of us who live under the new covenant. This term simply refers to God's people in a post-cross rather than pre-cross world. Read 2 Corinthians 3:4-6. Read in the margin *Strong's* definition of the following words from verses 5-6. Write a summary of the definitions.

Sufficiency _____

Able _____

Ministers _____

I love the NIV rendering of verse 6: "He has made us competent as ministers of a new covenant." I hope you noted that the word *ministers* encompasses the entire realm of servanthood, not just a pastor or a deacon. Beloved, God has a ministry for you, and in Him you are completely competent to receive it and fulfill it. Will you believe God?

faith Journal

Choose any one of three different elements of today's lesson to address with God in prayer. Perhaps you are withholding something you know God wants from you. Or perhaps you want to thank Him for the sprinkling of blood that speaks a better word over your life than justice or vengeance. You might want to pour out your heart to God over a lack of faith that you could ever be called or competent in an area of ministry.

Father Help me to come to a place where I completely trust you (Lisa) no matter what the outcome appears to be.

sufficiency
Greek Strong's Number: 2426
Transliteration: hikanotes
Phonetic Pronunciation: hik-an-ot'-ace
Part of Speech: n f
1) sufficient, ability or competency to do a thing

able
Greek Strong's Number: 2427
Transliteration: hikanoo
Phonetic Pronunciation: kik-an-o'-o
Part of Speech: v
1) to make sufficient, render fit
1a) to equip one with adequate power to perform duties of one

ministers
Greek Strong's Number: 1249
Transliteration: diakonos
Phonetic Pronunciation: dee-ak'-on-os
Part of Speech: n m
1) one who executes the commands of another, esp. of a master, a servant, attendant, minister 1a) the servant of a king 1b) a deacon, one who, by virtue of the office assigned to him by the church, cares for the poor and has charge of and distributes the money collected for their use 1c) a waiter, one who serves food and drink

 GodStops

BEDTIME MEDITATION

_____

_____

_____

_____

_____

_____

DAY 2
BY FAITH ENOCH

God's writing style versus my own reminds me of a letter of complaint I received from someone about one of my Bible studies. Her synopsis of my writing style? "So many words, so little said." And she was only in the first week! It still makes me laugh and say, "Amen!" God, on the other hand, says so many things in so few words. Today we'll see a perfect example in the biblical testimony of Enoch.

Testimony. That's the very word used in the *King James Version* of Hebrews 11:5. In the margin read the verse in its entirety. Of Enoch Scripture says, "He had this testimony, that he pleased God." Enoch did not have this testimony for himself. Stunningly, these words are God's testimony of Enoch. A commendation, as the NIV translates. One of the most frequent practices in my church upbringing is sharing testimonies. Simply put, our testimonies are our stories of God's faithfulness in our personal lives. Do you realize, however, that God also has testimonies? Are you ready for this? Based on the example of Hebrews 11:5 and the inference of the chapter as a whole, we might say that God's testimonies are stories of humanity's faithfulness in God's personal life. Hebrews 11 is a one-stop compilation of God's testimonies of faithful men and women. When all is said and done, God may likely have His own personal testimony of all who lived by faith. One primary goal of this Bible study is to ensure that God has a glorious testimony to share about each of us.

I'd like to suggest that God's testimony of Enoch represents the ultimate commendation. Short and sweet: he pleased God. You and I have already discovered that the entire purpose of our existence is to please God; therefore, Enoch crossed the finish line—not with a perfect life but with a perfect testimony. Not bad. In fact, I would like the same one. I don't have to be covetous to want it, because I don't have to take away from another soul's testimony to have it. Neither do you. Each of us has our own opportunity to please God.

So how did Enoch do it? Look for yourself in Genesis 5:21-24. List in the margin as many facts about Enoch from these verses as you can gather.

 Today's Treasure

By faith Enoch was taken from this life, so that he did not experience death; he could not be found, because God had taken him away. For before he was taken, he was commended as one who pleased God.
Hebrews 11:5

Enoch:
1. became a father to Methuselah at age 65.
2. he walked w/ God for 300 more yrs & had other sons & daughters
3. Altogether, Enoch lived 365 yrs.
4. he walked w/ God then he was no more.
God took him away

Don't miss the four-word testimony in Genesis: "Enoch walked with God" (v. 22,24). That's all we have to do to please God. Walk with Him. God wants our company, and the only way we can walk with Him is to walk by faith and not by sight. The law of Moses did not exist in Enoch's era. He had no rules and regulations. We have no grounds for believing that God appeared to Enoch or spoke aloud from the heavens. As we align Genesis 5:24 and Hebrews 11:5, Enoch clearly walked by faith, and faith is the evidence of things unseen.

Let's widen the lens on the Genesis passage for a moment and give the whole chapter a glance. I remember a Bible commentator saying that looking at Genesis 5 is like walking through an old cemetery reading gravestones (one of my favorite pastimes, by the way). Only one is missing. Enoch's. God appears to have enjoyed his company so much that He saved him the trouble of dying.

In a cold world Enoch had a feverish pursuit of God. Somewhere along the way Enoch took seriously those old stories handed down through the generations. Imagine the mighty Maker of heaven and earth forming mortals from the dust of the ground and then strolling with them in the cool of the day. Then came the unfortunate part. Obviously, to Enoch paradise may have been lost but not the divine company. Thankfully, God can also stroll among us outside the garden.

Enoch apparently walked for a while before he aligned his step with God's. Genesis 5:21-22 may mean that Enoch was 65 years old before he started walking with God. What changed? He and the Mrs. had Methuselah. (Keep in mind that life spans were very different when the earth's ecology was younger and kinder. Considering Enoch lived to be 365, he was only in the first quarter of his life.) Either the birth of his son made him sentimental and serious about the meaning of life, or Methuselah was such a fright that he scared his daddy right into a relationship with Jehovah. I've seen God use a number of children to drive their parents to Jesus. They are the ones who could make James Dobson cry! No matter what drove Enoch there, the relationship took. Enoch walked with his God for 300 years until, one day, God just walked him home. Apparently, they didn't pass a cemetery on the way.

Every morning I walk my two dogs. I take that back. Every morning my two dogs walk me. Together they weigh only slightly less than I do and have far more energy. One morning after days of rain, we hit a mud slick. I skidded for a good 50 feet, yelling my head off. When they are particularly unruly, I wonder why I put myself through the ordeal, but when I rise from my quiet time and they start dancing, turning in circles, and trying to high five one another, I know why: because they love it. And I love them.

On many a walk with my dogs I've asked God if His walking me is like my walking them. Do I keep trying my best to slip out of the leash without His noticing? Do my ears look as ridiculous as Beenie's when I do? Am I constantly trying to pull off the path and make God go where I want to go? Do I constantly chase rabbits instead of staying on course? We have so many good ideas. The world, even the Christian world, is full of options. Each of us could name a dozen different things we'd really love to do with our lives … sometimes all in the same day. We often suffer from spiritual schizophrenia or at least a serious case of attention-deficit disorder. Like the Israelites, who suffered from the potter-clay reversal syndrome (see Isa. 29:16), I sometimes forget that I didn't see Jesus in the distance and call Him to follow me.

Oh, if only we'd follow and not run ahead or lag behind! Just follow. Our perceptions have been so distorted by our world system that we fear God's path may be right and respectable, but it's sure to be boring. Does that sound like the life described in 1 Corinthians 2:9? The only way we will have an earthly experience with God that is more than ears have heard, eyes have seen, and minds have ever imagined is to walk

"No eye has seen,
 no ear has heard,
no mind has conceived
what God has prepared
 for those who love him."
1 Corinthians 2:9

with Him. God has promised never to leave us or forsake us. If we persist in our own way, the Spirit of God will accompany us (see Ps. 139:7-10), but we will walk ourselves right into a place we may as well call less-than land, the place of God's permissive will. When we choose to walk with God rather than off the path to handfuls of other options, we find His perfect will for our lives. We find our promised land.

I have discovered that if Satan can't get to me with destruction, he will try to get to me with distraction. We have only one turn on this green earth. We will never get to do this again. We cannot do a hundred things to the glory of God, but we can certainly do a few. What you and I need is focus. Day in and day out. Eyes on the goal. In our frenzied lifestyles we are desperate for simplicity: for a hundred things to narrow down to one.

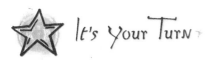 It's Your Turn

1. I can't imagine anyone experienced or achieved more than the Apostle Paul. I am convinced that he accomplished so much primarily because he adopted one goal. Read Philippians 3:12-14. In your own words, how did Paul describe his one-thing philosophy?

Keeping our eyes on Jesus & not looking back we run the race living up to what we already have been given. Eventually our final destination

Read in the margin *Strong's* definition of the following words. What do they mean to you?

Perfect *To make perfect - to complete*

Follow after (You will discover both negative and positive meanings. This context obviously calls for the positive.)

To press on

Apprehend *To lay hold of - Make one's own*

Reaching forth *To stretch towards*

Press (Which original Greek word is repeated here?) *epekteinomai*

Carefully look at the active verbs in these passages: *follow after, apprehend, reaching forth,* and *press.* What do these verbs suggest to you?

that this is an ongoing process

Dear One, God created us. He knows what satisfies our souls and fulfills us. Keep in mind that God created work before the fall. He created us with a need to contribute to and participate in the harvest. God could grant us victory and maturity without an ounce of participation on our parts, but He created us to be most satisfied by apprehending through diligent pursuit.

Our salvation is a free gift of grace that demanded the work of Christ Jesus alone. God made sure, however, that much of our fulfillment would involve the glorious

perfect
GREEK STRONG'S NUMBER: 5048
Transliteration: teleioo
Phonetic Pronunciation: tel-i-o'-o
Part of Speech: v
1) to make perfect, complete 1a) to carry through completely, to accomplish, finish, bring to an end 2) to complete (perfect) 2a) add what is yet wanting in order to render a thing full 2b) to be found perfect 3) to bring to the end (goal) proposed 4) to accomplish 4a) bring to a close or fulfilment by event 4a1) of the prophecies of the scriptures

follow after; press
GREEK STRONG'S NUMBER: 1377
Transliteration: dioko
Phonetic Pronunciation: dee-o'-ko
Part of Speech: v
1) to make to run or flee, put to flight, drive away 2) to run swiftly in order to catch a person or thing, to run after 2a) to press on: figuratively of one who in a race runs swiftly to reach the goal 2b) to pursue (in a hostile manner) 3) in any way whatever to harass, trouble, molest one 3a) to persecute 3b) to be mistreated, suffer persecution on account of something 4) without the idea of hostility, to run after, follow after: someone 5) metaph., to pursue 5a) to seek after eagerly, earnestly endeavour to acquire

apprehend
GREEK STRONG'S NUMBER: 2638
Transliteration: katalambano
Phonetic Pronunciation: kat-al-am-ban'-o
Part of Speech: v
1) to lay hold of 1a) to lay hold of so as to make one's own, to obtain, attain to, to make one's own, to take into one's self, appropriate 1b) to seize upon, take possession of 1b1) of evils overtaking one, of the last day overtaking the wicked with destruction, of a demon about to torment one 1b2) in a good sense, of Christ by his holy power and influence laying hold of the human mind and will, in order to prompt and govern it 1c) to detect, catch 1d) to lay hold of with the mind 1d1) to understand, perceive, learn, comprehend

reaching forth
GREEK STRONG'S NUMBER: 1901
Transliteration: epekteinomai
Phonetic Pronunciation: ep-ek-ti'-nom-ahee
Part of Speech: v
1) to stretch out to or towards 2) to stretch (one's self) forward to

pursuit of God and His goals so that our souls would be filled and thrilled in the constant discoveries. God is sovereign. When all is said and done, He knows what will thrill us most.

2. How can we be sure that we won't sacrifice something wonderful or something of value if we adopt the ultimate goal of walking with God? Matthew 6:33 answers the question for us. Rewrite it below in your own words as you personalize the meaning for your life.

All I need to do is continue to walk w/ God (seek His Kingdom) and He will take care of all my needs and more

Beloved, we could search the world over and never find another master who would deliver everything else of value as an added bonus.

faith Journal

Spend your journaling time today asking God to help you become a one-thing person. Talk to Him about areas in which you desperately need simplification. Conclude your journaling time by asking God to empower you to "follow hard" after Him and to persevere in "pressing on."

Lord Help me to "follow hard" after you - never slacking off which I have a tendency to do but pressing on to experience what you have already given me and then finally to come Home. Thank you Jesus

GodStops

BEDTIME MEDITATION

_____

_____

_____

_____

_____

BY FAITH NOAH

This week we focus on believing we are who God says we are and acting accordingly. Our means to that pivotal goal is studying the lives of others who believed that truth despite countless options and obstacles. God graciously compiled a concentrated list of such persons in Hebrews 11. It does not include all persons of faith in the Word of God. The inspired writer just made sure we had plenty of evidence throughout the generations to confront our tendency to believe that God could never greatly use someone like us. To such an idea the writer might respond with the profound original word *hogwash*.

Today's lesson has plenty of Scripture reading, but I never fail to find the details of Noah and the flood very interesting. I think you'll be intrigued by the review, too.

Please read Hebrews 11:7, then Genesis 6:5-22. You will find the very first mention of the word *covenant* in the Genesis passage. Where is it, and how did God say He would provide evidence of it?

Genesis 6:18

Now scan Genesis 7, but give attention to verse 23. Please fill in the following blank according to your KJV: "Every living substance was _destroyed_" (except, of course, those on the ark). The word you filled in will become important in It's Your Turn. Until then, let it steep in your soul a while.

Now read all of chapter 8. Where did the ark rest? _Mt Ararat_

How did Noah know that the waters had receded? _When the dove he sent out returned with an olive leaf in its beak He sent the dove out again waited 7 days- the dove didn't return_

What did Noah do when they finally departed the ark (see v. 20)? _He built an altar to the Lord and burnt animal sacrifices_

How did God respond, and what is our enduring evidence of His promise?

He promised to never again destroy all living creatures

The thought of Noah and his sons marching the beasts of the field into the ark has always thrilled me but never more than now. As I write, I sit on a stone overhang, pecking away on my battery-operated computer while overlooking a magnificent African plain. I taught all last week just outside Johannesburg. This week Keith and I are out in the bush, safe and sound in a wonderful little stone dwelling. This is no glorified zoo. It's the real thing. A river flows just below me, while mountains hem me in from both front and back. In between, however, is a huge plain teeming with beasts, most of which I had never seen. Many I didn't even know exist. I'll mention the most familiar so that you can picture them in reference to the account of Noah.

Today's Treasure

By faith Noah, when warned about things not yet seen, in holy fear built an ark to save his family.
Hebrews 11:7

All day yesterday I watched four hippos. Today I have not yet seen them, but I can clearly hear them gargling the river water and grunting rather unmannerly. In my eyesight this moment are two rhinos, a herd of wildebeests, ostriches, warthogs, and a variety of South African antelope. Yesterday Keith and I took a walk and happened upon five wonderful giraffes. I've seen more baboons than I could count and heard their screeching. I have marveled, laughed, and cried over God's creativity. Keith and I are such animal freaks that we are in a state of near euphoria. I so wish you were with me. Close your eyes and let your imagination take you to that ancient ark. Picture the beasts of the field and the birds of the air entering the world's oldest Titanic. If you've never researched the plentiful scientific evidence supporting a worldwide cataclysmic flood, you would be blessed to look into it, but for now let's focus on Noah's faith.

For our present purposes, Noah represents the following conditions.

1. *Being outnumbered.* If you think you and I struggle with being surrounded by worldliness and wickedness, take another look at Genesis 6:5: "Every inclination of the thoughts of [man's] heart was only evil all the time." I can't even imagine! Our society is shockingly depraved; yet many people of integrity inhabit our generation. Noah's world was completely wicked, and yet Noah was a righteous man, blameless among the people of his time, and he walked with God (see Gen. 6:9). We see the key once again: walking with God. Both Adam and Noah, 10 generations later, contrastingly ruin our theory that surroundings dictate character.

Do you ever feel outnumbered? In the midst of feeling outnumbered, do you ever wonder whether your unpopular, minority belief system could be right? Comment.

I personally don't feel outnumbered
but when I look at my daughter - I
recognize the pressure of the world she experience

Noah was the only man in his entire generation who held his exact conviction … yet he was right. Majority opinion holds utterly no security. Noah was right because God was right. Noah—simple flesh and blood—had the faith to agree with God. Mind you, a drop of rain had never fallen from the skies before. Glance at Hebrews 11:7 again. Noah believed God could do something no man had ever seen. Now, that's faith!

2. *Being scoffed at*. Please read 2 Peter 3:3-13 and note that scoffers will rise up vocally in the last days. Scripture intimates they will be similar to those who doubted the destruction of the flood. Can we be certain that the present heavens and earth will be destroyed and a new heaven and earth will take their place? ☑Yes ❑No Why?

Because God's word says this
will occur.

Beloved, one reason why we can be certain of future events prophesied in Scripture is that God has yet to be wrong in all the hundreds of biblical prophecies that have already been fulfilled. For now, why does God wait? (For a hint, see 2 Pet. 3:9.)

Because He doesn't want
any to perish

Glory to His merciful name! <u>Every day Jesus tarries, others are yet to believe and to be saved.</u> He does not will any to perish, but He leaves the choice to them.

※ <u>In the meantime, those who present-active-participle believe, like Abel, Enoch, and Noah, are liable to be scoffed at. We may as well be prepared in advance for others—sometimes other Christians—to ridicule us or think we are uneducated and unsophisticated to believe that God's Word applies to us today. Sometimes we may even be tempted to wonder whether we're wrong. Beloved, God is right. You can rest assured that He will prove it once again—sooner or later. Peer pressure is a powerful faith deterrent. Don't let it cheat you of your promised land.</u>

Important (margin)

 ## It's Your Turn

Today I will limit this section somewhat since you've already accomplished so much reading and answered many questions. Toward the very beginning of the lesson I asked you to fill in a blank to complete a Scripture verse. Please look up Genesis 7:23, the Scripture I used with the blank. Circle in the margin the original word for *destroyed*, and underline several of its English synonyms.

Now look up Isaiah 43:25. What is the original word for *blotteth out*?

Machah

Based on the use of this same Hebrew word in both contexts, what do you think God means when He says that He blots out all our transgressions?

1 to wipe out and
1c to blot out (from memory)

The cataclysmic death of God's Son and the crimson flood are enough to bring complete destruction to our histories of sin. Praise His name! The flood account is not only historical, but it is also highly symbolic. I want you to see one more jewel.

Carefully look at Genesis 6:14. Now read in the margin *Strong's* explanation of the Hebrew word for *pitch* in the phrase "shalt pitch it." What are several of its profound meanings in other contexts?

to make an atonement —
make reconciliation (to seal)

The vessel built to deliver Noah's family was covered with pitch to seal it. I love the potential symbolism of atonement in their protection from destruction. Like Noah's family, believers in Christ will be safely delivered from the coming destruction of the present heavens and earth. The atoning sacrifice of Christ has covered us for all eternity. Only our sins have been destroyed.

destroyed, blotteth out
HEBREW STRONG'S NUMBER: 4229
Transliteration: machah
Phonetic Pronunciation: maw-khaw'
Part of Speech: v
1) to wipe, wipe out 1a) (Qal) 1a1) to wipe 1a2) to blot out, obliterate 1a3) to blot out, exterminate 1b) (Niphal) 1b1) to be wiped out 1b2) to be blotted out 1b3) to be exterminated 1c) (Hiphil) to blot out (from memory) 2) (Qal) to strike 3) (Pual) full of marrow (participle)

pitch
HEBREW STRONG'S NUMBER: 3722
Transliteration: kaphar
Phonetic Pronunciation: kaw-far'
Part of Speech: v
1) to cover, purge, make an atonement, make reconciliation, cover over with pitch 1a) (Qal) to coat or cover with pitch 1b) (Piel) 1b1) to cover over, pacify, propitiate, 1b2) to cover over, atone for sin, make atonement for 1b3)to cover over, atone for sin and persons by legal rites 1c) (Pual) 1c1) to be covered over 1c2) to make atonement for 1d) (Hithpael) to be covered

faith Journal

Today express to God any way that practicing present-active-participle belief could be a challenge in your environment. Share with Him ways you feel outnumbered or even scorned.

I feel ridiculed by my mother and the world. But Lord, I can do all things through Christ who strengthens me. So I'm trusting you to help me stand strong & be bold for you. Thank you Lord Jesus

GodStops

BEDTIME MEDITATION

Someone came into the Church and asked Pastor Dave to pass on a check for $1000 to me. Thank you Jesus.

BY FAITH ABRAHAM

Prepare to be impressed. In a chapter of 40 verses, how many in Hebrews 11 are attributed to God's testimony about Abraham? _8_ Moses is second runner-up with six verses, but if the chapter had represented a competition, Abraham would have taken first place hands down. The fact that God esteemed Abraham so highly and spoke of him so often encourages me beyond words. Do you want to know why? Because not only does Abraham have a history of faith, but his record also bears the marks of some serious bouts with doubt and some remarkably foolish decisions. So does mine. A lump wells in my throat as gratitude floods my soul. Each of us doing this Bible study is still alive and kicking. No matter what our track record of doubt and foolishness has been in the past, we can still give God an opportunity to testify to our faith. We have today to believe God. Let's not put it off until tomorrow. Failure isn't terminal, Dear One. Faithlessness is.

What better time to recite our five-statement pledge of faith? Write it below:

God is who He says He IS

God can do what He says He can do

I am who God says I am

I can do all things through Christ

God's Word is alive and active in me

Today's Treasure

By *faith Abraham, when called to go to a place he would later receive as his inheritance, obeyed and went, even though he did not know where he was going.*
Hebrews 11:8

I hope you'll never forget it as long as you live. Our present stroll down the hall of faith allows us to stop at only one of several Hebrews 11 portraits of Abraham. I've chosen to highlight his first act of faith.

Carefully read Hebrews 11:8-10. What was Abraham's initial faith action?

He left his home and went where God told him to go.

List some of the obvious challenges Abraham confronted in his act of obedience as described in these verses:

He didn't know where he was going

He left his family behind

We might entitle the first portrait of Abraham in the hall of faith "The Obey-Now-and-Receive-Later Challenge of Faith." Please read Abraham's call in Genesis 12:1. What did God tell Abraham to do? *"Leave your country, your people and your father's household and go to the land I will show you."*

I love the KJV rendering of the first part of the command: "Get thee out of thy country." Of one thing I'm certain. Very few of us took our first leaps of faith without hearing God say with our spiritual ears, "Get thee out of thy comfort zone." Let's put it this way: if we were already where we are going, for all practical earthly purposes we'd be dead. We can rest assured what God has for us even in our earthly future is not identical to our present. Whether or not we like it, a fair amount of going is involved in following. I'm amused by a certain comparison between Abraham and us.

Compare Hebrews 11:9 with 2 Corinthians 5:1-8. While both Abraham and we have earthly promised lands where our callings are fulfilled on this planet, we've both been assigned to live in _____the body_____. Abraham's may have been skins while ours is our own skin, but both remind us that we are ultimately not at home here.

One of Abraham's monumental tests painstakingly challenges us: time. Between "go" and "receive" is more often than not the faith test of time. Allow me to rename the condition the Later Syndrome. Few of us will miss it, because it's too important.

Why is the Later Syndrome so important? Write as many reasons as you can think of.

① Helps us develop patience
② Makes us aware of how much we trust God
③ When the "Later Syndrome" comes to an end, it reaffirms our trust in God.

Time can test almost anything and undoubtedly anyone. We sometimes obey God and go where we believe He is sending us. We're not altogether certain what we expected, but after a while we ascertain, "This certainly can't be it." In fact, obeying God can initially seem to get us into a bigger mess than we left. Sometimes that's part of the test. Have you ever thought, "I may as well be an alien here"? Admittedly tongue in cheek, that may be your first indication you're in the right place. We can be in the bull's-eye of God's will for our lives, and things make utterly no sense until that ugly, five-letter word *later*.

Would it help to know that Christ also experienced the test of time? He didn't perform His first miracle until He was 30 years old. If we didn't know better, we might think God was running a little late, considering Jesus had only three years remaining in His earthly ministry. Nope. He was right on time.

Time by itself does nothing but grow us old. What we do with time makes the difference. We often say, "Time heals"; yet I've known just as many whom time embittered. Only God heals. Only God restores. Only God effectively prepares, teaches, equips, and matures, but you can count on Him to often use the test tube of time in which to accomplish it. We tend to argue, "God, why are you waiting so long? I don't have much time here!" We forget that God's primary objective for us on earth is to prepare us for a city for which He is architect and builder. In the meantime, God undoubtedly desires that our lives bear much fruit. He sees the whole picture.

First Corinthians 3:6-10 beautifully explains the process. What do these verses describe?

Our lives build on the faithfulness of the believing generations before us, and those after us will build on ours. Our ego says, *If I don't do the planting, sowing, growing, and harvesting, they won't get done.* We're mistaken. As much as we'd like to think otherwise, we have just one little piece, and our faithfulness with it is paramount. God uses time to prepare us to build only what lasts with what we're given. Based on Christ's example, God our Father calls us to make contributions of quality, not just quantity. Time is often where He tempers and tests us so that premature births of ministries don't result in lifelong handicaps.

God created time and never wastes it. We alone waste it when our impatience to receive our earthly inheritance hinders our preparation to know what to do with it.

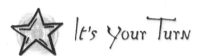 It's Your Turn

1. One of our challenges is watching others who seem to be operating effectively in their promised land, while we still feel like aliens in tents wondering whether we misunderstood. Adding insult to injury, some of those may be younger than we are! Have you found this frustrating?　❑ Yes　☒ No　If so, how?

_____

_____

Not only is comparison a waste of time, but it can also be deadly. We can allow resentment to kill our opportunity to grow. God reserves the right to handle us as individually as the prints He stamped on the ends of our fingers.

2. Don't discount the fact that sometimes we misunderstand where God told us to go. Thankfully, He knows our insecurities and uncertainties. Very often through Scripture we see God reconfirm His calling to His child. If God has granted you several reconfirmations of His direction, Dear One, persevere and walk with Him there, even if the full purpose eludes you. If He has never reconfirmed, ask Him to clarify. Then listen carefully over the days and weeks to come. Sometimes He will use a very wise person of the faith to help us discern God's direction. One thing is certain: we must be in His Word. Scripture is still the primary way He speaks. God does not begrudge our attempts to make sure we're on the right track. Let's just be sure we don't slip into practicing unbelief after reconfirmation.

important!

Do you feel that you may be in the right place or the wrong place in relation to God's present will for your life? Explain what you are sensing and why.

I think I am in the right place at the moment because I sense God's peace

Does Abraham's example help at all? If so, how?

I guess it confirms that when God speaks I need to not just listen but to obey immediately!

3. Galatians 4:1-2 offers a wonderful principle that helps us understand a few things about the time gap between "obey now" and "receive later." Carefully read these two verses. What do you think they are saying?

They are saying that if a child inherits his father's wealth, even though it is his legally, he can't touch it until he is of age & he is under the care of his guardian

You and I are joint heirs of Jesus Christ (see Rom. 8:17). We not only have a huge inheritance coming to us in heaven, but we also have gifts and riches to invest in kingdom work here on earth. These two Scriptures help us understand that sometimes God waits until we have a little maturity to place more important trusts in our hands. He also reveals the wisdom of the principle by allowing us occasionally to see what can happen when we are given more responsibility than we have the maturity to handle. I shiver at the thought of ways I unintentionally misused my gifts and responsibilities in my younger ministry years.

I experienced a terrible season of crisis in my early 30s. In retrospect I should have stepped out of leadership for a while and let God heal my shattered heart. I deeply regret that I didn't and have repented with much sorrow. Thankfully, He used that season to deliver me from bondage I had buried deep within me. He wasn't finished with me. On the contrary, I now understand we were just getting started; however, I still should have taken time to heal. My teaching (thankfully to a very limited audience at that time) was not erroneous, but I believe it was imbalanced. Beloved, the world will not stop and our true God-ordained ministries will not end when we take the time to let God make us healthier and better equipped.

No wonder He goes to such lengths and depths to prepare us as much as we'll permit Him. When the height of a ministry outgrows its depth, it will inevitably come tumbling down. Praise His merciful name, we can rebuild, but we are wise when we focus on the depth alone and from that time forward leave the length, breadth, and height to Him. As long as the latter dimensions matter most to us, we are not ready to build what lasts.

faith journal

Today I sense through the Holy Spirit that you know exactly what you want to write about to God and don't need a guided time of journaling. Use this space to respond to God about what today's lesson has quickened in you.

_____

_____

_____

_____

had you revealed yourself by having the Dr. at Clarkston Medical only charge me 80?? for Lisa plus he provided two months of samples for her meds and told her that he would give her samples whenever he had them.

DAY 5

BY FAITH ISAAC

Life is complicated, isn't it? I am so glad God didn't limit Holy Writ to high and lofty subjects. From the birth of family life, He revealed how entangled and awry human natures can grow in relationship to one another. Our personalities, replete with their insecurities and strengths, collide with another and enmesh at times into a tangled mess. We are a complex lot wired with DNA that often seems woven from spun gold and splintered twine. Few of us are thoroughly good … or thoroughly bad. Most of the time, our inner self is at war, just as the Apostle Paul grieved (see Rom. 7:23).

I have yet to find the story of a fully healthy and functional family in the Word of God. So that we wouldn't lose heart or hope, He graciously made sure we'd know that in things pertaining to the sons of the earth, abnormal is more normal than normal. That doesn't mean we should surrender to dysfunction. It means we don't have to hang our heads as we surrender and let Him sort out our tangled mess.

Somewhere along the way, Jacob needed a good paddling. Not that Rebekah was going to give it to him. After all, she taught him most of his tricks. And who taught her? Ah, the futility of hunting a final resting place for blame. Because all else is out of his hands, the pointer is better off pointing at self.

Please read all of Genesis 27 and give this saga a title and a subtitle.

Today's Treasure

By faith Isaac blessed Jacob and Esau in regard to their future.
Hebrews 11:20

Look at Today's Treasure. Under the inspiration of the Holy Spirit, the writer of Hebrews gives a one-sentence testimony of the faith of Isaac. What is it?

By faith, Isaac blessed Jacob & Esau in regard to their future

Now that you've read the account, how could such circumstances result in a commendation for Isaac's faith? Share your thoughts.

_____

_____

_____

As I shared with you early in our series, God willing, the next Bible study I believe He is appointing me to write is on the patriarchs of Genesis. I have not begun official research, but I am already intrigued by the concept of the blessing given to one person by another. I have much to learn, but I can already tell you that the Hebrews understood the blessing to mean much more than Gentiles comprehend. We throw blessings around over the least sneeze. That's not the kind of blessing the Hebrews learned from God. The account of Isaac and the blessings of his sons is a perfect example. Isaac was obviously devastated that he was tricked into granting to Jacob the blessing ordinarily entitled to the firstborn. Why couldn't he just render it null and void since he unknowingly gave it under false conditions? Take a look at another occasion when something comparable happened, and let's see if we can find our answer.

league
Hebrew Strong's Number: 1285
Transliteration: beriyth
Phonetic Pronunciation: ber-eeth'
Part of Speech: n f
1) covenant, alliance, pledge 1a) between men 1a1) treaty, alliance, league (man to man) 1a2) constitution, ordinance (monarch to subjects 1a3) agreement, pledge (man to man) 1a4) alliance (of friendship) 1a5) alliance (of marriage) 1b) between God and man 1b1) alliance (of friendship) 1b2) covenant (divine ordinance with signs or pledges) 2) (phrases) 2a) covenant making 2b) covenant keeping 2c) covenant violation

Read Joshua 9:3-6,14-19. These verses will become more significant to us later, so I hope you'll remember it. Noting verse 15, read *Strong's* definition for the word *league*. What is the original word, and what does it mean?

beriyth — treaty / alliance / covenant

You have seen this word before, haven't you? Covenants are never to be entered into lightly. You no doubt noticed that because everything appeared legitimate, they did not bother to receive counsel from the Lord. Big mistake and one I've made too many times, based on appearances.

How was this treaty formed, and why did the Israelites consider themselves bound by it (see Josh. 9:19)?

They formed this treaty w/o consulting God. A broken oath was considered a serious offense in the ancient world especially if it had been made to God

Look again at Isaac's blessing over Jacob (who he thought was Esau) in Genesis 27:27-28. Although one example involves a blessing and the other a treaty, the binding common denominator was the name of the Lord invoked in each vow. Ancient devout Hebrews never used the name of God haphazardly. They would be appalled by our societal slurs, likely falling to the floor and covering their heads, fearful of holy reprisal. The ancient Hebrews so revered their God that they feared saying YHWH aloud, generally substituting the synonym Adonai. If they invoked the name of the

Lord God in a vow, they believed God alone had the power to break it. Because the Israelites understood Him to be a covenant God and knew that He was faithful, they more readily assumed that the vow was utterly binding. I am convicted by how thoughtlessly I petition something "in the name of Jesus" without really seeking the heart and will of God in the matter. I feel if we really had faith to believe that we would more times than not receive what we ask, we might be more careful what we pray. Sometimes our hasty, popcorn prayers reveal a lack of conviction in the true power of the name of Jesus.

Back to Isaac. Where did his faith enter the picture? Isaac was old, and his eyes were weak. He believed the day of his death was approaching. Isaac had a very important choice to make, like many of us. He could fret himself into an earlier grave, or he could trust in the sovereignty of God. As a parent of young adults, I am terribly impressed by his faith. I'm afraid I personally blend my faith with a healthy dose of fretting. I have a feeling that God sees fretting faith as faithless fretting.

Another piece of information helps fit this puzzle together, but we don't know whether Isaac ever knew it existed. Take a good look at Genesis 25:19-26 and briefly describe the events. _Rebekah was barren, Issac prayed to the Lord & she conceived twins, The babies were very active within her, she inquired of the Lord & He told her that two nations were growing inside her_

Celebrate the fact that God indeed spoke to women, as well as men, from the very beginning of Scripture. I love first mentions. Don't you like knowing this is the first biblical mention of twins? Don't you imagine when Rebekah's back was aching and her tummy was rolling, the thought of two babies within her womb never occurred to her? What had God told Rebekah about the jostling within her (see v. 23)? _So that she would understand that her two children would be separated and be two nations and that the older child would serve the younger_

Our having this piece of the puzzle makes Rebekah's impending actions and partialities no less wrong, but they don't require a psychiatric evaluation. Rebekah appeared to do exactly what we're prone to do. She volunteered to help God accomplish His will or fulfill His own prophecy. You can be sure He dealt with Rebekah's deceit and manipulation at some point. He always does. It's not our business how.

Notice that in His thorough foreknowledge God stated before the boys were born that the younger would dominate the older. God's sovereign plans for the future are based on the foreknown. When Isaac grew old and the time came to pass on the blessing, he chose to respect God's name and sovereignty even though he had been deceived. I believe Isaac knew God well enough to discern when more might be at work than met the eye. After all, he had looked at life from the top of an altar on Mount Moriah, seeing his own reflection in his father's knife (see Gen. 22).

Thus far in our study we've viewed faith primarily from the standpoint of action. In other words, we believe; therefore, we act. Today we see a different and oftentimes harder dimension of faith: when faith requires us to do nothing at all, while our human nature screams to interfere. In these cases we believe; therefore, we do not act. Wisdom is knowing the difference between the two.

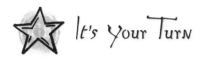 It's Your Turn

1. The dimension of faith we've studied today can be seen on several occasions in Christ's life. Trusting in the sovereign plan of God also necessitated at times that Jesus not act when He certainly had the power. How does each of the following passages reveal faith not to act?

Matthew 26:47-56 _Jesus could have called on His Father and he would have put legions of angels at Jesus' disposal_

Matthew 27:41-43 _Jesus was on the cross voluntarily — He could have come off the cross when the people (chief priests, elders, & teachers) mocked Him_

What do you suppose could have happened if Christ had acted in His power rather than trusting God and refusing to be goaded into action?

we would all be going to hell

2. If we've walked with God for any length of time, we've each probably faced times when faith required us not to act when everything within us wanted to take action. Like me, you may be action-oriented. You may have failed some of those faith tests but later learned to sit on your hands a little more effectively. Share one of your experiences and what you learned.

When Mike's parents moved Lisa out of my house — I wanted to go after her.

When she decided to go back to N.C. — I didn't persuade her to stay & I stayed out of God's way & didn't ask questions about her life down there.

 faith Journal

Begin your journaling time reverencing God's name. Then consider the following: Which do you believe your most pressing faith challenge is presently calling you to do—act or not act? Journal with God about your need for His wisdom and empowerment to be obedient one way or the other. If you're unsure, use this space to ask God how to exercise faith in your present challenge.

To not act!

_____

_____

_____

_____

_____

_____

_____

GodStops

BEDTIME MEDITATION

_____

_____

_____

_____

_____

_____

_____

Believing You Can Do All Things Through Christ

Sessions 4, 5, and 6 focus on God's priority work in the lives of believers. Each builds strategically on the one preceding it. As you view them in relationship to one another, picture session 4 as who, session 5 is the what, and session 6 as how.

1. God is in the process of raising _____ _____ among His people.

2. The common denominator will not be _____ _____, _____,

_____, or _____. The common denominators will be consistent with

those throughout biblical history (see Eph. 6:10-18).

- _____

- _____ (see Josh. 1:8 figurative; 6:21 literal)

- _____ (prayer)

3. The church also has an _____ promised land that precedes her heavenly land of promise.

The New Testament tells us that before the end of times the church will be _____,

_____, _____, and _____ to _____ (or proclaim truth).

4. God warned the children of Israel not to fall for two of the biggest obstacles any of us will have about the

fulfillment of God's personal promises: _____ and _____. Hatat—"to be

discouraged, _____; be afraid, be dismayed … The meaning of the term ranges from

a literal breaking to military _____ to _____."

5. God will never _____ us. The word *rapah* means "to be _____, be remiss,

be _____, be _____. … The basic idea of _____ the hand."

6. Our responsibility is to be _____ and courageous. Strong—*chazaq*—"to be _____ fast,

be _____, to make firm, … be valiant, … to _____." Our success will be

_____ tight to the One who has us in His _____.

WEEK

5

Believing You Can Do All Things Through Christ

BY FAITH JACOB

Session 5 launched this week's emphasis on the present-participle belief that we can do all things through Christ. This week's homework will follow our previous week's approach. As we continue our walk through the Hall of Faith museum, the stories of flesh-and-blood mortals who believed God over what they saw and felt will convince us that we can do the same. Read Today's Treasure. Even though our walk down the corridors of this biblical museum is hurried, I hope you're blessed by the family portraits we're viewing. Yesterday we looked at a family portrait of Isaac, Rebekah, Esau, and Jacob. Today we'll get to see a much older Jacob; his younger son, Joseph; and his two grandsons.

Let's read the original record to which Hebrews 11:21 refers, where we will find Jacob called by the new name God gave him: Israel. Savor every word of Genesis 48. The scene is so tender and powerful. Oh, how I wish we had time to approach this chapter expositionally. If this chapter raises questions in your mind, you are welcome to do your own research by using the Internet or library tools you may have available. For now let's keep our eyes on the goal: viewing the faith of Jacob, also called Israel.

What similarities do you see between this record and the previous record of Isaac's blessing on Esau and Jacob?

Today's Treasure

By faith Jacob, when he was dying, blessed each of Joseph's sons, and worshiped as he leaned on the top of his staff.
Hebrews 11:21

_____

_____

I hope you noted several, but surely among them you saw that the blessing ordinarily reserved for the firstborn went to the secondborn. How did Israel demonstrate which grandson was receiving the dominant blessing?

_____

Though we see this obvious similarity, don't miss the very different circumstances. Was any trickery or deception used in this reversal of blessing? ❏ Yes ❏ No

I see an important point surfacing here. We like the security of rules that have no exceptions, but God can do whatever He wants in keeping with His perfect character. Certainly the primary practice of ancient fathers was to give the dominant blessing to the firstborn; however, God had a different plan for both sets of sons: Esau and Jacob,

Ephraim and Manasseh. The significant point is that when God seems to be prompting something out of the ordinary, we don't have to manipulate things to make it happen and cause people to accept it.

In some strange ways and on a far lesser scale, I can relate to the challenge of wanting to explain some of God's unseemly choices. My mother tried to bear children for many years. She finally joyfully adopted my beloved oldest sister. Four years later my mother unexpectedly became pregnant (the first of four times!). She was so thrilled and awed to bear a son that she dedicated him to the Lord. As he grew, he showed great potential for future ministry. He was a gifted musician and could play the piano long before his feet reached the pedals. He could also sing and write music and dramas. From all appearances my brother was a true psalmist. A son of David. The problem was, when he grew up, he adamantly rejected Christ.

God heard my mother's prayer of dedication, but His sovereignty and His foreknowledge proved to be inseparable. The mantle for vocational ministry fell to me. I am by far the least naturally talented of all my brothers and sisters. I have also sinned grievously and have been terribly foolish at times in my life. I have no idea why God would make such a decision. Ironically, my mother went to her grave without giving me her blessing in ministry. She certainly gave me her love, but the tone my ministry took toward the freedom of captives proved too much for her. As she often said (and I grin as I write it), she liked me better when I was funny. Sometimes I do too, Mom, but lots of people are in bondage out there just as I was. The only thing funny about it is the thought of Satan steaming while Christ sets them free. I love you so much, Mom, but I want to be there when it happens.

Perhaps you have also felt pain when someone important to you didn't give you a blessing in the area where you feel most called to serve God. Yours may or may not be a parent. We can also deeply desire the blessing of mentors or others we respect and love in ministry.

Do you have an example? If so, please share. (As you discuss your homework in small group, remember not to use names.)

_____

_____

For the sake of application, let's think of Ephraim and Manasseh receiving a call of sorts, only far more profound. Carefully look at Genesis 48:5-6. Jacob or Israel didn't intend to take the boys from their father. Keep in mind that he was very near death. His intention was that Ephraim and Manasseh be among his sons and also become heads of the twelve tribes of Israel.

What was Joseph's reaction in verse 17?

_____

Did Jacob/Israel budge (see v. 19)? ❏ Yes ❏ No

Hence his faith. Jacob was so convinced of the will and the dependability of God's good plans that he was willing to displease his beloved son. Looking more closely at the circumstances, we also see that Jacob could have felt obliged to do as Joseph wished. After all, Jacob's son had saved them all from famine. Now take a look again at Hebrews 11:21. Jacob not only blessed Ephraim and Manasseh according to God's will instead of his son's, but he also worshiped God for the privilege.

Misunderstandings can initially result as we exercise enough faith to do what we're convinced is God's will. Sometimes those misunderstandings can involve people whose opinions are very important to us. If we are convinced that God has willed the action, let's go the extra faith mile and believe that God will handle the consequences. Years ago He taught me a principle I've never forgotten. The consequences of our (humble) obedience are His problem, not ours. Let's just be sure not to develop an attitude that would make anyone want to withhold blessing. We are wise to prayerfully discern whether the cause of withheld blessing is something in them … or in us.

In one last glance at today's portrait we see Jacob, old and very near death, leaning on his staff and worshiping God. Though his son was displeased and his grandsons were sure to experience friction, Jacob knew his God was faithful. Time would tell.

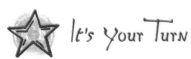 It's Your Turn

1. Read in the margin the definitions of *blessed* and *worship* from Hebrews 11:21 in *Strong's*. Circle each word and underline their meanings.

As you can see, the original word for *worship* implies postures of either kneeling or being prostrate before God. It is also associated with blowing kisses toward a superior as an expression of affection, as well as awe. Perhaps the fact that Jacob worshiped while leaning on his staff indicates that he was too old and feeble to fall prostrate or even bow before God. Something about picturing the worship of the old man just before he died is precious. Close your eyes for a moment and imagine what he may have been doing to express his worship. Also picture his son and grandsons as they watched him. Whether or not they appreciated it, they were blessed in more ways than one, weren't they? Few things could be more priceless than a generational heritage of worship. Ephraim and Manasseh weren't the only boys with a grandfather who was a true worshiper.

At the most challenging moment of his life, what are we told about Jacob's grandfather, Abraham, in Genesis 22:5?

_____

Many of us are either grandparents or grandparents-to-be. What a wonderful example to keep tucked in our hearts.

2. Please read Ephesians 1:3. With today's lesson in mind, how does this verse speak to you as a person blessed by God?

_____

_____

God's blessing on us is one of the most important reasons we can do all things through Christ.

Hebrews 11:21; blessed
GREEK STRONG'S NUMBER: 2127
Transliteration: eulogeo
Phonetic Pronunciation: yoo-log-eh'-o
Part of Speech: v
1) to praise, celebrate with praises 2) to invoke blessings 3) to consecrate a thing with solemn prayers 3a) to ask God's blessing on a thing 3b) pray God to bless it to one's use 3c) pronounce a consecratory blessing on 4) of God 4a) to cause to prosper, to make happy, to bestow blessings on 4b) favoured of God, blessed

worshiped
GREEK STRONG'S NUMBER: 4352
Transliteration: proskuneo
Phonetic Pronunciation: pros-koo-neh'-o
Part of Speech: v
1) to kiss the hand to (towards) one, in token of reverence 2) among the Orientals, esp. the Persians, to fall upon the knees and touch the ground with the forehead as an expression of profound reverence 3) in the NT by kneeling or prostration to do homage (to one) or make obeisance, whether in order to express respect or to make supplication 3a) used of homage shown to men and beings of superior rank 3a1) to the Jewish high priests 3a2) to God 3a3) to Christ 3a4) to heavenly beings 3a5) to demons

 *faith Journal*

Respond to God based on the privilege of being His blessed child. Spend time worshiping and praising Him.

_____

_____

_____

_____

_____

_____

GodStops

BEDTIME MEDITATION

_____

_____

_____

_____

_____

_____

_____

_____

_____

BY FAITH JOSEPH

Begin today's lesson by reading Hebrews 11:21-22. If only we had time to read between those lines! A fascinating saga unfolds between them. Our tour through the Hall of Faith necessitates that we step to the next portrait in order to stay on our schedule, but I urge you to read the story of Joseph and his brothers on your own time if it's unfamiliar. I promise that you won't be bored. I am constantly reminded in my study of God's Word that fact is far more captivating than fiction. Joseph's story is just one of many examples.

In a nutshell, after Joseph was betrayed by his brothers and suffered numerous injustices, God purposed that His faithful charge would rise to a position of power in Egypt second only to Pharaoh. True to His usual mode of operation, God had many purposes in mind. He made sure Joseph was in a strategic position and was given the wisdom to provide for coming years of famine. God used Joseph to deliver the entire family of Israel (Jacob) from starvation, but the plan also necessitated their relocation to Egypt, the bread bowl of their world.

Today Your Turn and mine will intermingle for the most benefit. The Book of Genesis concludes with Jacob's death and Joseph's full reconciliation with his brothers.

Mentally fast-forward many years and read Genesis 50:22-26. Which part of the story is highlighted in Hebrews as an act of profound faith?

Read Exodus 1:1-13. What would make us question whether Joseph was mistaken?

Now read Exodus 3:1-10. What was God preparing to do?

Look back at Genesis 15:12-18 to read the specific prophecies God spoke over Abram when He cut covenant with him and his descendants. Generally speaking, how long had this plan obviously been in the works? _____ Compare the carefully inspired wording of Acts 7:17. What insight does it give?

God hadn't experienced unexpected turbulence that prolonged His plan. Nothing was accidental or incidental. Everything proceeded like clockwork on the kingdom calendar. (It still does, by the way.) So how do we reconcile Joseph's faith-filled prophecy to his brothers in Genesis 50:24? Didn't he say that God would take them out of Egypt to the land God promised them? Absolutely. Joseph spoke with the same faith through which he received his father's prophecy over him.

By faith Joseph, when his end was near, spoke about the exodus of the Israelites from Egypt and gave instructions about his bones.
Hebrews 11:22

Carefully look at Genesis 48:21-22. What had Israel (Jacob) clearly told Joseph (v. 21)?

_____

Yet Genesis ends with Joseph dying in Egypt, never making it back to the land of promise alive. Furthermore, he died making a promise to his brothers that did not come to fruition in their lifetimes. Either folks are pitching around false prophecies, or there's more to these blessings than meets the eye! God would never affirm faith in misunderstandings or in misleading prophecies, so the former is out of the question. Both Jacob and Joseph were esteemed faithful in the final blessings and pronouncements they made. Obviously, the answer lies in God's much broader view of you.

Look again at Genesis 50:24-25. If you are reading these verses from your own Bible, consider circling every reference to *you* or *your* in these two verses.

Read Exodus 13:17-19 and let's see what insight the verses offer. What action reminiscent of today's subject matter do these verses describe?

_____

I grin as I picture Moses with a staff in one hand and a bag of bones in the other. Actually, we'd more accurately picture Moses overseeing the transport of a coffin containing Joseph's mummified bones.

Read Joshua 24:28-32. The Book of Joshua tells the story of the Israelites taking possession of the promised land. What do the concluding verses describe?

_____

As you can see, events happened just as foretold in the faith-filled blessings. They just didn't happen in the time frame or to the exact generation of people the hearers might have presumed. That's where the broader view of you enters the picture.

Actually, we also use *you* in similar ways. Picture a classroom setting. The visiting economics professor from Japan makes a bold prediction: "After much research I predict that you will experience across-the-board financial disaster." As the students gather their books and begin departing, the professor looks at one student who has skipped a number of classes and says, "You are going to fail this class." Sure enough, the student fails. Fifty years later the United States experiences the financial disaster the professor predicted though some of those students never live to see it.

In each statement the professor employed the word *you*, but the word was directed differently. What did the professor intend by the two uses of *you*?

_____

We see this principle often in Scripture. *You* sometimes means an individual. Other times God uses the *you* to mean the nation of Israel. Still other times, the church. Often the word *you* means the people of God as a whole. According to the context, we personally may apply the corporate *you*. Students in God's classroom should realize the desire to make God's every *you* mean *me alone* rises from an ego that says, "I prefer *me* to *we*."

I don't think we can begin to grasp God's encompassing love and plan for Israel, His nation, and the body of Christ as a whole. Our human affections and interests are so narrow in comparison that we cannot comprehend the depth, length, and breadth of God's. Our tendency is to think that if He loves us all the same and has a corporate plan as important as the individual, He must be spread pretty thin. God's love is measureless. His plans are infinite. He loves each of us and plans for us with limitless extravagance.

With this understanding, turn to Genesis 50:24-25 and read the words of Joseph that Hebrews 11:22 hails as faith-filled. Review each *you* and *yours* in the two verses.

Based on our earlier research of the fulfillment of Joseph's statements, to whom did the *you* and *yours* obviously refer?

_____

We don't know whether Joseph even knew to whom his words would specifically apply. Remember the wording of Hebrews 11:22? "By faith Joseph ... spoke." Joseph knew that God had placed the words on his heart, and he knew that he could also trust God to bring them to pass. And indeed He did.

After years of study, I have much left to learn but I have come to understand a number of things about God's heart that have transformed my approach to life. One of them is the profound importance of lineage to God. That's why you see numerous references to family lines. Because I cut my teeth biblically on the KJV, I like to refer to them as the begats because they record who begat whom. Knowing that many of you are single without children or married without children, please apply the point I will make momentarily to your spiritual offspring, based on Isaiah 54:1.

Summarize this wonderful verse. _____

I am convinced that God calls those who have no physical children to concentrate more fully on spiritual offspring. Whether you apply this consideration physically and/or spiritually, accept the monumental importance of future lineage. Ultimately each generation is responsible to all those that follow. Each generation is directly responsible to their children and children's children. The question is not whether our parents, grandparents, or great-grandparents (physically or spiritually) did their job. God will hold each person accountable. The question is whether we will do our job.

God's view of lineage has made my view dramatically swell in recent years. Keith and I wear simple silver bands on our right hands. Inscribed on the inside is a verse we believe God has given us for our family line. Amanda gave it to us on her wedding day so that we'd always remember to pray that each generation will allow God to fulfill the promises we believe He has given us. I may never see the fruition of some of the things I believe God has promised directly to me, but I will dance for joy when I hear from heaven that they were fulfilled in the lives of our children and theirs. I regularly pray for our descendants, unwaveringly believing God to circumcise their hearts to love and serve Him passionately. (I will share this approach in our next unit. Please be encouraged that you don't have to have a faith-filled heritage. You can start one! I'll show you how in week 6.)

Oh, Beloved, if you only realized the depths of the pit from which our lives have been pulled, you would understand what prompted me to write this Bible study. We had enough family baggage to pass down to subsequent generations until the return of our Lord, no matter how long He tarried! Somewhere along the way, we began believing that God could do what He said He could do and that we could do what He said we could do. God told us He could give us beauty for ashes. To our human eyes, our heaps looked bigger than our God, but He said we were believing a lie. Beginning with only a mustard seed of faith, we decided to try believing Him instead.

Not long ago I sat in an evening service at my church. My spiritual mentor, Marge Caldwell, and her husband—both very young in their 80s—were sitting on one side of me. Keith was sitting on the other. Melissa, who surrendered to ministry last summer, was sitting right behind me. Two of my spiritual daughters were sitting in front of me. Amanda, who is already very busy in ministry, was sitting on Keith's left. The seat on the other side of her was empty because her young husband was standing at the pulpit preaching his heart out to us all. My heart floods with emotion as I think of it.

Beloved, God cares no more about *me* than *we*. But will we believe Him? Nothing is impossible for those who believe!

faith Journal

I hope you have come to see in the past few weeks that God has made "you" many promises. On the lines provided, would you pray that God will apply that precious "you" to include also "your" descendants, whether spiritual, physical, or both?

_____

_____

_____

_____

_____

GodStops

BEDTIME MEDITATION

_____

_____

_____

_____

_____

BY FAITH MOSES

I can't wait to meet Moses. He's one of the heroes of the faith I'm most anxious to know personally. I also can't wait to see the reruns of all he and the children of Israel experienced … starring Moses, not Charlton Heston. I just know God has His own glorious rendition of the Visual Bible in heavenly Technicolor, with multidimensional graphics that would baffle the most brilliant human imagination. And Lord, I would consider it a personal favor if you would provide buttered popcorn in heaven. A movie's just not a movie without it. And a good fountain Coke—not diet! And maybe some chocolate-covered raisins. On second thought, make that almonds. The only reason I ever chose the raisins was to save the fat. And as long as we won't have to think about fat, do You think I could also have …

Oh, you'll have to forgive me. I almost forgot you were there. Let's see if I can get my mind off concessions and back on convictions. Now, where were we? Ah, Moses. A complex character indeed. When he was most impressed with himself, he blew it badly. But just about the time he was smallest in his own eyes, dimmed by the scorching sun at the far side of a desert, God called to him from a burning bush. We read a bit of the story in our previous lesson. Our purposes today leave room for only glimpses.

Please read Hebrews 11:23-29. Help me with the motif we've chosen for our approach in weeks 4 and 5. We've imagined ourselves walking down the corridor of Hebrews' Hall of Faith, and we've stopped at one portrait after another. Like Abraham, Moses is one of the few with several portraits on the wall. Use your imagination, based on the exact text in Hebrews 11:23-29.

How many portraits in our Hall of Faith do you think would include Moses? Briefly describe what each pictures.

_____

_____

_____

_____

I love to do that kind of thing. Our Creator deliberately gave us vivid imaginations, and He delights when they are captivated by the knowledge of God (see 2 Cor. 10:5). Step down the hall with me to the next-to-last portrait that includes Moses, captured in Today's Treasure. Imagine the portrait. Stare at it with me. This portrait is troubling, isn't it? Yet at the same time, it is gloriously symbolic and full of hope.

What colors from the Artist's infinite palette do you imagine most brilliantly in the painting, and how are they used?

_____

_____

_____

Today's Treasure

By faith he kept the Passover and the sprinkling of blood, so that the destroyer of the firstborn would not touch the first-born of Israel.
Hebrews 11:28

Perhaps the original text will help us picture the colors even more vividly. Let's read the passage that describes what is happening in the painting. Please read Exodus 12:1-36. How did God calendar the Passover, according to Exodus 12:2?

_____

_____

_____

Oh, how I praise Him that our deliverance begins a whole new first in our lives! What would we do without new beginnings? Exactly how and with what were the children of Israel to mark their homes so that death would pass over them?

_____

_____

_____

Try to place yourself in Moses' position. You are mortal flesh and blood. You have virtually no confidence in yourself. You've faced terrible failure in your past. (Murder, no less!) You have heard the audible voice of God. He has unmistakably called you, though you have no idea why. He has performed wonders before your eyes; yet your vast insecurities incited His anger because you persisted in your resistance. He relented only enough to raise your brother to stand beside you, even though God was all you needed. In obedience to God, you have repeatedly approached a stubborn and powerful pharaoh to demand the release of the mistreated nation of Israel. To complicate matters, you probably know this pharaoh intimately because you grew up with him in your adoptive home. You know his priorities and his prejudices all too well. You are also well aware of his power to slay you and your people. God has given you instructions to prepare the nation of Israel for the wonder that will result in a mighty deliverance. Your mind is whirling. In moments you must tell your people.

With all these feelings and considerations conjured in your heart and mind, read Today's Treasure once more. As you try to place yourself in Moses' position, think of as many reasons as you can why these events required a faith great enough for God to esteem in Hebrews 11. In other words, why did this act of Moses require so much faith? Write your reasons below.

_____

_____

_____

The potential reasons are almost innumerable. Who could imagine that something as horrendous as death would lead to deliverance? And why in the world would the blood of a simple lamb swept with hyssop on the tops and sides of their doorframes offer them protection from the plague of death? Moses had been a shepherd for years.

The blood of lambs killed by their predators had been on his hands a hundred times. He never knew it to have any power. What would make this terrifying night any different? And what about the others who would hide behind their crimson doors, dressed and ready to leave at a moment's notice? How were they to resist becoming paralyzed by fear as wails pierced the midnight air? They too were imperfect people. They too had sinned. They hated their persecutors as much as they were hated. They were victims of oppression, but what man was innocent of all transgression? Would the blood of lambs be enough to cover the homes of the guiltier ones? Oh, the questions! How could any such light come from this dark night?

By faith Moses kept the Passover and the sprinkling of blood. Moses believed God, even though his human mind could not fathom how sprinkling lamb's blood could deliver them from a force as powerful as death. He had no idea of the ultimate work of deliverance that was depicted that night.

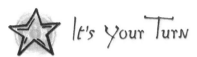 ## It's Your Turn

I'd like for you to consider several representations of the Passover, ranging from strong possibilities to absolutes. Those that Scripture clearly associates are the absolutes.

1. What does 1 Corinthians 5:7 call Christ? _____

2. Please read Luke 22:7-20. Before Christ demonstrated the fulfillment of the Passover through His death on the cross, He illustrated its fulfillment at the Last Supper. Explain how.

_____

_____

_____

3. Recall the specific instructions for sprinkling the blood on the doorframes in Exodus 12. In the margin please draw a doorframe. Then mark it where you think the blood would have been.

Go back to your illustration of the doorframe and draw a cross within it. I imagine the blood on the top of the frame also inevitably dripped on the ground. If you mentally connect the blood on the top, on the ground, and on the sides, you can easily envision a cross.

4. Surely all of us are moved by the death of the firstborn in the Passover account. Read Colossians 1:18-20. What kind of firstborn is Christ?

_____

_____

_____

 faith Journal

Psalm 51 is David's cry of repentance after he committed adultery and murder, then tried to cover them up. Please read David's words in Psalm 51:7. Why is this kind of plant familiar to us in today's lesson?

_____

_____

_____

When David voiced this prayer of repentance, he knew that hyssop had no power to cleanse him from sin. He spoke symbolically. The hyssop represented the painting of the blood on the door-frames that covered the inhabitant from the plague of death. In your journaling today, behold the Lamb of God, who takes away the sin of the world.

_____

_____

_____

_____

_____

GodStops

BEDTIME MEDITATION

_____

_____

_____

_____

_____

BY FAITH THE WALLS OF JERICHO

Joshua would be the first to tell us that God's methods may not make common sense, but boy, are they effective! Because we've already discussed God's faithfulness through the Passover era, quickly glance at the Hebrews 11:29 portrait of the Israelites crossing the Red Sea and step down to the next one. Its caption appears in Hebrews 11:30 or, if you'd rather, Today's Treasure.

I once read a newspaper article titled "The Walls of Jericho Really Did Come Tumbling Down." According to the article, significant archaeological findings indicated an implosion rather than an explosion, suggesting that something happened from outside the walls to make them crumble inward. Imagine that. I know a much more reliable resource.

Please read Joshua 6:1-20 and then record the basic strategy for taking one of the most powerful cities in Canaan. Please be specific. It is most concisely described in verses 3-5.

_____

_____

We've talked a little about the importance of biblical first mentions. Would you like to see the first mention of Joshua? Find it as you read Exodus 17:8-16. Joshua wasn't just a warrior; he was the head of the Israelite military.

What weapon was his specialty, according to Exodus 17:13? _____

Mind you, Joshua was unaware of the arm issue Moses was having on top of the hill. At the time he led the children of Israel in the battle, he simply knew that sometimes they were winning and other times they were losing. Been there. Before Joshua could take any credit toward the end result, God made sure he understood.

Take a close look at Exodus 17:14. What did God expressly tell Moses about Joshua?

_____

_____

I like both the KJV and the NIV translations of this phrase. The former says, "Rehearse it in the ears of Joshua," while the latter cuts to the chase: "Make sure that Joshua hears it." Two days ago we considered different uses of the word *you*. Keeping in mind how many people God can address at once, we should be even more impressed when He uses names! This word was to Joshua. At that time the young man had no idea that before he was born, God had chosen him to lead the conquest of Canaan. Joshua also had no idea he was already in training. Scripture implies that he was both a warrior and a worshiper (see Ex. 33:11) long before he led the Israelites into the promised land. None of his training was wasted, nor is ours, Dear One. If we try to skip our training and jump to the thrill of leveling the walls of Jericho, all the huffing and puffing in the world won't even blow the dust off our boots. We'll end up shouting, all right—more than likely at one another.

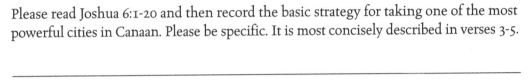

Today's Treasure

By faith the walls of Jericho fell, after the people had marched around them for seven days.
Hebrews 11:30

Considering what lay ahead of Joshua, why do you think God made such a point of his knowing what ultimately happened in the Amalekite battle (see Ex. 17:14)?

_____

_____

Now read in Joshua 5:13-15 what happened just before God gave Joshua his instructions about Jericho. Based on his prior experience in battle with the Amalekites, how does this scene seem to fit into the picture?

_____

_____

_____

Do you see the significance, Beloved? God certainly wasn't telling Joshua that his efforts were pitiful and meaningless. He wanted Joshua to know exactly what He wants us to know: we can do amazing things! In fact, Philippians 4:13 says we can do all things, but here's the catch: through Christ, who makes us strong. Old Testament or New, the common denominator in any victory has remained consistent. God doesn't try to make us feel worthless so that He can be more highly esteemed. Only insecure people approach others that way, and God has no security issues. He simply wants us to understand who empowers every victor.

Years earlier, while he wiped the sweat from his brow and Moses rehearsed the means to the Amalekite victory in his ears, Joshua had no idea what battles lay ahead. As he stood on the hill overlooking the tightly shut city of Jericho, he probably began to get a clue. God then graced Joshua with a face-to-face encounter with the Commander of the Lord's army, and the warrior became a worshiper once again. Then, just about the time he had sharpened his sword to perfection, God presented Joshua the strategy: "First, you're going to shout the walls down." By now you know that Joshua was himself a battle strategist. You can believe that God's plan didn't resemble a single one in his weekly war planner. Imagine how the conversation might have gone had Joshua been in a questioning mood:

"We're going to do what?"

"Circle, then shout, Joshua. Then I'm going to bring the walls down. This battle will not be won with muscle, Mighty Warrior. This battle will be won by faith."

I can't wait to ask you to write 1 John 5:4 from the translation of your choice.

_____

_____

As the old hymn says, faith is the victory!

Now read again Joshua 6:1-2. Carefully look at God's words to Joshua: " 'See, I have delivered Jericho into your hands.' " Picture Joshua gazing at that imposing city "tightly shut up" and God saying " 'See, I have delivered Jericho into your hands.' " Jericho couldn't have looked very delivered to Joshua. Yes, the people of Jericho had shut themselves inside because of the Israelites, but days had passed since word got out that they were melting with fear. These were sophisticated people, not wilderness wanderers. They could have planned an ambush or called another Canaanite army to their aid. Joshua might have had the faith to believe victory was coming, but did he have faith to believe it was already in his hands? That was the question of the moment. Surely Joshua was much like us. Our insecurity tends to overwhelm us on the brink of something big.

Look more closely at the text and hear the words of God again. When Keith is trying to show me wild game camouflaged in the distance, he always says, "Look right down my arm to the point of my index finger, Elizabeth, and see what I see." Imagine the outstretched arm of God before Joshua as He pointed to a city already defeated in His eyes. "See, Joshua! Look closer, My son! Look closer!" Picture Joshua squinting, but nothing looks different. Then he rubs his eyes, but it still looks the same. "No, Joshua, not with eyes of man. Look with eyes of faith! See? See it My way! It's already accomplished. I have delivered Jericho into your hands! Just go get it, Son."

And as Joshua looked with eyes of faith, he saw. Then conquered.

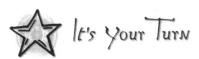 It's Your Turn

1. Let's look at a few words we might have stumbled over in our walk through the Hall of Faith today. Read in the margin three words from the KJV with *Strong's*. (I think you'll especially like *steady* in view of the theme of our study.)

2. Read the awesome words of 2 Corinthians 2:14. How does this New Testament verse align with the Old Testament accounts we've considered today?

_____

_____

_____

_____

I think you'll be blessed by Strong's definition of the word *thanks* in this verse. Read the definition in the margin and describe its meaning in your own words.

_____

_____

_____

I hope you noted how closely our triumph is associated with grace. Glory to His name! Victory is not about what we deserve. It's about who we follow.

Steady (*see Ex. 17:12*)
HEBREW STRONG'S NUMBER: 530
Transliteration: 'emunah
Phonetic Pronunciation: em-oo-naw'
Part of Speech: n f
1) firmness, fidelity, steadfastness, steadiness

Discomfited (*see Ex. 17:13*)
HEBREW STRONG'S NUMBER: 2522
Transliteration: chalash
Phonetic Pronunciation: khaw-lash'
Part of Speech: v
1) to be weak, be prostrate
1a) (Qal) to be prostrate
2) to weaken, disable, prostrate
2a) (Qal) to disable, prostrate

Overcometh (*see 1 John 5:4*)
GREEK STRONG'S NUMBER: 3528
Transliteration: nikao
Phonetic Pronunciation: nik-ah'-o
Part of Speech: v
1) to conquer 1a) to carry off the victory, come off victorious 1a1) of Christ, victorious over all His foes 1a2) of Christians, that hold fast their faith even unto death against the power of their foes, and temptations and persecutions 1a3) when one is arraigned or goes to law, to win the case, maintain one's cause

thanks
GREEK STRONG'S NUMBER: 5485
Transliteration: charis
Phonetic Pronunciation: khar'-ece
Part of Speech: n f
1) grace 1a) that which affords joy, pleasure, delight, sweetness, charm, loveliness: grace of speech 2) good will, loving-kindness, favour 2a) of the merciful kindness by which God, exerting his holy influence upon souls, turns them to Christ, keeps, strengthens, increases them in Christian faith, knowledge, affection, and kindles them to the exercise of the Christian virtues 3) what is due to grace 3a) the spiritual condition of one governed by the power of divine grace 3b) the token or proof of grace, benefit 3b1) a gift of grace 3b2) benefit, bounty 4) thanks, (for benefits, services, favours), recompense, reward

 faith Journal

I wonder if God is trying to get you to see what He sees about something in particular. I know He is with me. Let's imagine standing next to God before our own personal Jerichos and leaning in closely so that we can see all the way down His outstretched arm until we gaze on the place where His index finger is pointing. What would God be pointing out to you? Hear Him say to you, "See, Child? Would you please see this the way I do? No, not through your eyes. Through eyes of faith!" Today pinpoint what this particular Jericho may be for you. Don't quickly assume. Keep in mind that we sometimes misdiagnose our own problems and fight the wrong foes. Ask God to give you insight into any Jericho that stands between you and your promised land. Then ask Him for the grace to follow Him there in triumphal procession.

_____

_____

_____

_____

_____

GodStops

BEDTIME MEDITATION

_____

_____

_____

_____

_____

_____

_____

BY FAITH THE PROSTITUTE RAHAB

Any given day of the week I love something different about God best of all. Today I love best of all what He's willing to do for a damsel in distress. I am a hopeless romantic, and I fall in love with Him all over again every time I see that Prince Charming side of Him. In this story He rides in on a white horse, but you won't find a fairy godmother in a single scene. Come to think of it, this Cinderella is not only PG-13 but also maybe a little farfetched. Maybe that's what I love best of all about God. We've never gone so far that we can't be fetched.

Today we have one more portrait to view in the Hall of Faith. A myriad of fascinating snapshots are framed on the wall from here to the end of the corridor, but we've arrived at the last painting, and it has a Scripture caption all its own. Read Hebrews 11:31. Then glance at the remainder of the chapter and see what I mean. The inspired writer started running out of time (see v. 32), and the pace picks up considerably. How I praise God that He paused on this one and made sure Rahab was included in the longer strokes of the chapter's paintbrush. Step up and gaze on a wonderful work of art. Are you surprised? Were you expecting someone a little less rough around the edges? Now glance up and down the Hall of Faith portraits. Does she seem to be a misfit? Ah, but she's supposed to … for the sake of all the rest of us who do.

You might be amused to know that some well-meaning Bible tour guides through the centuries have tried to smooth the rough edges on this story by explaining what the Bible "really meant." They pontificate that Rahab was actually just a tavern keeper. A hostess of sorts. God suspected as much. That's why He made sure He repeated the label she lived by often enough to remove all doubt.

Take James 2:25 for instance, an inspired book written by Christ's little (half-) brother. How does this verse refer to Rahab?

_____

_____

Yep. That's what she was, all right. Vocationally challenged, you might say. We can't tidy this one up, Dear One. If you already know that Rahab's an Old Testament figure, you may wonder why she has to carry such a brand name in the New Testament. The reason is very important. Rahab is mentioned a number of times in Scripture, but the association with her former profession is made only where her testimony of faith is told. Both Hebrews 11:31 and James 2:25 make the point that her exercise of faith did not come after Rahab went to rehab. She was actively making a living as a prostitute when she decided that she might just believe God over her own press. You see, that's the beauty of the story! How could a woman like her among Jericho's teeming population believe that she could be delivered from death? Strictly by faith.

Somehow Rahab rings Romans 5:8 like a liberty bell—so loudly that I can hear it all the way from the Old Testament. Please write it below.

_____

_____

While Rahab was yet a sinner. While Beth was yet a sinner. And while _____ was yet a sinner. (If you put your spouse's name in that blank, I need to see you after class.) We want tidier stories than these, don't we? But all the tidying up without God's

> By faith the prostitute Rahab, because she welcomed the spies, was not killed with those who were disobedient.
> Hebrews 11:31

grace is just pressed and folded filthy rags. Rahab was like me and a few others I know. She couldn't seem to clean up her act, then believe God. She believed God first and then let Him clean up her act. Let's take a look at her story. Let's pick up exactly where we left off in our previous lesson. Remember, the walls of Jericho have just collapsed, and the entire city is under the sword.

What does Joshua 6:22-26 tell us about Rahab?

_____

_____

If you glance once again at the sequence of the portraits in the Hall of Faith, you will see that they are in biblical order. Rahab is no exception, since the results of her faith weren't realized until after the walls of Jericho came down. Her entrance into the epic of conquest, however, is back in Joshua 2.

Please read the entire enthralling account and don't miss the details. What part do you like best?

_____

_____

_____

Me too. How do I know? I told you already. I have a new best-of-all virtually every day, and today I like yours. The story offers a variety from which to choose. First of all, I like the fact that the king of Jericho knew the spies were there. God intentionally made the Israelites, like the body of Christ, a peculiar people. Ordinarily, the devout of the Lord stick out like a June bug in January. After wandering in the desert for 40 years wearing the same old clothes, conspicuous tassels on their garments, and their hair in certain ordained styles, they didn't exactly fit in. Their disguises didn't work. (Mine didn't work, either, no matter how good they were.) The king was on to them, and he knew the one place strangers might not seem so out of place: the local brothel. (I'm sorry. I didn't write the history.)

We might say Rahab lied. I can almost picture Christ looking at His Father and saying, "OK, maybe We should work on that rough edge next, but first things first."

Carefully look at Joshua 2. What do you imagine the "first things" of Rahab's faith were? In other words, based on the text, how did her faith in the one true God begin?

_____

_____

What promise did Rahab beg the spies to make her?

_____

I appreciate God reminding us that deeply injured hearts can still love their families deeply. What did the spies promise to do if she wouldn't divulge their actions (see v. 12)?

_____

The next question highlights the part I really like best of all. What was the condition for binding the oath (see vv. 17-18)?

_____

_____

What about this mark for deliverance from death is similar to the markings on the doorframes of the Israelites on the first Passover?

_____

_____

Inspired Scripture pays too much attention to detail for the color and purpose of the cord (or KJV thread) to be incidental. Jesus Christ is the scarlet thread that sews every book of the Bible together. Only faith could make Rahab and her family gather in that former brothel, hear the walls collapse and the people scream, and rely on a simple scarlet cord tied in her window to mark them for deliverance. Oh, the creative consistency of our God and His ways!

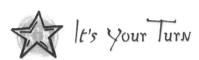 It's Your Turn

1. Read in your Bible the promise made to Rahab in Joshua 2:14. Then read in the margin meanings of *kindly* and *truly* from *Strong's* . Note that the word *kindly* is a wonderful and very important Hebrew word. In very exceptional cases it could be used negatively, based on the context. Obviously, this is not one of those times.

How often do you think a woman like Rahab had been treated " 'kindly and faithfully' " (NIV)? This situation reminds me of a certain Samaritan woman at a well who came face-to-face with the Scarlet Thread Himself (see John 4).

2. Something else I love best of all about God is that He not only delivers but also redeems. Go back to where our lesson began in Joshua 6. Just as the Israelites promised, Rahab and her family were spared, but that's not all. She was obviously still alive when the Book of Joshua was written. What does Joshua 6:25 imply happened to her?

_____

Glance at Matthew 1:1-16. What are these verses? (see v. 1) _____

Carefully look through the important list of names. Do you find anyone we've come to know in today's lesson? If so, how is she identified?

_____

_____

Beloved, not only was Rahab's life spared, but she was also embraced by the holy nation of Israel and married an Israelite. I'm grateful for men like Salmon who believe a woman is who she can be. Not just who she was. And how like my God to make sure Rahab was right there in the very genealogy of Jesus Christ! Grafted into His family line! God gave a painted woman dignity and honor. Then He painted her picture among the greatest heroes in the Hall of Faith. I like His style.

kindly
Hebrew Strong's Number: 2617
Transliteration: checed
Phonetic Pronunciation: kheh'-sed
Part of Speech: n m
1) goodness, kindness, faithfulness
2) a reproach, shame

truly
Hebrew Strong's Number: 571
Transliteration: 'emeth
Phonetic Pronunciation: eh'-meth
Part of Speech: n f
1) firmness, faithfulness, truth 1a) sureness, reliability 1b) stability, continuance 1c) faithfulness, reliableness 1d) truth 1d1) as spoken 1d2) of testimony and judgment 1d3) of divine instruction 1d4) truth as a body of ethical or religious knowledge 1d5) true doctrine; adv 2) in truth, truly

faith Journal

Meditate on one more dimension in the life of Rahab to discover something that will prompt your journaling today. Who was Rahab's son, according to Matthew 1:5? _____ In the Old Testament Book of Ruth, Boaz is the kinsman redeemer. He too came to the rescue of a woman in terrible distress and allowed her to become the love of his life. I wonder where he got such a redemptive heart and a faith to believe that what seems plan B might just have been plan A all along. From his mother, perchance? At one time Rahab must have felt destined to leave a legacy of shame. The day she first believed that the God of Israel was the true God of heaven and earth, all that began to change. She didn't just have the faith to be delivered. She had the faith to be redeemed. Then accepted. Then made a bride. Then she exercised the faith to rear one of the finest men captured in the annals of Bible history. Generations later, drops of her spiritual blood could be found in the veins of the holy Son of God. Oh, the infinite implications of believing God! That should give you something to write about, Beloved.

_____

_____

_____

_____

_____

GodStops

BEDTIME MEDITATION

_____

_____

_____

_____

_____

_____

_____

Believing God's Word Is Alive and Active in You

"The Word that God speaks is _____ and _____ _____ _____ [making it active,

_____, _____, and _____]" (Heb. 4:12, AMP).

Take to heart the first and foremost equipping for success in the promised land: the _____ in our mouths.

How to Become _____ and _____

1. In first person: I _____, and therefore I _____. Without exception the most

   powerful built-in instrument God has given us is our _____.

2. We are created in the image of God; therefore, His words are _____, and our words are

   _____. Using our instruments _____ is an effective way to stay _____

   of our promised lands.

3. For reasons ultimately known to God alone, He has ordained that _____ words carry a power,

   authority, and effectiveness that exceed words we simply _____. "Renounced"—*apeipon*—

   "literally, to _____ out against."

4. By far, the most explosively effective thing we can believe and therefore speak is _____.

   "It is _____: 'I believed; therefore I have spoken.' With that same _____ of faith we

   also believe and therefore speak" (2 Cor. 4:13). *Pneuma* means *spirit,* but it also means _____.

   Consider how we can live off the _____ of God: as we believe, we _____ His words, and as

   we speak, we _____ His words. Cast the _____ upon God and His Word. Not our

   _____ to pray.

5. Perhaps more than anything else, Satan wants to hinder us from ever learning how to use our

   _____. *Stenochoreo* means "to _____ into a narrow space, … figuratively, to be

   constrained, reserved, be unable to _____ oneself."

6. In the Old Testament oil can symbolize the _____ _____ (see Isa. 61:1).

   Jeremiah 23:29 says, " 'Is not my _____ like _____,' declares the LORD."

Believing God's Word Is Alive and Active in You

THE POWER OF THE TONGUE

Today's Treasure

Out of the same mouth come praise and cursing. My brothers, this should not be.

James 3:10

I hope you have viewed or heard the session 6 video before starting today's homework. The goal of this unit will be unclear and incomplete without it. I don't want you to miss a thing! I want God's Word to be alive and active in you. Assuming that you heard the video presentation, allow me to remind you of several vital concepts.

- God's words are omnipotent; because we have been created in His image, our words are potent.
- Our words are potent no matter how we use them.
- God desires not only that His children believe truth but also that we speak it: " 'I believed; therefore I have spoken' " (2 Cor. 4:13).
- God ordains that words of faith have more power than thoughts of faith alone: " 'Say to this mountain, "Move from here to there" ' " (Matt. 17:20).

You and I want to function in the full throttle of power God desires to give us. Ideally, our faith can become voice, and our voice can become power when we're operating in God's will. When we're actively trying to do what God says we can and we don't get the results God's Word says we can expect, we need to ask what might be wrong. Scripture tells us that if Christ's words dwell in us, we can use our mouths to speak or pray over situations, and the Holy Spirit will often bring powerful results. God may bring forth those results through different means and on a different timetable than we pictured, but His Word says power is applied when we pray and speak with faith in His name.

So what if our reality doesn't reflect a powerful-voice theology? What if we are doing everything we know to do and yet what we voice through faith often proves ineffective? Unbelief may not be our primary obstacle on this issue. The hindrance could possibly be what we might call double talk or what the Native Americans dubbed the forked tongue. Let's consider the possibility even if we think it is remote. Our goal today is to identify and remove hindrances to practicing the powerful voice God's Word tells us we can. Feeling guilty or defeated is not the goal. Whenever we are confronted by a hard truth, God's purposes are always redemptive.

How does James 3:2-12 reflect the first two bullet points in today's lesson?

_____

_____

Based on verse 2, how many people do you imagine rarely struggle with their tongues?

_____

This Scripture intimates that one of the most outstanding signs of spiritual maturity is a controlled tongue. Let's be frank. Our tongues are huge challenges for all of us. I'm suggesting not only that they are challenges but also that they can be tremendous hindrances to power.

What is the answer to every question asked in verses 11-12?

_____

When Christ empowered His disciples to speak under His authority and produce certain results, He treated the tongue as an instrument. The muscle itself has no supernatural power. The Holy Spirit infuses power through the instrument. Likewise, when we believe and speak (see 2 Cor. 4:13), the Holy Spirit can use our tongues as instruments or vessels of supernatural power and can bring about stunning results, whether immediately or over time. However, God is not nearly as likely to powerfully and regularly infuse an instrument that is also employed for opposing purposes. That's double talk. In other words, the wrong use of the instrument can dramatically hinder its effectiveness in the right use.

We want to be persons to whom God can entrust a spiritually powerful voice. Let's allow the Holy Spirit to alert us to misuses of the tongue that can diffuse its spiritual effectiveness:

- Gossip
- Lying
- Profanity
- Rudeness or unkindness
- Inappropriate humor
- Misuse of God's name

Gossip can be such a part of our life that we don't even recognize it. We can rationalize it as concern or even a prayer request. The temptation and opportunity to gossip are so rampant that if we don't deliberately make a choice not to gossip, we probably do!

Lies come in many forms ranging from slight exaggerations and excuses to complete fabrications. Their primary motivations are self-protection and self-exaltation. Unfortunately, the tendency of the natural man toward deception is as deep and pulsing as the heart within us (see Jer. 17:9). Because the mouth speaks from the overflow of the heart (see Luke 6:45), an untreated heart will easily give way to a lying tongue. Each of us could regularly use a fresh work of healing and purification at the very source of our deception problem. God desires truth in our inmost parts (see Ps. 51:6). I have come to the conclusion that we will never have it accidentally. A truth-filled heart is so unnatural that we must pursue it to have it.

Profanity is common and extremely habit forming. Thank goodness, the weapons we fight with are not the weapons of the world. On the contrary, they have divine power to demolish strongholds (see 2 Cor. 10:4). If you struggle with profanity, please be encouraged that you can be extremely honest with God about it. I'd hate for you to know the habits He has empowered me to break. Openly dialoguing with God about my strongholds and telling Him in advance when I felt that old, familiar setup for failure are two of the most vital practices God ever taught me. I still don't hesitate to tell Him when I'm feeling weak, insecure, or vulnerable to attack. I've found that I can talk to God without shame and expect Him to come to my aid. Be honest! He will never turn you away.

What does Psalm 145:18 tell us about the approach that draws God most readily?

_____

Few things destroy our witness like rudeness or unkindness. I fear that a misinterpreted sense of superiority makes this shortcoming rampant among our religious ranks. Interestingly, the same Christian who might be appalled over a profane word someone else says might be totally oblivious to ways she misuses or abuses her own tongue. Perhaps you've heard someone pray at a restaurant, then become so insolent to the waitress that you wanted to crawl under the table. Sins that differ from ours always seem worse.

Inappropriate humor implies not only off-color jokes but also humor at someone else's expense. The latter used to be a big temptation to me. I love to laugh, and in my flesh I can think something is hilarious about someone that the person would not find at all humorous. Perhaps you can relate. Ordinarily, I'm not as given to temper as I am to laughter; therefore, the switch in the nature of my humor is one of my first signals of departure from the control of the Holy Spirit. Don't misunderstand me. Godliness doesn't preclude humor. Laughter is good medicine! We just want to make sure our humor is appropriate and doesn't quench the Spirit's presence and power.

Lastly, we can't even calculate the costs of misusing God's name. I'm talking not only about taking God's name in vain but also about using it loosely, inappropriately, or casually. We can only imagine how reluctant God might be to infuse our prayers or statements said "in His name" when we have a tendency to misuse that same name.

Can you think of any other misuses of our tongues that could hinder their becoming vessels of supernatural power? If so, share.

_____

_____

_____

_____

Beloved, no matter how stubborn the tongue or how habitual our problem, God can sanctify it and make it a vessel of honor and power. The psalmist wrote,

> Before a word is on my tongue
>   you know it completely, O Lord (Ps. 139:4).

God is quick to help us. When we deliberately invite Him, He can intervene in the split second it takes for a word to travel from our brains to our tongues and stop it before it leaves our mouths. God can also sanctify our minds—our unparalleled battlefield—where every word originates. Let's believe the power of God over the power of our own tongues and fight fire with Fire. How do we do that? We'll talk about that tomorrow.

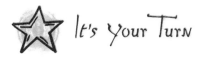 It's Your Turn

1. Read James 3:2,8,9. Then read in the margin selected words and their definitions. What will you do to bring your life into line with what God desires for you?

offend _____

perfect _____

bridle _____

poison _____

bless _____

curse _____

2. Read Galatians 5:15. Does this Scripture create a mental picture to which most of us can sadly relate? ❑ Yes ❑ No   Below are selected words from Galatians 5:15. Circle each original word and underline the meaning you think best fits the verse.

bite: *Transliteration: dakno;* 1) to bite with the teeth 2) metaph., to wound the soul, cut, lacerate, rend with reproaches

devour: *Transliteration: katesthio or kataphago;* 1) to consume by eating, to eat up, devour 1a) of birds 1b) of a dragon 1c) of a man eating up the little book 2) metaph. 2a) to devour ie. squander, waste: substance 2b) to devour i.e. forcibly appropriate: widows' property 2c) to strip one of his goods 1c1) to ruin (by the infliction of injuries) 2d) by fire, to devour i.e. to utterly consume, destroy 2e) of the consumption of the strength of body and mind by strong emotions

take heed: *Transliteration: blepo;* 1) to see, discern, of the bodily eye 1a) with the bodily eye: to be possessed of sight, have the power of seeing 1b) perceive by the use of the eyes: to see, look descry 1c) to turn the eyes to anything: to look at, look upon, gaze at 1d) to perceive by the senses, to feel 1e) to discover by use, to know by experience 2) metaph. to see with the mind's eye 2a) to have (the power of) understanding 2b) to discern mentally, observe, perceive, discover, understand 2c) to turn the thoughts or direct the mind to a thing, to consider, contemplate, to look at, to weigh carefully, examine 3) in a geographical sense of places, mountains, buildings, etc. turning towards any quarter, as it were, facing it

consumed: *Transliteration: analisko;* 1) to expend 1a) to consume, e.g. spend money 2) to consume, use up, destroy

What is the exhortation immediately following in Galatians 5:16?

_____

James 3:2; offend
GREEK STRONG'S NUMBER: 4417
Transliteration: ptaio
Phonetic Pronunciation: ptah'-yo
Part of Speech: v
1) to cause one to stumble or fall 2) to stumble 2a) to err, make a mistake, to sin 2b) to fall into misery, become wretched

James 3:2; perfect
GREEK STRONG'S NUMBER: 5046
Transliteration: teleios
Phonetic Pronunciation: tel'-i-os
Part of Speech: adj
1) brought to its end, finished 2) wanting nothing necessary to completeness 3) perfect 4) that which is perfect 4a) consummate human integrity and virtue 4b) of men 4b1) full grown, adult, of full age, mature

James 3:2; bridle
GREEK STRONG'S NUMBER: 5468
Transliteration: chalinagogeo
Phonetic Pronunciation: khal-in-ag-ogue-eh'-o
Part of Speech: v
1) to lead by a bridle, to guide 2) to bridle, hold in check, restrain

James 3:8; poison
GREEK STRONG'S NUMBER: 2447
Transliteration: ios
Phonetic Pronunciation: ee-os'
Part of Speech: n m
1) poison (of animals) 1a) poison of asps is under their lips, 1b) spoken of men given to reviling and calumniating and thereby injuring others 2) rust

James 3:9; bless
GREEK STRONG'S NUMBER: 2127
Transliteration: eulogeo
Phonetic Pronunciation: yoo-log-eh'-o
Part of Speech: v
1) to praise, celebrate with praises 2) to invoke blessings 3) to consecrate a thing with solemn prayers 3a) to ask God's blessing on a thing 3b) pray God to bless it to one's use 3c) pronounce a consecratory blessing on 4) of God 4a) to cause to prosper, to make happy, to bestow blessings on 4b) favoured of God, blessed

James 3:9; curse
GREEK STRONG'S NUMBER: 2672
Transliteration: kataraomai
Phonetic Pronunciation: kat-ar-ah'-om-ahee
Part of Speech: v
1) to curse, doom, imprecate evil upon

faith Journal

As James 3:2 says, "We all stumble in many ways. If anyone is never at fault in what he says, he is a perfect man." All of us struggle with our tongues in one way or another. Openly dialogue with God about the area that is most challenging to you and ask Him to alert you and help you when temptation arises. Let's ask God to help us form holy habits to replace carnal ones.

_____

_____

_____

_____

_____

_____

_____

GodStops

BEDTIME MEDITATION

_____

_____

_____

_____

_____

_____

_____

LIVE COALS TO OUR LIPS

I begin this lesson with emotion clutching my throat and the Spirit of God weighing on me. I read today's text afresh and looked up many of the original words. I neither read further commentary in preparation for today's lesson nor looked up a word in a more detailed lexicon. Because I've included the information for you to use as well, I have done nothing you can't do. For that reason I'm going to ask you to start today's lesson exactly the way I did so we will begin in a similar spiritual place when we proceed to the commentary section. Please know that being in a similar spiritual place doesn't mean you have to be on the verge of tears as I am. We may each process the information differently, but my prayer is that we will all process it deeply. Therefore, It's Your Turn will precede my turn today. Stop now and pray that God's presence will fall on you afresh and will make this a living, trembling word in your marrow.

Today's Treasure

With it he touched my mouth and said, "See, this has touched your lips; your guilt is taken away and your sin atoned for." Isaiah 6:7

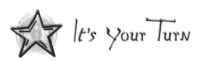

It's Your Turn

1. Please read Isaiah 6:1-8 slowly and meditatively. Do your best to picture and hear the activity to the fullest reaches of your imagination. Record your thoughts.

_____

_____

2. Read the following words from KJV with *Strong's*. Underline the essence of their meanings. Please don't skip this exercise. I don't want you to miss the treasures. Note any insights you receive or pictures that come to mind.

VERSE 1: **high:** *Transliteration: ruwm*; Phonetic Pronunciation: room; Part of Speech: v 1) to rise, rise up, be high, be lofty, be exalted 1a) (Qal) 1a1) to be high, be set on high 1a2) to be raised, be uplifted, be exalted 1a3) to be lifted, rise 1b) (Polel) 1b1) to raise or rear (children), cause to grow up 1b2) to lift up, raise, exalt 1b3) to exalt, extol 1c) (Polal) to be lifted up 1d) (Hiphil) 1d1) to raise, lift, lift up, take up, set up, erect, exalt, set on high 1d2) to lift up (and take away), remove 1d3) to lift off and present, contribute, offer, contribute 1e) (Hophal) to be taken off, be abolished 1f) (Hithpolel) to exalt oneself, magnify oneself 2) (Qal) to be rotten, be wormy

_____

VERSE 3: **cried:** *Transliteration: qara'*; Phonetic Pronunciation: kaw-raw'; Part of Speech: v 1) to call, call out, recite, read, cry out, proclaim 1a) (Qal) 1a1) to call, cry, utter a loud sound 1a2) to call unto, cry (for help), call (with name of God) 1a3) to proclaim 1a4) to read aloud, read (to oneself), read 1a5) to summon, invite, call for, call and commission, appoint, call and endow 1a6) to call, name, give name to, call by 1b) (Niphal) 1b1) to call oneself 1b2) to be called, be proclaimed, be read aloud, be summoned, be named 1c) (Pual) to be called, be named, called out, be chosen

_____

VERSE 3: **holy:** *Transliteration: qadowsh or qadosh; Phonetic Pronunciation: kaw-doshe' or kaw-doshe'; Part of Speech: adj;* 1) sacred, holy, Holy One, saint, set apart

---

VERSE 3: **hosts:** *Transliteration: tsaba' or tsaba'ah; Phonetic Pronunciation: tsaw-baw' or (fem.); tseb-aw-aw'; Part of Speech: n m;* 1) that which goes forth, army, war, warfare, host 1a) army, host 1a1) host (of organized army) 1a2) host (of angels) 1a3) of sun, moon, and stars 1a4) of whole creation 1b) war, warfare, service, go out to war 1c) service

---

VERSE 3: **full:** *Transliteration: melo' or melow; Phonetic Pronunciation: mel-o' or rarely; mel-o'; Part of Speech: n m;* 1) fulness, that which fills; 1a) fulness, handful 1b) mass, multitude 1c) fulness, that which fills, entire contents 1d) full length, full line

---

VERSE 3: **glory:** *Transliteration: kabowd or kabod; Phonetic Pronunciation: kaw-bode' rarely or kaw-bode'; Part of Speech: n m;* 1) glory, honour, glorious, abundance 1a) abundance, riches 1b) honour, splendour, glory 1c) honour, dignity 1d) honour, reputation 1e) honour, reverence, glory 1f) glory

---

VERSE 4: **moved:** *Transliteration: nuwa`; Phonetic Pronunciation: noo'-ah; Part of Speech: v;* 1) to quiver, totter, shake, reel, stagger, wander, move, sift, make move, wave, waver, tremble 1a) (Qal) 1a1) to wave, quiver, vibrate, swing, stagger, tremble, be unstable 1a2) to totter, go tottering 1a2a) vagabond (participle) 1b) (Niphal) to be tossed about or around 1c) (Hiphil) 1c1) to toss about 1c2) to shake, cause to totter 1c3) to shake, disturb 1c4) to cause to wander

---

VERSE 5: **woe:** *Transliteration: 'owy; Phonetic Pronunciation: o'-ee; Part of Speech: interjection* 1) woe! alas! oh! 1a) passionate cry of grief or despair

---

VERSE 5: **undone:** *Transliteration: damah; Phonetic Pronunciation: daw-mam'; Part of Speech: v;* 1) to cease, cause to cease, cut off, destroy, perish 1a) (Qal) 1a1) to cease 1a2) to cause to cease, destroy 1b) (Niphal) 1b1) to be cut off 1b2) to be undone, be cut off at sight of the theophany

---

VERSE 5: **unclean;** *Transliteration: tame'; Phonetic Pronunciation: taw-may'; Part of Speech: adj;* 1) unclean, impure 1a) ethically and religiously 1b) ritually 1c) of places

---

VERSE 6: **live coal:** *Transliteration: ritspah; Phonetic Pronunciation: rits-paw'; Part of Speech: n f;* 1) pavement 2) glowing stone or coal, live coal

---

VERSE 7: **touched:** *Transliteration: naga`; Phonetic Pronunciation: naw-gah'; Part of Speech: v;* 1) to touch, reach, strike 1a) (Qal) 1a1) to touch 1a2) to strike 1a3) to reach, extend to 1a4) to be stricken 1a4a) stricken (participle) 1b) (Niphal) to be stricken, be defeated 1c) (Piel) to strike 1d) (Pual) to be stricken (by disease) 1e) (Hiphil) to cause to touch, reach, approach, arrive 1e1) to cause to touch, apply 1e2) to reach, extend, attain, arrive, come 1e3) to approach (of time) 1e4) to befall (of fate)

VERSE 7: **iniquity:** *Transliteration: `avon; Phonetic Pronunciation: aw-vone'; Part of Speech: n m;* 1) perversity, depravity, iniquity, guilt or punishment of iniquity 1a) iniquity 1b) guilt of iniquity, guilt (as great), guilt (of condition) 1c) consequence of or punishment for iniquity

---

VERSE 7: **taken away:** *Transliteration: cuwr; Phonetic Pronunciation: soor; Part of Speech: v;* 1) to turn aside, depart 1a) (Qal) 1a1) to turn aside, turn in unto 1a2) to depart, depart from way, avoid 1a3) to be removed 1a4) to come to an end 1b) (Polel) to turn aside 1c) (Hiphil) 1c1) to cause to turn aside, cause to depart, remove, take away, put away, depose 1c2) to put aside, leave undone, retract, reject, abolish 1d) (Hophal) to be taken away, be removed

---

VERSE 7: **sin:** *Transliteration: chatta'ah or chatta'th; Phonetic Pronunciation: khat-taw-aw' or khat-tawth'; Part of Speech: n f* 1) sin, sinful 2) sin, sin offering 2a) sin 2b) condition of sin, guilt of sin 2c) punishment for sin 2d) sin-offering 2e) purification from sins of ceremonial uncleanness

---

VERSE 7: **purged:** *Transliteration: kaphar; Phonetic Pronunciation: kaw-far'; Part of Speech: v;* 1) to cover, purge, make an atonement, make reconciliation, cover over with pitch 1a) (Qal) to coat or cover with pitch 1b) (Piel) 1b1) to cover over, pacify, propitiate 1b2) to cover over, atone for sin, make atonement for 1b3) to cover over, atone for sin and persons by legal rites 1c) (Pual) 1c1) to be covered over 1c2) to make atonement for 1d) (Hithpael) to be covered

---

VERSE 8: **send:** *Transliteration: shalach; Phonetic Pronunciation: shaw-lakh'; Part of Speech: v;* 1) to send, send away, let go, stretch out 1a) (Qal) 1a1) to send 1a2) to stretch out, extend, direct 1a3) to send away 1a4) to let loose 1b) (Niphal) to be sent 1c) (Piel) 1c1) to send off or away or out or forth, dismiss, give over, cast out 1c2) to let go, set free

1c3) to shoot forth (of branches) 1c4) to let down 1c5) to shoot 1d) (Pual) to be sent off, be put away, be divorced, be impelled 1e) (Hiphil) to send

---

3. Based on insights of the definitions, record your immediate response to the verses.

You may have suspected the connection between today's lesson and our previous lesson. Yesterday James reminded us of the overwhelming destructive power of the tongue. In fact, he called the tongue a fire, a world of evil among the parts of the body. It corrupts the whole person, sets the whole course of his life on fire, and is itself set on fire by hell (see Jas. 3:6). James is not one to mince words, is he? He reminds me of his big Brother.

The tongue has staggering potential to wreak havoc; yet not coincidentally, it also has potential to reap the stuff of heaven on earth. We can be sure that God and Satan are both vying for authority over our mouths. Nothing threatens the enemy more than a believer with the Word of God living and active on her tongue, ready to apply it to any and every situation. James 3:2 tells us that no part of the body is harder for the person to submit to godly authority than the tongue. Therefore, we should not be surprised that nothing possesses more power to reap benefit.

Yesterday we faced the fact that our tongues have been misused and misappropriated countless times. As if our own tongues weren't bad enough, we, like Isaiah, also live among a people of unclean lips. You may work in an environment where backbiting, gossip, lying, profanity, and off-color remarks and jokes are pandemic. My precious husband would not mind my telling you that he has really struggled to get control of his mouth. I'm so proud of him because he's made tremendous progress, but he's told me, "Elizabeth, you can't imagine what it's like to work in the blue-collar world where I spend my days. Profanity is so continual that you become desensitized to a lot of it. It's also terribly habit-forming. It's like trying to give up cigarettes in a room full of smokers." Many believers who work in the white-collar world may face the same challenge.

God wants to send us, like Isaiah, into our world in His name. Our tongue is the instrument of His greatest potential use. Think how many of Christ's New Testament commands involve our mouths. We've been called to share Jesus with the lost and give our testimonies anytime we have the opportunity to tell another person of our hope. We've been called to pray. Yes, we can and do pray silently, but some of our most explosively powerful praying will be aloud. We've been called to disciple others, teaching God's Word and His ways. We've been called to resist the devil so that he will flee. If we're going to resist the devil as Christ did, we are going to strike with the spoken Word of God. Beloved, we've also been called to speak to some mountains and tell them to move!

While on earth, Christ possessed the power to do anything He wanted. He could have thought people to wholeness, and they would have been healed, but He didn't. He used His mouth and spoke healing. Likewise, God could have thought the world into existence, but He didn't. He said, "Let there be," and there was. The spoken word of God seems to accomplish what our merely mental words and prayers do not.

Certainly, many Christian practices don't involve our mouths, but we can hardly discount those that do. We have been called to believe and therefore to speak. We have been commissioned to proclaim the greatness of the King of all creation; yet our mouths aren't even fit to utter His name. Our tongues have corrupted our whole person (see Jas. 3:6) innumerable times through gossip, backbiting, lying, criticism, profanity, perversity, and/or cursing. Then in an instant we can switch masks and speak blessings from the same mouth. "My brothers [sisters], this should not be" (see Jas. 3:10)!

So what's the solution? We desperately need God to sanctify our mouths! And praise His name, He is willing and able. Beloved, through God's Word and prayer, let's go to the throne of grace as Isaiah did and walk the passages one step at a time. Read Isaiah 6:1-4 very carefully and picture the scene again. Don't proceed until you do.

Now read Isaiah's reaction again: "Woe is me! for I am undone!" (Isa. 6:5, KJV). Confess to the Father right now what has you most undone in His presence.

"Woe is me! For I am _____."

Now read verse 6. Where did the seraph get the live coal? _____

Nothing is more important in the atoning scene of Isaiah's vision than the altar from which the live coal was taken. The *Strong's* definition of the word *altar* is very brief, but my *Old Testament Lexical Aids* tells me the original word *mizbeach* comes from the word *zabach*, meaning "to … sacrifice."[1] *Mizbeach* means "an altar, a place of sacrifice."[2] Remember, other kinds of altars existed among the ancient people. The altar of incense was also in the temple, but I believe the live coals in this vision could have come only from the altar of sacrifice. Why? Because coals, no matter how consumed with fire, have no power to take away guilt or to atone for sin.

What insight does Hebrews 9:22 lend?

_____

I am convinced that the God-appointed power the coals had to purge and atone came from the blood of the sacrifice laid on the altar. God's Word never veers from the concept that all remission of sins comes through the shedding of sacrificial blood. Jesus Christ, the one and only Son of God, graced earth's guilty sod to offer Himself as the perfect sacrifice and to fulfill every requirement of the law once and for all. He shed His precious blood on an altar constructed of two pieces of wood and fashioned into a cross. The fire of holy judgment met with the blood of the spotless Lamb; our guilt was purged and our sins atoned. Glory to His name! We need no further act of atonement, but we are desperate for the continuing work of sanctification.

Today you and I stand before the same throne the prophet Isaiah approached in his glorious vision. God is just as holy. Just as high and lifted up. The train of His robe still fills the temple, and the seraphs still cry, "Holy!" But the writer of Hebrews 4:15-16 tells us that because we have Jesus as our great high priest, we boldly approach a throne of grace. The same grace that saves also sanctifies, and we could use a fresh work of consecration, couldn't we? In one way or another, we too are a people of unclean lips, and we undoubtedly live among a people of unclean lips. How God wants to use our mouths! But He is calling us to a fresh consecration and willingness to cease misusing our mouths.

We need not hang our heads and beg. All we need to do is lift up our faces and ask. May Jesus touch our lips with coals from the altar and set our tongues aflame with His holy fire.

 *faith Journal*

Use these lines to ask God to consecrate your mouth to His glory. Believe by faith that you receive what you ask in His name.

_____

_____

_____

_____

_____

_____

_____

GodStops

BEDTIME MEDITATION

_____

_____

_____

_____

_____

_____

_____

_____

_____

_____

DAY 3
BLESSING OTHERS

I can't decide if a person is more or less weird if she knows she's weird. In case this helps you, even I think I'm weird. I can hardly sit at my computer to begin today's lesson because I'm so excited about a discovery we're going to make together. My heart is literally pounding. I guess you don't have to wonder whether I get emotionally involved in the lessons and whether what we do together is real to me. But I'm still weird. The good news is, I have not yet developed a taste for locusts and wild honey. Nor have I purchased a homestead in the wilderness. Of course, I did go to Africa and eat hippo.

Today I want to introduce you to a wonderful Greek word. The KJV with *Strong's* word and definition come from Today's Treasure (Eph. 1:3). The Greek word (transliteration) for *blessed* in the phrase "who hath blessed us" is *eulogeo*. It means to praise, celebrate with praises; to invoke blessings; to consecrate a thing with solemn prayers; to ask God's blessing on a thing; pray God to bless it to one's use; pronounce a consecratory blessing on; of God; to cause to prosper, to make happy, to bestow blessings on; favoured of God, blessed.

Eulogia is a very similar Greek word for *blessings*, as in the phrase "spiritual blessings" (also in verse 3). Its definition is: praise, laudation, panegyric: of Christ or God; fine discourse, polished language; in a bad sense, language artfully adapted to captivate the hearer: fair speaking, fine speeches; an invocation of blessing, benediction; consecration; a (concrete) blessing, benefit.

Can you think of an English word that seems similar to these Greek words? If the word *eulogy* came to mind, we're on the same track. If it didn't, go ahead and hop on this track with me. From the onset, get any association with a funeral out of your mind and share my conviction that we more often praise the dead than the living. According to Webster's dictionary, a eulogy is simply "high praise." Even Webster, however, cites the original Greek word *eulogia*.[3] Carefully look back at the two Greek words above. *Eu* means *good* or *well*. In the remainder of the word you should be able to recognize a form of *logos*, meaning *word*. In other words, to be blessed with this kind of blessing is to have God speaking a good word over us. *Eulogeo* means "to bless, speak well of."[4]

Two primary Greek words are translated *bless* or *blessing* in the New Testament. The other one is *makarios*, a wonderful word that also involves an acknowledgment or pronouncement of blessedness.[5] For our purposes today I want you to center on the word *eulogeo* because we are focusing on the power of the tongue. As we established in the session 6 video, we are created in the image of God, whose words are omnipotent. Our words are not omnipotent, thank goodness. Can you imagine the destruction we would have caused? But our words are certainly potent.

The Greek root word we're focusing on is also used of man toward God, as the first word in Ephesians 1:3 suggests: "Blessed be the God and Father of our Lord Jesus Christ" (KJV). I'd like to suggest that we might not realize just how much we want to bless God until we grasp how much He's blessed us. So let's start with Him first.

I want you to understand and celebrate today, Dear One, that God has used His powerful mouth to call you by name and speak blessing over you. Absorb this: God has been talking about you. That's right. Behind your back. And God has been talking over you. Eulogizing you, of all things. Look at one segment of the definition of *eulogeo* from *The Complete Word Study Dictionary of the New Testament:* "Of God toward men, to bless, i.e., to distinguish with favor. ... When the subject is God, His speaking is action, for God's speech is energy released."[6]

Today's Treasure

Praise be to the God and Father of our Lord Jesus Christ, who has blessed us in the heavenly realms with every spiritual blessing in Christ.
Ephesians 1:3

I don't think I can keep from shouting, "Hallelujah!" I can't imagine what the orthodontist next door to my office thinks of my sudden outbursts of "Glory!" and "Amen!" I think he agrees with my initial self-diagnosis of weirdness. Right now I'm too caught up in the Spirit to care. Get up here with me, Sister. Look at those words again: God speaks favor over us. And His speaking is action, for God's speech is energy released. Lord God, I welcome You to release Your energy over my life anytime You want. Speak on, O King eternal!

Imagine it. God could simply think words of kindness and blessing, but one of the main ideas wrapped up in *eulogeo* is that He chooses rather to speak those words. Just imagine Him saying your name!

Now think about some of the most specific blessings you've received from God in the past year or so. Write them down. Use the margin if you need more space!

_____

_____

Now imagine God opening wide His powerful mouth and speaking those blessings into existence over your precious life. All I can do is sit here and shake my head in amazement. Oh, Lord, how good You are. How active! How involved! Look back at the definition I gave you a few paragraphs earlier and note the "…" in it. Now I want to tell you what was in that space. Part of God's spoken blessing over our lives involves the following: "to act in man's life and accomplish His purposes instead of allowing men to have their own way."[7] At first we might grimace, but give the concept a few more thoughts. God has a calling on each of our lives (see Rom. 8:30; Eph. 1:18). He is determined to perform a good work in each of us (see Phil. 1:6). He has set aside good works for each of us to accomplish in our tenures on earth (see Eph. 2:10). It is to Christ's Father's glory that our lives bear much fruit (see John 15:8). God's plans for those who love Him are beyond what eye has seen, ear has heard, or mind has conceived (see 1 Cor. 2:9). Let's face it. We don't always cooperate.

Take me, for starters. If I had gotten everything I wanted, I would have married my eighth-grade boyfriend. Then my eleventh-grade boyfriend. Then my boyfriend in my sophomore year of college. Then my boyfriend in my junior year of college. (I was getting increasingly serious about marriage by then and was officially having tryouts.) I would also have divorced and remarried my husband at least 12 times by now. I also originally wanted—and asked God for—six children. Count them. Six! Furthermore, I would never have begun teaching the Word, because all I wanted to do at my church was play in the handbell choir—and they rejected me. I, for one, am ecstatic that God often refuses to let us have our own way. Let's face it. We cannot bless our own lives the way God can. Thank goodness He does not bow to our pressure. (Have you ever considered that God never has to endure peer pressure because His Highness simply has no peers?) Aren't we thankful that much of what we've spoken over our own lives has not come from a speech that is energy released? Let's leave that kind of power to the all-wise God.

Name a few occasions for which you're thankful that God did not give you your way.

_____

_____

Here's where today's lesson on spoken blessing turns to us: as a people created in His image, then born again by His Spirit to be called by His name, God wants to make us blessings to those around us. This week we've centered on having mouths sanctified by God so that they can be empowered by God. God wants to make us people who speak well over others. People who bless. Earlier in the week we talked about vocal practices we want to omit, such as gossip, lying, profanity, rudeness, inappropriate humor, and any measure of disrespect toward God. However, we don't just want to omit bad things from our mouths. We want to commit our mouths to blessing!

Name a few ways we can become this kind of blessing to others. _____

_____

_____

I always try to anticipate your questions. Right now I'd want to make this inquiry if I were you: "How can I speak sweetly all the time when serious issues must occasionally be addressed?" Let's not misunderstand blessing. If we say something we don't mean, our blessing just turned into deception. Blessing is never false flattery. Blessing can never be deceiving. Blessing runs the gamut from encouraging others, to praying for one another, to speaking the truth in love. Remember the "…" portion of the earlier definition of *eulogeo* on page 127? Read it again; then consider how we might occasionally take God's example. As parents, for instance, sometimes we bless our children more by not letting them have their own way. As employers and supervisors in work positions, we usually aren't wise to release those under our authority to do whatever they want. In either scenario, we are wrong to speak unkindly or abusively to them in the process.

I have often been blessed by someone graciously and lovingly helping me teach a better lesson by correcting something I've said or done. How well I can receive their words is always connected to the heart with which they approach me. Thank goodness, I also have those who bless me with pure encouragement. Dear One, all of us could use a few others to speak good words over us. More importantly, you and I can become people who speak good words over others. And if we do, can you even imagine how God will talk behind our backs?

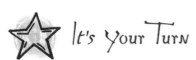 It's Your Turn

1. In light of our lesson's conclusion, please read Malachi 3:16. How does God respond when those of us who reverence Him speak good words to one another?

_____

_____

2. Find each one of the following verses in the KJV. Each includes an English translation of the Greek word *eulogeo*. Record the context of each kind of blessing and any insight you receive.

• Matthew 5:44 _____

- Matthew 14:19 _____

- Matthew 25:34 _____

- Luke 1:28 (Imagine God talking behind her back and planning this blessing.)

  _____

- Luke 2:27-30 _____

- 1 Corinthians 4:11-12 _____

- James 3:9 (This verse means a little more to us now, doesn't it?)_____

  _____

- 1 Peter 3:8-9 _____

faith Journal

Let's spend our journaling time blessing God today. Let's also ask Him to bring to our minds anyone He wants us to bless. Perhaps someone could also use the blessing of our apology for times when we've used our mouths inappropriately. I don't want this journaling time to infuse us with feelings of condemnation, but we want the way cleared to start using our mouths with power and blessing. Humbling ourselves and apologizing to someone we may have hurt with our mouths is a small price to pay. If God brings anyone to mind, go forward in obedience, knowing the harvest ahead!

_____

_____

_____

_____

_____

_____

_____

_____

_____

_____

_____

_____

_____

_____

_____

_____

_____

_____

DAY 4
THE PRACTICE OF BLESSING

In week 5 I shared a testimony about lineage and the astounding work God continues to accomplish in my family. I also promised that I'd share some of the ways God has taught me to pray and believe Him to bring forth a harvest through our family line. In the session 6 video I described the most powerful means God has given me to pray. The basic concept is taking applicable, topical Scripture and turning it into prayer over loved ones or circumstances. All week we'll address the why and how of God's desire to use our mouths powerfully to His glory. Undoubtedly, prayer is a primary discipline of the faith that God wants to infuse with supernatural power.

I want to show you how the concept works and lead you to practice it for yourself and those on your priority prayer list. Remember, prayer occurs anytime we communicate with God. We never want to become legalistic about our prayer lives. I pray in all sorts of ways, just as you do. The concept we'll practice is my most common approach toward my highest-priority requests. Please know in advance that I am far from an expert in prayer. I'm not sure we ever develop prayer lives that don't leave room for growth. My only desire is to share a few practices that have proved helpful to me. Consult others who have experienced significant affirmative answers to prayer and reap from their experiences, too.

We'll start with an inventory of your life, your loved ones, and your greatest concerns. For now fill out only the information and not the possible Scripture references. We'll come back to those later.

On him we have set our hope that he will continue to deliver us, as you help us by your prayers.
2 Corinthians 1:10-11

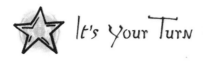 *It's Your Turn*

1. Briefly describe this present season of your personal life. Are you momentarily experiencing a break from the usual challenges, or are you enduring difficulty, strife, physical illness, pain (whether emotional or physical), indecision, or confusion? Get as specific as possible in several sentences. Specify whether the greatest challenges are at home, at work, or elsewhere.

_____

_____

_____

_____

Possible Scripture references to apply in prayer: (Include references only. You will write selected Scriptures on your index cards.)

_____

_____

2. List the names and relationships of loved ones you most want to prioritize in prayer. Include any specific requests you might have. I have included room for five, but feel free to add more on additional sheets of paper.

Name _____ Relationship to you _____

Specific requests _____

_____

Possible Scripture references to apply in prayer _____

_____

Name _____ Relationship to you _____

Specific requests _____

_____

Possible Scripture references to apply in prayer _____

_____

Name _____ Relationship to you _____

Specific requests _____

_____

Possible Scripture references to apply in prayer _____

_____

Name _____ Relationship to you _____

Specific requests _____

_____

Possible Scripture references to apply in prayer _____

_____

Name _____ Relationship to you _____

Specific requests _____

_____

Possible Scripture references to apply in prayer _____

_____

3. Now list one or two circumstances in or around your life that you believe God wants to change according to your understanding of His will.

Circumstance _____

_____

Possible Scripture references to apply in prayer _____

_____

Circumstance _____

_____

Possible Scripture references to apply in prayer _____

_____

Let's begin applying the concept by using the first question in our inventory about this specific season of your life. From the time God first began imploring me to believe Him, I have recorded on index cards a set of approximately 8 to 15 Scriptures addressing each season of my life. For instance, just before I wrote *Breaking Free*, my heart was shattered over losses I had endured, so my stack of Scriptures spoke to suffering and persevering. Not surprisingly, when I proceeded to write the study on freedom, I went through a terrible time of spiritual warfare, so I knew I needed to change to a new set of Scriptures that addressed standing firm against attack. In His mercy, God followed that ferocious season of warfare with a season of peace, harvest, and relative ease. You might be surprised to know that I was also highly concerned about victoriously enduring the easier season. I never want to grow distant from the God I love or become dull of spiritual hearing. Furthermore, I want God to know that He can trust me with a few days, weeks, or months of relative ease every now and then! That season was followed by enormous work and ministry pressure, so my prayer focus took a suitable turn.

When I sense a shift in seasons, I know the time has come for a new stack of Scriptures. How do I compile the Scriptures? I ask God to give them to me. Then I try to be alert during my devotional times or Bible-study times to any relevant Scripture I might sense Him highlighting. I also listen for preachers or other teachers to address Scriptures that address my prayer needs. You have probably seen a cartoon in which a light bulb suddenly goes off in someone's head. Ordinarily, I sense God equipping me with a Scripture much like the cartoon character suddenly receives a bright idea. I have an "aha" moment in which I realize that God is supplying me with an applicable Scripture. I then write it down on an index card in the form of a prayer and keep it with my daily prayer materials. I usually compile a small stack. Then, depending on the level of desperation or seriousness of the need, I may pray them daily or every couple of days. Soon the Scriptures have moved from ink on an index card to a truth abiding in my heart, and I can pray them from memory while driving or taking a walk. When the season begins to shift, I ask God for another set of Scriptures.

Now review inventory questions 2 and 3, which address loved ones and circumstances. I practice the same approach for each of these areas. In fact, when I write the Scripture on the index card, I often insert the name of the person or the kind of circumstance in the reference. I'll give you an example.

Deuteronomy 30:6 is a Scripture I often pray for myself and my family. What does this Scripture say?

_____

_____

Based on this reference, very often I pray something like the following: *God, You desire nothing more than our love, and You willingly and graciously prepare our hearts to love You. According to Your Word, I ask You to circumcise my heart, Keith's heart, Amanda's heart, Melissa's heart, and Curt's heart so that we each will love You with all our heart and soul and live the abundant life You chose for us.*

I am also very aware of Satan's attacks on our minds. I believe that women deal with insecurity issues and desperation for love more than men. For this reason I love to pray Scriptures like Psalm 90:14 over the women among my loved ones.

Turn Psalm 90:14 into a prayer. _____

_____

_____

Certainly, women deal with sexual temptations, but I believe that men in our culture are under severe and exceeding attack in this area. Therefore, I like to pray Scriptures like Psalm 101:3-5 over the men I love. Turn these verses into prayer for someone (unnamed on this page) who could be dealing with sexual temptation.

_____

_____

_____

The Word of God is full of Scriptures to apply to our workplace. God doesn't promise wealth to every believer, but He certainly promises to meet our needs. He can also delight in granting us a surplus when our hearts can handle it. He knows our finances are huge concerns to most of us.

Proverbs 30:7-9 is a great Scripture for prayer. What is its main idea?

_____

For conceptual approaches, use the Search tool in your online Bible library or in your own Bible concordance to find verses that include words like *harvest* or *plentiful*. Remember, God can always say no if what we're asking would ultimately harm us, but how silly we would be to "have not, because ye ask not" (Jas. 4:2, KJV). Remember, God looks on the heart of our desire more than the desire of our heart. I generally ask God to give us what we can humbly handle and what would glorify Him.

God can speak through any Scripture, but Psalms, Proverbs, the Gospels, and the Epistles are full of Scriptures that can be easily turned into prayers.

To end today's study, look at two chapters from Scripture and see if any "light bulbs" appear for any points on your inventory list. If so, write the references below. Over the days to come, be alert to any others God leads you to add. Then start making index cards and praying with confidence! I think you'll love it!

Read Proverbs 14 and Ephesians 1. Look for any Scriptures that might apply to the inventory you completed today. Record the references here.

_____

_____

_____

 *faith Journal*

Practice what we've learned today by turning some of the Scriptures you discovered into prayer for yourself, your loved ones, or your circumstances.

_____

_____

_____

_____

_____

_____

_____

_____

GodStops

BEDTIME MEDITATION

_____

_____

_____

_____

_____

_____

_____

_____

RENOUNCING WORDS

Several thousand years ago a Hebrew son by the name of Jabez had no idea that God would record a prayer from his mouth in Holy Writ and that a million people in the 21st century would repeat it. I have an idea that today's confident prayer approach might bear very little resemblance to the original, but we won't know for sure until we ask Jabez in heaven. If word of the earthly phenomenon tagged with his name has reached his mansion, I hope someone snapped a picture of his facial expression when he heard it. I don't doubt he's thrilled to share the prayer with us, but I imagine that he will have quite a story to tell us about what prompted the prayer. Just in case one of us has been on another planet over the past few years, perhaps we'd better stop and read the passages before we go any further. Please read 1 Chronicles 4:9-10. You might be blessed by reading it in several different versions.

Read in the margin *Strong's* definitions of selected words in 1 Chronicles 4:9-10 and complete the following.

The name *Jabez* means _____.

Strong's tells us that *sorrow* is translated elsewhere in the KJV (under "English Words Used in KJV") as _____.

Compare the meanings of *sorrow* and *grieve*. Which definitions are similar?

I love the NIV translation of these verses. I believe it best reflects the heart of Jabez and his prayer. I'd like to consider it in sections so that we can grasp what may have been the original motivation of the petition.

"His mother had named him Jabez, saying, 'I gave birth to him in pain'" (v. 9). This verse jolts any semblance of parental sensibility in me every time I read it. I don't know whether the woman had a severe case of postpartum depression or a general mean streak, but she basically named the boy Pain. My Bible translation tells me that the word *Jabez* sounds like a Hebrew word for *pain*. Just imagine. She called Pain in for dinner. She fed Pain his vegetables. And every time she called his name, she reminded him how much pain he'd caused. Thanks, Mom.

Did you catch the intriguing translation of the same Hebrew word (translated *sorrow* in the KJV) found elsewhere in Scripture? The word is also translated *idol*. I'm certainly no scholar and can't explain intellectually why a word translated *pain* one place is translated *idol* in another. However, I've lived long enough to know two things:

- Nothing ultimately causes more pain than our idols.
- Our pain can become our idol.

In the story of Jabez a blatant association occurs to me. In my opinion his mother made an idol of the pain associated with his birth. I wonder how many of us have also made an idol of our past pain. Not only did she bow down to it, she also inflicted the same sentence on Jabez—until one day when he decided maybe his God was bigger than his name. Bigger than his pain.

"Jabez cried out to the God of Israel" (v. 10). I think the NIV likely captured the scene most literally when it suggested that he cried out. In my estimation his prayer was one of absolute desperation. Where the KJV says "bless me indeed," the Hebrew language simply repeats the plea: "Oh, that You would bless me! Bless me!" Adjust

Today's Treasure

"Oh, that you would bless me and enlarge my territory! Let your hand be with me, and keep me from harm so that I will be free from pain."
1 Chronicles 4:10

Jabez
HEBREW STRONG'S NUMBER: 3258
Transliteration: Ya`bets
Phonetic Pronunciation: yah-bates'
Part of Speech: n pr m
Jabez = "sorrow"
1) the head of a Calebite family
n pr loc 2) a town in Judah apparently near Bethlehem

sorrow
HEBREW STRONG'S NUMBER: 6090
Transliteration: `otseb
Phonetic Pronunciation: o'-tseb
Part of Speech: n m
English Words used in KJV: sorrow, wicked, idol
1) pain, sorrow 2) idol

grieve
HEBREW STRONG'S NUMBER: 6087
Transliteration: `atsab
Phonetic Pronunciation: aw-tsab'
Part of Speech: v
English Words used in KJV: grieve; displeased ; hurt; made; sorry; vexed; worship; wrest
1) to hurt, pain, grieve, displease, vex, wrest 1a) (Qal) to hurt, pain 1b) (Niphal) to be in pain, be pained, be grieved 1c) (Piel) to vex, torture 1d) (Hiphil) to cause pain 1e) (Hithpael) to feel grieved, be vexed 2) to shape, fashion, make, form, stretch into shape, (TWOT) worship 2a) (Piel) to shape, form 2b) (Hiphil) to form, copy, fashion

your spiritual ears and see if you denote desperation. We have no idea what the additional circumstances may have been. Without a doubt, however, one of the chief motivations for his petition to God is well captured in the conclusion of the prayer: " 'Keep me from harm so that I will be free from pain' " (v. 10).

If you compare the original word in verse 9 for the mother's "sorrow" (or "pain," NIV) with the original word in verse 10 for "grieve" (or "pain," NIV), you will find them very similar. Jabez asked to be free from pain: the very thing his mother had associated with him. I am convinced Jabez asked God to bless him, break the boundaries set around him, and release him from the curse of pain that had ridden him all his days. I know one thing for certain: the prayer was not arrogant or self-aggrandizing.

James 4:3 is the basis of my certainty. What does it say? _____

_____

First Chronicles 4:9 tells us that Jabez was honorable. God doesn't honor requests motivated by the lusts of our flesh.

What does the prayer of Jabez have to do with our study on the power of our tongues? Look how powerful his mother's words had been over his life! Behold the power of a name! My brothers and sisters and I have often given our parents a playful piece of our minds over saddling some of us with the names of ancient Arkansan kinfolks, but the names our parents gave us weren't our problem. I well remember times, however, when I was called other kinds of names at school as I grew up a very confused and hurting adolescent. Whoever said, "Sticks and stones may break my bones, but words will never hurt me" lied.

This week we have been talking about God's desire to sanctify our mouths and infuse them with God-given power and authority. We confronted how often we've misused the vessel God wants to use. We then met the Lord at the altar in Isaiah 6 and asked Him spiritually to touch our lips with the coals from His altar and give us mouths to speak blessing. We spent four days addressing how we need to use our mouths more carefully. Before our week of study concludes, however, we need to address the detriment that has come to us through other mouths, renounce any hold they might retain, forgive their owners, and ask God to heal our hearts and minds of their damage. Words like …

- "You'll never amount to anything."
- "No one will ever want you now."
- "You'll never get over that."
- "You've missed your chance."
- "God can't use you now."
- "You're finished."
- "You're no good."
- "You're hopeless."
- "You're just like your father, and we all know what he was like."
- "You're a drunk, and that's all you'll ever be."
- "You're a _____."

Or maybe the person wasn't gutsy enough to say it to your face. Maybe it was said behind your back, and you weren't hard of hearing. Words hurt. Words influence. Words echo in the canyons of our memories and reflect in the mirrors of our minds. If you still remember clearly and the thought conjures a stab, the statement retains a hold and wields a certain amount of power.

Beloved, what is the third statement in our five-statement pledge of faith?

The more thoroughly convinced we become that we are who God says we are, the more we will begin to act like who He says we are. Our daily lives demonstrate what we really believe about ourselves. Most of us have bought more of what others have said than we'd like to admit. Dear One, the time has come to believe God. The time has come to renounce words others have spoken over us that don't line up with the truth of God's Word. And while we're at it, let's give others the same privilege. They get to be who God says they are, too.

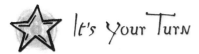 It's Your Turn

Read 2 Corinthians 5:17-21 and then the following original words and meanings from *Strong's*. Record any insights you receive.

new: *Transliteration: kainos; Phonetic Pronunciation: kahee-nos'; Part of Speech: adj* 1) new 1a) as respects form 1a1) made, fresh, recent, unused, unworn 1b) as respects substance 1b1) new kind, unprecedented, novel, uncommon, unheard of

---

all things: *Transliteration: pas; Phonetic Pronunciation: pas; Part of Speech: adj* 1) individually 1a) each, every, any, all, the whole, everyone, all things, everything 2) collectively 2a) some of all types

---

ministry: *Transliteration: diakonia; Phonetic Pronunciation: dee-ak-on-ee'-ah; Part of Speech: n f* 1) service, ministering, esp. of those who execute the commands of others 2) of those who by the command of God proclaim and promote religion among men 2a) of the office of Moses 2b) of the office of the apostles and its administration 2c) of the office of prophets, evangelists, elders etc. 3) the ministration of those who render to others the offices of Christian affection esp. those who help meet need by either collecting or distributing of charities 4) the office of the deacon in the church 5) the service of those who prepare and present food

---

reconciliation: *Transliteration: katallage; Phonetic Pronunciation: kat-al-lag-ay'; Part of Speech: n f;* 1) exchange 1a) of the business of money changers, exchanging equivalent values 2) adjustment of a difference, reconciliation, restoration to favour 2a) in the NT of the restoration of the favour of God to sinners that repent and put their trust in the expiatory death of Christ

---

What are we called in verse 20? What does the title means in context with the verse?

_____

_____

❦ faith Journal

Your faith-journaling section is profoundly important today. Before you write anything in this section, please find a private place where you can pray aloud. No matter how much the process temporarily stings, verbalize every statement contrary to God's Word that has wielded significant power over you. Tell God how the words hurt and any effect you feel they have had on you. In Jesus' name renounce every statement one by one, along with any hold it has had on you. Then believe God to completely release you.

On the lines provided, thank God for His truth and ask Him to replace all hurtful words with words of healing. Thank Him that none of those injurious statements have further authority over you. Ask Him to empower you to forgive those who said them, in the same way He has forgiven you for detrimental words you have said over others.

_____

_____

_____

_____

❦ GodStops

B E D T I M E   M E D I T A T I O N

_____

_____

_____

_____

---

[1]"Lexical Aids to the Old Testament," in Warren Baker, gen. ed., *The Complete Word Study Old Testament* (Chattanooga, TN: AMG Publishers, 1994), 2312.

[2]Ibid., 2330.

[3]*Ninth New Collegiate Dictionary* (Springfield, MA: Merriam-Webster Inc., 1988), s.v. "eulogy."

[4]Spiros Zodhiates, gen. ed., *The Complete Word Study Dictionary* (Chattanooga, TN: AMG Publishers, 1992), 677.

[5]Ibid., 678.

[6]Ibid., 677.

[7]Ibid.

Believing God Has Been There All Along

1. God has assigned each generation a tremendous _____ to its _____

   and its _____ .

   • As the spiritual seed of Abraham, we are called to be far more _____ about building

   a _____ of _____ into our children. .

2. The Hebrew word for "cut off" is karat, meaning "to cut, cut off; to make a _____."

   • Through the concepts in Joshua 4, God seems to say, "Because I have cut covenant with you, I will also

   cut a _____ through any _____ that stands between you and the

   fulfillment of My covenant promises."

   • "I will _____ the path, but you must _____ the path"

3. Consider the significance of the memorial stones coming from the middle of the Jordan. The middle can

   represent the _____ point, the place of sudden _____ and _____ .

4. Sometimes we are wisest to _____ _____ .

   • The Israelites: _____ _____ !

   • Moses: _____ _____ !

   • God: _____ _____ !

5. Conclude with 1 Peter 2:4-5. You and I are living _____ . We are living

   _____ to the world that _____ was here.

Believing God Has Been There All Along

DAY 1
A DIFFERENT KIND OF MEMORY RETRIEVAL

Today's Treasure

"The Counselor, the Holy Spirit, whom the Father will send in my name, will teach you all things and will remind you of everything I have said to you."
John 14:26

In video session 7 we joined the Israelites in the middle of the Jordan riverbed and watched them draw forth stones of remembrance. We are going to follow suit for the next week of homework and for the next two weeks of Faith Journal. Our specific objective will be to remember God.

The brain's ability to remember has never been more thoroughly explored than by current research. God deliberately created the human mind so complex that modern medicine would seek many answers in vain. The brain retains a vast measure of mystery and commands a deep respect, compliments of the One who formed a clump of gray matter from the dust of the ground.

As one who grew up with unexplainable gaps, memory has special meaning to me. I am grateful to live in an age when people who have experienced childhood abuses can rather safely reveal what happened. I can't imagine how different my life would have been had I been saddled with the taboos of generational yesteryears and left to internalize my victimization for the rest of my life. Traumas surface one way or another. If we're unable to bring them to the surface in healthy ways, they will float to the top in a myriad of destructive ways. Based on my behavior prior to divulging the truth, I am quite sure I would have eventually imploded with self-destruction.

The psychiatric field says much about memory retrieval. I am far from an expert, but I know that a person can repress many memories until something releases them so that they rise to the top. I personally experienced the phenomenon, but it did not catch me totally off guard. I had been haunted all my young life by a certain awareness that bad things had happened. I was painfully aware of the tip of the iceberg. I simply had never had the courage to duck my head below those waters and face the mountain beneath. Every person I know whose memory retrieval has proved valid over time has a similar testimony.

I am concerned that the attempt to retrieve repressed memories has become almost faddish in our culture. I also know several women who feel they were talked into memories they never had. I fear that if behavior can be explained in no other way, a patient is sometimes guided into grasping imaginative straws. The doctor or counselor may have no idea that he or she is suggesting the images. I am a great supporter of sound, godly counseling. I most assuredly sought it and recommend it, but I urge caution where this phenomenon we call memory retrieval is concerned.

The human imagination is very active, so we can't believe just any picture that comes to our minds. Consider that every fairy tale, fictional story, and sci-fi movie was conjured in the human mind. Though we are created in the image of a very creative

God, our minds obviously differ from God's in many ways. For starters, we can't call our every imagination fact. I am certainly no counselor, but I tend to think that retrieval of deeply repressed memories can be considered most accurate when they fit in the life like a missing puzzle piece. My pieces fit because I demonstrated many classic childhood behaviors of a victim of molestation. I was terribly insecure, was on the verge of tears much of the time, was afraid of my own shadow, feared being alone with men, and pulled out my hair by the handfuls. Any single symptom may not mean much, but together they spell trouble.

I am glad many of those old, repressed memories surfaced, even though I hated the trauma that forced me to deal with them. I could finally allow the God of my heart, mind, and soul to begin treating me with His healing balm. Late into the difficult process something wonderful happened. I began experiencing a different kind of memory retrieval. I started remembering various interventions and activities of a God who was with me all along. I began to remember afresh that significantly wonderful things also happened to me as a child and a youth. My life also had some good in the midst of the bad and ugly.

Whether the scales in your life tipped toward the negative or the positive, you and I are going to practice a different kind of memory retrieval. Through the leadership of the Holy Spirit, we are going to go back and retrace God's goodness to us. Perhaps you've never forgotten, but have you ever carefully recorded His faithfulness toward you over the course of your life? That's exactly what we're going to do.

Read Psalm 77:11-12. What kinds of things did the psalmist want to remember?

_____

_____

_____

We're going to personalize the psalmist's words, applying his historical reference to "long ago" to our personal long ago. We're going to look back and see what treasures we can find, sometimes even in the midst of rubble. Like detectives searching for evidence, we'll look for the fingerprints of our invisible God interspersed throughout our lives. Beloved, God has been there all along—even before we acknowledged Him as Savior. He is the infinite, eternal, omnipresent God who woos to His heart those who will draw near. It's time for some positive memory retrieval, Dear One. The kind that edifies rather than terrifies. I can hardly wait!

We're also going to retrace some of the most powerful life lessons and truths God taught us along the way. Do you remember when we first began this Bible-study journey and I told you that God often allows me to see order in the things He has done in my life? Over the next two weeks in the Faith Journal section you are going to write your own book of your personal journey with God. Whether or not you realize it, you have a book inside you! Let's get some of it down on paper. Please participate fully. I hope you'll at least do what is requested, but you can go into far greater detail than I'll suggest if you desire. I pray that this journal will become priceless to you and your children in the years to come.

I love what the *World Book Encyclopedia* offers on the subject of remembering: "Memory is a vital part of the learning process. Without it, learning would be impossible. If your brain recorded nothing from the past, you would be unable to learn anything new. All your experiences would be lost as soon as they ended, and each new situation would be totally unfamiliar. Without memory, you would repeatedly have the same experiences for the 'first time.' Memory gives a richness to life—the pleasure of happy remembrances as well as the sorrow of unhappy ones."[1]

What spiritual applications can you draw from these thoughts?

_____

_____

_____

Take a look at John 14:26. This verse is going to become our watchword over the next two weeks. What activities of the Holy Spirit are described in this verse?

_____

_____

_____

When you and I received Christ, the Holy Spirit took up immediate residence inside us. He has many roles, but one targeted in John 14:26 is most involved in the task before us. The Holy Spirit is the blessed Reminder. Guess what else the verse says He is? The Counselor! I believe we can make an application to our present goal of remembering God. The Holy Spirit is the divine Counselor we can thoroughly trust to evoke memories that are true, edifying, and steeped in Jesus. Right now I ask you to enter distinctly directed prayer. Ask God to cause His Holy Spirit to remind you of Jesus' works throughout your life: His presence, His activity, and things He has taught and revealed to you along your journey.

Like a river spilling into an ocean, actively remembering God in our past spills into believing God for our future. Beloved, whether or not we're able to discover palpable evidence, we can be certain that God was faithful even when we were faithless (see 2 Tim. 2:13). He was making GodStops long before we started to notice. You and I are about to go on a GodStop-hunt in the jungle of our pasts.

These next few weeks will mean as much to you as you'll let them. I don't want you to miss a single blessing God may have for you. Commit to active participation!

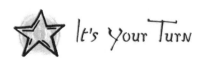 It's Your Turn

1. Place your current age in this blank: _____ . Divide your age by 5: _____ . (If the number doesn't divide evenly, round it to the closest number.) In the Faith Journal sections of weeks 7–8 you will be interviewed about and encouraged to remember God's apparent activity in each fifth of your life. Because 10 days of homework will be involved, you will take two days to consider each fifth. For instance, I am 45 years old as I write this study, and 45 divided by 5 is 9. Therefore, on days 1–2 of this week I'll respond to the interview based on the first 9 years of my life. On days 3–4 I'll respond

according to the second 9 years of my life and so forth. No matter what your age is, this math model will work. Even if you're 20, you can consider your life story in 4-year increments. Fill in the blanks below so that you will know in advance how to group the years of your life in the interviewing process.

Week 7, days 1–2: first fifth of your life (birth to _____)
Week 7, days 3–4: second fifth of your life (ages _____ to _____)
Week 7, day 5, and week 8, day 1: third fifth of your life (ages _____ to _____)
Week 8, days 2–3: fourth fifth of your life (ages _____ to _____)
Week 8, days 4–5: fifth fifth of your life (ages _____ to _____—record present
    month and year)

2. Read each of the following Scriptures and describe God's specific involvement in human life.

Psalm 139:13-16 (record every involvement listed by the psalmist)_____

_____

_____

Jeremiah 1:5 _____

_____

Acts 17:26-27 _____

_____

faith Journal

We will now begin the interview process on the first fifth of your life, and it will continue in tomorrow's Faith Journal. Please complete the following inquiries in complete sentences, when possible, as if you are being interviewed for a magazine article or documentary.

Reflections on the First Fifth of My Life: Birth to _____

Did any kind of wonders surround your birth? If so, explain. (If you were conceived outside marriage, Dear One, consider the wonder of a sovereign God who made sure you made it to this earth when abortion is such a frequent practice today.)

_____

_____

_____

_____

Describe the emotional and spiritual climate of your family of origin at the time of your birth. Include where you fell in the birth order of your siblings and whether both parents remained in the family unit throughout the first fifth of your life.

_____

_____

_____

What, if any, is your spiritual heritage from your great-grandparents forward? If you don't have a spiritual heritage, please meditate and then write on the wonder of being among the first in your family line born of the Spirit of God. Please read John 1:12-13.

_____

_____

_____

As you look back on your life from a GodStop perspective, do you believe that God placed you among your family members for your sake or for theirs or both? Please explain.

_____

_____

_____

Who if any among your extended family members had the most impact on early seeds of Christian belief planted in your life? (For now don't answer for anyone outside the family.) Ask God to reveal to you even the least hints toward faith in Christ.

_____

_____

_____

_____

Conclude by thanking God for all He's going to show you in the days to come.

_____

_____

_____

_____

GodStops

BEDTIME MEDITATION

_____

_____

_____

_____

_____

_____

DAY 2

HOW GOD REMEMBERS

Yesterday we talked about the power of memory, the imagination, and the fact that our creative minds were fashioned in the image of a very creative God. We have the ability to remember because our Maker remembers. He equipped us with a reflective capacity for our blessing and benefit. Try to imagine the infinite mind of God. Do you realize that He remembers things that haven't even happened yet? His memory is eternal and unconfined by time. He remembers the future as actively as He remembers the past. Ouch. My brain hurts. Let's try to think more finitely in terms we can understand from God's Word. What can we comprehend about how God's memory works? Let's find out together. Travel with me to the first place in Scripture we see a reference to memory.

Today's Treasure

God remembered Noah and all the wild animals and the livestock that were with him in the ark, and he sent a wind over the earth, and the waters receded.
Genesis 8:1

Grab your galoshes and turn to Genesis 8:1. Whom and what did God remember?

_____

Do you find a sudden mention of God remembering a little unsettling? Wouldn't you hope that after God commanded you to build an ark for your family and a host of beasts and birds, then sent a flood to destroy all other life, He might not forget you were there? I can't imagine anything more terrifying than believing I could be forgotten by God, particularly when I was tossing about on an angry sea.

Read Isaiah 49:15-16. How serious is God's assurance that we never leave His mind?

_____

If God never forgets His children, what does He mean when He says He remembers us? I'd like to suggest to you that for God _remembered_ isn't the opposite of _forget_. Later in the week we will view some very specific things God chooses to forget, but God's practice of remembering entails something far broader than the antonyms of those things. I'd like to interject Your Turn at this point in the lesson so that you can discover the biblical evidence to support the direction this lesson will take. This lesson will intentionally be brief and abruptly concluded because I want the final concept to whirl around in your mind like a funnel cloud until we settle the dust tomorrow.

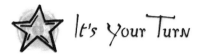 It's Your Turn

Please read each of the following Scriptures that first introduce us to the memory of God. Record in the columns what or whom God remembered and any subsequent action He took or promised.

	God Remembered	Then God …
Genesis 8:1	_____	_____
	_____	_____
	_____	_____
Genesis 19:29	_____	_____
	_____	_____
	_____	_____
Genesis 30:22	_____	_____
	_____	_____
	_____	_____
Exodus 6:5-6	_____	_____
	_____	_____
	_____	_____
Numbers 10:9	_____	_____
	_____	_____
	_____	_____

Based on these Scriptures, what can you conclude about how God remembers?

_____

_____

The vast majority of references to God remembering also record a subsequent action or promise of action. Beloved, God never forgets His people. When the Word says that God remembers, we can assume a subsequent action on His part, even if it is not specified. Almost every time we see a reference to God remembering, He is about to stretch forth His mighty arm and swing into action. And when He stands, His enemies scatter (see Ps. 68:1). Glory! As you discovered in the previous Scriptures, most of the time the action is included, if not implied, in the context of God's remembrance. Hear this carefully: God acts on what He remembers.

My concluding suggestion? Beloved, so do we.

faith Journal

Today we will continue our focus on the first fifth of your life: from birth to _____. Respond to the following inquiries accordingly. Recheck yesterday's journaling to recapture the mood and context.

Were you exposed to any religious education through church or school during this period of your life? Describe the way you view it in retrospect.

_____

_____

_____

Who, if anyone, outside your extended family had the most influence on you spiritually during this time? Please explain how.

_____

_____

_____

What major or pivotal events occurred in this season, and how did they influence your life and the lives of close family members? Record any relocation, divorce, or death in the family and any birth or influential/consequential event. If you received Christ as Savior during this season of your life, document and date this experience. No matter what fifth of your life included your acceptance of Jesus, give a brief testimony of your understanding at that time. Also include any immediate impact it may have had on your life. Give your age at the time of each pivotal occurrence.

_____

_____

_____

_____

As you view this period of your life in retrospect, can you see any ways Christ revealed Himself or showed any level of activity? List every example that comes to your mind.

_____

_____

_____

Did any life lessons emerge from this season that you realize in retrospect were dimensions of God's character (for instance, truth, grace, justice, compassion, etc.)? If God can speak through Balaam's donkey and pagan kings, He can speak through anyone. God can teach us lessons reflecting dimensions of godliness through teachers who may themselves be oblivious to His activity.

_____

_____

_____

Explain in your own words what John 1:17 says. _____

_____

What does this verse tell you about the ultimate origin of those characteristics in our otherwise dark and depraved world?

_____

_____

First John 4:7 tells us to love one another, for love comes from God. Name every person you know for certain truly loved you during the first fifth of your life. Include how you knew they loved you.

_____

_____

_____

Whether or not they knew Jesus personally and taught you about Him, can you accept that even their ability to love you and demonstrate their love was born in the heart of God? God can love us through people who don't even know He exists. All true love originates in God. How did those individuals confirm God's love for you?

_____

_____

_____

 GodStops

B E D T I M E   M E D I T A T I O N

_____

_____

_____

_____

_____

_____

DAY 3
HOW WE REMEMBER

I'm so glad you're back. Grant me this opportunity to tell you the great joy you are to me. Thank you so much for allowing me the privilege to serve you and join you on this walk of faith. If I were you, I suppose I'd have trouble fathoming how a person I'd never met could love me and feel so close to me. Conceivable or not, it's a fact: a miracle of the heart that God performs on servants who desire their offerings to be acceptable rather than rendered null and void by the absence of love (see 1 Cor. 13:1-3). I constantly think of all of you, picture your faces, and imagine your challenges. God places you ever before me and uses you in countless ways to keep me pressing on in the Lord Jesus even when my physical body is weary. I desire nothing more than to wash your feet with the water of God's Word. "To this end I labor, struggling with all his energy, which so powerfully works" in any of us who let it (see Col. 1:29).

Recall yesterday's lesson. What insight did you gain from the Scriptures pertaining to God remembering?

_____

_____

 Today's Treasure

I remember my affliction and my wandering, the bitterness and the gall.
I well remember them, and my soul is down cast within me.
Lamentations 3:19-20

I hope you grasped the concept that, as shown in every verse we considered, when God remembered, He acted. Our concluding suggestions were these: God acts on what He remembers. So do we.

Like every other part of (at least) our immaterial being, our memories were created in the image of God's. Though ours are imperfect and often highly selective, make no mistake: we act on most what we remember most. At first glance you might think I'm contradicting the points I made about repressed memories earlier this week. You'll remember that I said I very actively behaved from the horrible things that had happened to me, even though I diligently tried not to actively picture them. Like all victims of repression, my memories remained. Just because I didn't look them in the face doesn't mean I didn't act on them daily. The constant nagging of something negative and frightful constitutes a viable measure of memory even before the specifics take form. Repressed and suppressed memories do not equal amnesia. They are still memories. In fact, mine were very much with me before I faced them. Thankfully, not everyone can relate to my experience, but we are going to consider a memory practice we can all apply.

Read Lamentations 3:17-20 and try to relate to the emotions implied and expressed. Surely the prophet Jeremiah spoke for all of us at one time or another. The words and their meanings are so clear in verses 19-20 of the NIV. Please be sure to read Today's Treasure on the previous page, as well as from any other version you are using. Then answer the following questions completely candidly for your benefit in the Lord.

How actively do you remember your previous affliction(s)? If you're like most of us and have lived long enough to have plenty of them, which come to mind most often?

_____

_____

Have you had a season of wandering? Remember Isaiah 29:13. We can wander in our hearts even if our mouths remain close to God and our bodies still occupy a church pew. If you have had a season of wandering, what can you remember about it?

_____

_____

Let's get really honest. What memories bring the most bitterness and gall to you?

_____

_____

How often does your mind turn to these memories or to their effects?

_____

_____

Read again Lamentations 3:20. When you remember these things well, does your soul, like Jeremiah's, sometimes become downcast within you? Mine surely does! Describe what these kinds of memories can do to you if you let them.

_____

_____

When we meditate on our afflictions and wanderings—the bitterness and the gall of life—we can depend on our souls feeling downcast. You see, even our inner self will act on what we remember most.

Now let's watch Jeremiah deliberately (albeit temporarily) refocus his mind. Read Lamentations 3:17–25. and describe the specific ways he refocused.

_____

_____

_____

Let's watch the same back-and-forth shift in focus displayed by the psalmist in Psalm 42. Read the entire psalm, noting the mood and mental shifts of the psalmist throughout his honest if not totally accurate portrayal. (Take note of v. 6. We have already learned that God cannot forget His children, but sometimes His children can honestly, though not accurately, feel forgotten.) Like Jeremiah in the Book of Lamentations, the psalmist also suffered from a downcast soul and one that was disturbed within him.

Based on the context, can you surmise what you think motivated his downcast estate?

_____

_____

_____

In Psalm 42:5 the psalmist had a talk with his own soul. What did he say to it?

_____

_____

_____

Have you ever had a talk with your own soul? ❏ Yes ❏ No If so, what did you say?

_____

_____

_____

_____

⭐ It's Your Turn

Read Psalm 42:5 in your Bible. Consider and underline several synonyms for each of the following words. Note any insights or points of interest.

Cast down: _Transliteration: shachach; Phonetic Pronunciation: shaw-khakh'; Part of Speech: v; English Words used in KJV: bow down, cast down, bring down, brought low, bow, bending, couch, humbleth, low, stoop;_ 1) to bow, crouch, bow down, be bowed down 1a) (Qal) 1a1) to be bowed down, be prostrated, be humbled 1a2) to bow (in homage) 1a3) to bow (of mourner) 1a4) to crouch (of wild beast in lair) 1b) (Niphal) to be prostrated, be humbled, be reduced, be weakened, proceed humbly, be bowed down 1c) (Hiphil) to prostrate, lay low, bow down 1d) (Hithpolel) to be cast down, be despairing

_____

Disquieted: *Transliteration: hamah; Phonetic Pronunciation: haw-maw'; Part of Speech: v* *Vines Words: Multitude; English Words used in KJV: roar, noise, disquieted, sound, troubled,* *aloud, loud, clamorous, concourse, mourning, moved, raged, raging, tumult, tumultuous, uproar,* *1)* to murmur, growl, roar, cry aloud, mourn, rage, sound, make noise, tumult, be clamorous, be disquieted, be loud, be moved, be troubled, be in an uproar; 1a) (Qal) 1a1) to growl 1a2) to murmur (fig. of a soul in prayer) 1a3) to roar 1a4) to be in a stir, be in a commotion 1a5) to be boisterous, be turbulent

---

Hope: *Transliteration: yachal; Phonetic Pronunciation: yaw-chal'; Part of Speech: v;* *English Words used in KJV: hope, wait, tarry, trust, variant, stayed;* 1) to wait, hope, expect, 1a) (Niphal) to wait 1b) (Piel) 1b1) to wait, await, tarry 1b2) to wait for, hope for 1c) (Hiphil) to wait, tarry, wait for, hope for

---

Help: *Transliteration: yeshuw`ah; Phonetic Pronunciation: yesh-oo'-aw; Part of Speech: n f;* *Vines Words: Deliver (To), Save (To); English Words used in KJV: salvation, help, deliverance,* *health, save, saving, welfare;* 1) salvation, deliverance 1a) welfare, prosperity 1b) deliverance 1c) salvation (by God) 1d) victory

---

Countenance: *Transliteration: paniym; Phonetic Pronunciation: paw-neem' pl. (but always* *as sing.) of an unused noun; Transliteration: paneh; Phonetic Pronunciation: paw-neh'; Part of* *Speech: n m; Vines Words: Face; English Words used in KJV: before, face, presence, because, sight,* *countenance, from, person, upon, of, me, against, him, open, for, toward;* 1) face 1a) face, faces 1b) presence, person 1c) face (of seraphim or cherubim) 1d) face (of animals) 1e) face, surface (of ground) 1f) as adv of loc//temp 1f1) before and behind, toward, in front of, forward, formerly, from beforetime, before 1g) with prep 1g1) in front of, before, to the front of, in the presence of, in the face of, at the face or front of, from the presence of, from before, from before the face of

---

In Psalm 42:6 the psalmist deliberately refocused his memory, much the way Jeremiah did. What did the psalmist decide to remember?

I recently heard a wonderful song confessing that we humans don't have a sea of forgetfulness. Been there. You and I don't have a sea of forgetfulness we can cast things into. Much of it is all right here. Jeremiah and the psalmist knew they had complete freedom to pour out their hearts before God. They also knew that the more they focused on bad or hard memories, the more downcast they felt. We saw that both of them deliberately refocused and reframed the difficult memories in the goodness and faithfulness of God. Mind you, they didn't throw away the memories. They couldn't.

Neither can we, short of a lobotomy. We have to deal with them before God just as they did. We have to get the old pictures a new frame.

Like Jeremiah and the psalmist, we can reframe difficult memories against the backdrop of God's attributes. We can also call on His ability to change the course of our futures, no matter the pattern of our pasts. In these ways we practice the very essence of 2 Corinthians 10:3-5, taking captive our difficult memories to the knowledge of our powerful God. He breaks the strongholds of our negative meditations when we reframe our old memories with God in the picture. Anytime we agree to see God accurately in any portrait, all else dwarfs—bows down—in His presence. The difficulty soon becomes little more than a short measuring stick by which we estimate the size of a huge God.

Beloved, both freedom and faith emerge from deliberate acts of the will to shift our focus from all that begs to differ to the great and glorious truth of the living God. Neither freedom nor faith is ever accidental. As we refocus on the God of our past and remember His goodness, we are far more inclined to believe Him in our present and future. Be deliberate, Dear One. Remember, we're going to act on that which we remember most. God has been faithful to each of us. He cannot be otherwise. Let's shift our focus to the memory of His overriding faithfulness, then begin acting on that. How about an upcast soul for a change?

faith Journal

We will now begin the interview process on the second fifth of your life and continue in tomorrow's Faith Journal. You will notice that many of the inquiries will be similar, if not identical, because I want your thoughts to be organized when the time comes to draw our final conclusions.

Reflections on the Second Fifth of My Life: Ages _____ to _____

How would you characterize your home life through this period of time?

_____

_____

_____

_____

What did you learn about God during those critical years that you realize in retrospect was accurate?

_____

_____

_____

_____

Did you perceive or were you taught anything about God in those years that you realize in retrospect was not accurate?

_____

_____

_____

_____

How did God later make sure you knew the truth? Please don't miss the fact that any clarified misconception about God originates with Him, not with man. Truth comes only from the Spirit of truth, no matter the instrument He employs.

_____

_____

_____

_____

Could you perceive God at all in nature at these ages? If so, how?

_____

_____

_____

_____

See Romans 1:20 and Psalm 19:1-4.

Did you have any belief in miracles? If so, why?

_____

_____

_____

_____

_____

_____

In retrospect, can you pinpoint any areas of God's intervention or activity in your life during those years? In other words, can you find any GodStops in the scenes of your second fifth of life? If so, please list them.

_____

_____

_____

_____

How would you respond if God told you that He never took His eyes off of you during those years?

_____

_____

_____

_____

GodStops

B E D T I M E   M E D I T A T I O N

_____

_____

_____

_____

_____

_____

_____

_____

_____

_____

THE IMPORTANCE OF
DEVELOPING A GOD-MEMORY

Today's Treasure

*Then they believed his
promises and sang
his praise.
But they soon forgot what
he had done and did
not wait for his counsel.*
Psalm 106:12-13

This week we focus on remembering God. Let's travel in our imaginations once more to the shore on the other side of the Jordan, where in our session 7 video we watched 12 Israelites retrieve 12 stones from the Jordan riverbed.

Fill in the following blanks. If you don't remember the details, check Joshua 4:4-7.

Each of the 12 Israelites took up a stone on his _____.

Joshua told the Israelites that in the future their _____ would ask

them, _____.

The stones were to be a _____ to the people of Israel forever.

You and I committed to follow suit. Whether or not you realize it, you have been returning to your own Jordan riverbed retrieving rocks all week in your Faith Journaling sections! The primary goal of this Bible study is to call the willing to their personal promised lands to walk by faith and live in victory. I refuse to believe you are the exception. You didn't just wander into a Bible study meant for others but not for you. You aren't the one believer who has no promised land equivalent for your New Testament life. First Corinthians 2:9 and Ephesians 1:18; 2:10 were written as surely for you as for anyone else.

That you've traveled so far into this journey of faith testifies to your tenacity, especially considering that this Bible study is only one piece of your adventure with God. I am believing God for your promised land, Beloved. God wired me strangely. I can't be satisfied with simply finding my own. I won't rest until you find yours, too. Listen carefully, Dear One: you have not gotten this far in your journey with God without His footprints planted all over your path and without His fingerprints all over the doorknobs to every new season. You have not arrived accidentally in your present place on the map of your Holy Land. You have had an amazing ride with God, whether or not you realize it.

The primary purpose of your Faith Journaling section this week and next is to help you arrive at a fresh realization. Every now and then someone says, "Beth, I wish I had an exciting story like yours. Mine has been so boring." Beloved, listen up. If you know Jesus Christ, you have embarked on an amazing adventure. He is never boring. The only difference between you and me is that I have been forced to analyze and articulate my journey with Him. When you do the same, you will also wake up to the realization that you have been on a wild ride all along. Perhaps you've just been napping through part of it. Let's wake up and feel the wind in our face!

One of my favorite old hymns begins with the words:

> Blessed assurance, Jesus is mine!
> Oh, what a foretaste of glory divine![2]

The chorus rings, "This is my story, this is my song." Dear One, if you have Jesus, you have a story. My prayer is that the Holy Spirit will help you articulate it as He reminds you of Jesus and His works throughout your life. Bride of Christ, you were already on the great adventure of faith even when Jesus was wooing you, drawing you, and if I may be so bold, flirting with you. He was there long before you asked Him to make your heart His home. I'm hoping God is going to help you recognize and remember all the chess pieces He moved to get you across that board, into His hand, and into your land.

You're not just organizing your story for your sake: "In the future, when your children ask you …" (Josh. 4:6). Every believer is called to bear the fruit of spiritual offspring, born of God through your living witness, but perhaps you also have physical offspring. The ancient Hebrews considered sharing their heritage of faith with children and grandchildren their most important responsibility (see Deut. 6). Have you organized your faith adventure with God into stories you can share with your children and grandchildren? Writing them on paper allows you to leave documentation they can share with the next generation after you've gone to live with the Lord.

Don't feel that your stories have to be dramatic to be important. Years ago in the peak of the Arkansan racial riots, my father crossed invisible lines and served in the African-American community by helping with one of their churches. Today he takes bread to hungry people one day a week. These treasures are priceless to me. If no one left those kinds of faith stories to you, you should have an even greater motivation for leaving yours to your offspring, whether spiritual or physical. You may want to go much further than the simple questions in Faith Journaling. I hope you'll write your own book! Who would read it? Hopefully, your children and your grandchildren. That's the meat. Everything else is gravy. You see, if my own children don't emotionally and spiritually buy those books I've written, they mean nothing. My authenticity to them is more important than what any number of others think.

Every question in Faith Journaling throughout weeks 7 and 8 is an opportunity for you to go back to that Jordan River, draw out a stone of remembrance, and retrace the path that God paved from your wilderness to your promised land. Even if no one else ever reads it, Beloved, you need to know your own story. God has done so much behind the scenes in your behalf. My prayer is that He will divulge a few of those hidden treasures through His Holy Spirit as you look back.

Today in It's Your Turn we're going to discover one huge reason to remember God's faithfulness. I'll meet you there.

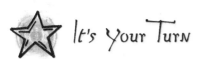 It's Your Turn

Psalm 106 is unparalleled in tracing the familiar cycle of remembering and forgetting. Read the entire psalm very carefully. Then roughly outline the chapter on the following lines. The key words you want to notice are forms and tenses of the words *remember* and *forget*. Your notes will help you draw a diagram of the obvious behavioral cycle later.

_____

_____

_____

_____

_____

What invariably happened after the Israelites forgot God's mighty acts and kindnesses on their behalf?

_____

_____

Dear One, if you and I really start believing God, we will undoubtedly see His mighty acts as never before. I can testify that I have seen more explicit divine action in the past five years than in the sum total of many previous years. At times God has been so palpable that He nearly scared me death. Perhaps you can relate as I share that I've spent most of my life pursuing God, and if I believe anything at all, I believe that He exists and is who He says He is. But every now and then for just a moment He does something that removes all doubt, and I find myself in near physical pain, wanting to cry out, "Woe is me!" I almost can't handle the exposure.

My point? As we begin really believing God and He rewards us with various revelations of Himself or His activity, God forbid that we'd grow casual in a few years and forget what we have seen. When He appoints us to wait on Him in an important matter, God forbid that we'd return to our whining and complaining that He never does anything for us. I still have so much to learn about believing God, but of two things I'm certain: God means to be noticed, and God means to be remembered. If we receive surpassing revelations from Him and don't prove grateful and mindful, I don't think we'd be off base to imagine that we could end up in a future bondage exceeding any past bondage we have experienced. Praise God, He won't break His covenant with us, and He will still hear us when we cry, but the meantime could be painful. Fair warning. Lest we ever forget it, responsibility accompanies revelation.

Now that you've had the benefit of more time to organize your thoughts on Psalm 106, please draw and label the cycle you see in the psalmist's pictorial chapter. Keep in mind that you are simply diagraming your impressions of the forget-remember cycle of the Israelites and their God. Don't try to come up with "right" answers.

Will you humbly go with me one more step? I promise that this step is for our benefit and not our self-condemnation. Human nature naturally falls into behavioral cycles until we invite God to graciously and powerfully break them. We've all practiced negative behavioral cycles. As I consider mine, can you think how the most common cycle of your past has looked? If you're willing, draw the basic cycle below.

Dear One, if by any chance you still feel caught in that cycle, your realization and confession to God represent the biggest leap to freedom. Believe Him to break that cycle and create a new one that spirals up instead of down!

faith Journal

Today we continue with inquiries based on the second fifth of your life: ages _____ to _____.
What pivotal events, traumas, or life markers occurred during those years of your life? Please document
anything of importance on the lines below and approximate your age as accurately as you can.

_____

_____

_____

_____

_____

_____

_____

_____

_____

Has retrospect allowed you to see any GodStops among those markers? If so, describe them.

_____

_____

_____

_____

Identify the people who had the most profound spiritual impact on you during this period of your life and describe how. Perhaps you weren't a believer at this time and didn't know any Christians. In retrospect, can you think of anyone who demonstrated the character of Christ to you? How?

_____

_____

_____

_____

If you attended church during those years, what was the level of its impact and your involvement?

_____

_____

_____

_____

How would you characterize your relationship with or view of God during those years?

_____

_____

_____

_____

What was the most powerful life lesson God taught you during this period of your life?

_____

_____

_____

Beloved, keep drawing forth those stones of remembrance and reframing some of those hard memories with the God who never took His eyes off you.

 **GodStops**

B E D T I M E   M E D I T A T I O N

_____

_____

_____

_____

_____

_____

REMEMBERING NO MORE

Sometimes I chide myself for being so forgetful. Other times I berate myself for remembering something far too long. Humans often forget what we need to remember and remember what we need to forget.

Can you relate? In what ways do you tend to be forgetful?

_____

_____

In what ways do you tend to have a memory that works too well?

_____

_____

This week in our study we've somewhat redefined remembering according to God's apparent practice of the term. From the context of many Old Testament references to God remembering, what have we discovered about the biblical term?

_____

_____

Today's Treasure

"I, even I, am he who
   blots out
   your transgressions,
   for my own sake,
   and remembers your
   sins no more."
Isaiah 43:25

As people created in His image, what similarities to God have you discovered in yourself this week?

_____

_____

I hope you answered the previous two questions without hesitation: When God remembers, He acts, and we too most often act on what we most remember. Our memories were given for us. Not against us. Our challenge is to pursue the appropriate practice of memory. How would we define such a thing? It means remembering the vastness of a powerful and sovereign God most of all in every situation we recall. Remembering God makes up a vital part of believing God. Our past-tense faith feeds our present-active-participle believing God.

When we talked about God's memory being unlimited by time, I suggested that God can remember the future as well as the past. For example, all fulfilled prophecy is a way God remembers the future. You and I obviously don't have the capability to remember the future. We can, however, go back into our pasts through the power of the Holy Spirit and find God there. We're not just imagining His presence. God's Word gives us complete assurance. Our attempt is to see if we can recognize Him in the rearview mirror.

In a peculiar way we are indeed getting to step over the confines of time. Backwards. We are walking back through our imaginations into situations we may have viewed as hopeless or faithless at the time. By believing God was there all along—wooing us, planning for us, loving us, and contending with those who contended with us—we are getting to infuse our pasts with present-active-participle faith. Who said we can't change the past? Beloved, when we allow God to change the way we see our pasts, the power of our pasts changes dramatically. In a wonderful way we are also getting to go back to situations in which we feel we've been unfaithful to God and fill them with retroactive faith: belief that God can do miraculous good even with terrible failure. I am certainly proof of that. Seeing even my worst failures through God's sovereignty and faithfulness dramatically changes their impact on me.

Several of the things I hate remembering most are the very motivators to obedient servant living today. I remember where I've been, and I assure you I never want to go back. That, my dear friend, is precisely why God remembers our sins no more but we remember many of them to the death. Do you recall the wonderful remarks on memory we read in day 1 from the _World Book Encyclopedia_? One statement reads, "If your brain recorded nothing from the past, you would be unable to learn anything new."[3] Frankly, Beloved, I have most effectively learned to walk around the pit because I have such a vivid memory of falling into it.

I'd like to suggest, however, in light of our new concept of biblical remembering that we can forget in one of the same ways God does.

What good news does Today's Treasure bring us?

_____

_____

That's not the only place we'd find the concept. Without a doubt, Scripture consistently teaches that when God's people turn back to Him, He forgives us and remembers our sins no more. Hallelujah! But how does His apparent ability to drop something out of His mind like dirty clothes through a laundry chute fit into His omniscience? His infinite ability to know all things? I've talked over my past with God a hundred times. Even my past sins. I desperately needed to hash out some whys and hows before God, cry to Him, tell Him how they haunted me. I didn't need God to act as if He had no idea what I was talking about. Long after I was forgiven, I still needed to talk about the pain and to process the situation with my divine Counselor. What if I had gotten a blank stare from God as though He had no idea what I was talking about?

I'm going to warn you that you may not like my theory. Your consolation will be knowing that I could be off base and that the concept you want to believe about God's forgetfulness may well be doctrinally accurate. With that loophole in place, hear me out for a moment. If God's primary way of remembering is to act on behalf of what He remembers, could it be that His primary way of remembering no more is to no longer act on the memory? Thankfully, in most cases our sin is what God has committed to remember no more. You and I are recipients of the new covenant. Our atonement is in the sacrificial death of the Lamb of God, Christ Jesus.

Please read Hebrews 10:11-18 very carefully in view of the work of the cross. What is the main idea embodied in this passage of Scripture?

_____

_____

What does Hebrews 10:17 say God will do with our sins? _____

_____

What does Hebrews 10:18 say? _____

_____

Do you see any hint of the theory I've suggested? God remembers our sins no more because the work of the cross already has. No further sacrifice remains for sin because the work has already been accomplished. God need never act again on behalf of those sins. Christ remembered them on the cross and already acted on their behalf. Therefore,

> "Their sins and lawless acts
>   I will remember no more" (Heb 10:17).

Does all memory of my past sins suddenly drop out of the all-knowing mind of God, or does His satisfaction in the work of the cross prevent His acting on them again? Either way, Beloved, we win. The effects are the same. I have come to trust the loving heart and faithful thoughts of my God. One way or another, God will never act in judgment over my sins or yours again. Chastisement is another matter. Keep in mind that the original meaning of the word discipline is inseparable from disciple. Chastisement or discipline is always about instruction. Any discipline we receive is always to teach us and protect us in our present and our future, never to condemn our past.

Earlier I suggested that we might also have the ability to forget in a way similar to God's. If remembering no more could mean no longer acting on a memory, you and I are capable of forgetting the most traumatic and painful events of our lives. How? By no longer acting on their behalf! In other words, by no longer allowing them to have power over us. For the longest time I thought renewing the mind meant that every terrible thing I'd ever experienced or done would drop out of my thoughts, never to rise again. When something would occasionally bring an old, painful picture to mind, I'd berate myself and wonder when I would ever forget. Sound familiar? Yet I can tell you that after much concentrated time with *Jehovah Rapha*, though old pictures occasionally pop back in my mind, I no longer act on their behalf. I am convinced this is the essence of forgiving and forgetting.

Try telling a victim of childhood abuse that forgetting is the heart of forgiving. Try telling a husband or a wife whose spouse committed adultery that forgetting is the heart of forgiving. Try telling the mother of a victim of drunk driving that forgetting is the heart of forgiving. They'll never forget. But does that mean they can never forgive? Hardly! The human mind is a storehouse. The profound and pivotal events of our lives are there. Only the unhealthy repressive and suppressive mind forces them from sight while ironically acting on them more than ever.

Beloved, consider that the essence of forgetting is allowing God to heal you and cause you no longer to act on behalf of negative, hurtful, or destructive memories. Biblical forgetting can defuse their negative power of influence. Unfortunately, I'll never forget that I was victimized as a child, but to the glory of my healing God, I can honestly tell you that I never act on it anymore. It no longer empowers my behavior. And because the memories get so little behavioral cooperation these days, they come to the surface less and less. To me, that's forgetting. In that way alone is forgetting the heart of forgiving.

Let God use the truths we have discovered this week to transform your memories:
- Remembering is acting on behalf.
- Forgetting is no longer acting on behalf.
- Remember God. Act on behalf of His constant presence and infusing power.
- Who we remember will always dictate how we remember.
- Remember God in your past. Believe God in your present. This is the stuff of transformation.

 It's Your Turn

Because today's commentary was so lengthy, our time here will be brief. Throughout our study we've compared ourselves to the children of Israel crossing the Jordan and living victoriously in the promised land. We also noted from the beginning that some of the literal applications of the Old Testament commands to the nation of Israel have spiritual applications for us. Please read all of Deuteronomy 8. Its relevance to our subject matter this week will become immediately obvious. On the lines provided, apply several of its priority principles to us and our promised lands.

_____

_____

_____

 faith Journal

Today we begin our responses to inquiries on the third fifth of our lives.

Reflections on the Third Fifth of My Life: Ages _____ to _____

How would you characterize this period of your life? Please write a paragraph description.

_____

_____

_____

_____

_____

_____

If not included above, where did you live during this time, and what was the emotional and spiritual climate of your home?

_____

_____

_____

_____

_____

_____

Who had the most profoundly positive influence on your life during these years and how?

_____

_____

_____

_____

_____

Did you have a relationship with God at this time? If so, how would you describe it, and how did you perceive Him?

_____

_____

_____

_____

_____

In retrospect, can you see ways God revealed Himself or expressed His love and care for you during these years? In other words, as you look back, what GodStops can you find during this time?

_____

_____

_____

_____

_____

_____

_____

_____

_____

_____

_____

_____

¹*The World Book Encyclopedia*, (Chicago: World Book Inc., 2001), s.v. "memory."

²Fanny J. Crosby, "Blessed Assurance, Jesus Is Mine," in *The Baptist Hymnal* (Nashville, TN: Convention Press, 1991), 334.

³*The World Book Encyclopedia*, s.v. "memory."

Believing God to Get You to Your Gilgal

Joshua 5:6 recaptures the basic premise of our study: God has made solemn _____ to His children and desires that we live in the place where we get to enjoy their fulfillment. He requires our faith-induced _____.

See Hebrews 3:18-19 for the association of the following two words:

• Unbelief: *apistia*—a—_____ *pistia*—_____

• Disobedience: *apeitheo*—_____ on our _____

1. Joshua 4–5 retraces Israel's new _____ and an entirely new _____.

2. The word *Gilgal* means _____.

3. Gilgal was the place God brought the Israelites _____ circle and broke the old _____.

   See the dating in Joshua 4:19 (also see Ex. 12:3) and Joshua 5:10 (also see Ex. 12:6,18).

   On a separate piece of paper, please diagram a typical circle or cycle of defeat and another of victory, based on Israel's experience in the wilderness.

4. Gilgal was the place where _____ was reinstated. Circumcision was the sign that they were _____ because they were in covenant with God. Remaining uncircumcised was their way of _____ their _____. *Herpah*—"reproach, shame, scorn, contempt," is often translated _____ in the Old Testament.

5. At Gilgal God cut away the sign of their _____, and they wore the mark of their new _____. Often a _____ precedes our full reception of God's promises, but healing always follows. Joshua 5:8: "Healed"—hayah—"to live, exist, _____ _____; to live anew, recover, be well; … to … refresh, _____." Paradoxically, by this _____ they were _____.

6. God wants to _____ away the _____ of our Egypts from us. "Roll away"—*galal*— "to roll, turn, drive away; … roll upon _____; to be rolled (___ blood), be _____ red."

WEEK

8

Believing God to Get You to Your Gilgal

ONE BELIEVING MAN

Today's Treasure

He said to them all: "If anyone would come after me, he must deny himself and take up his cross daily and follow me."
Luke 9:23

In our session 8 video we circled around the children of Israel in a place of profound significance. Gilgal was their first stop in the promised land, just west of the Jordan River. There they set up 12 stones of remembrance and bore the mark of God's covenant by observing the rite of circumcision. No longer could they be called an unbelieving generation. When the nation of Israel reached Gilgal, a name meaning *circle*, they had indeed come full circle. God removed their reproach, and they could finally put Egypt behind them.

In some dimension a *Gilgal* exists for any child of God who is willing to follow Him there by faith. Consider our Gilgals the places where we realize that God has rolled away our reproach, proved us victorious in a do-over (an opportunity to go back and get something right), or taken us full circle in a significant way. The Apostle Paul is a perfect example of a man who reached his Gilgal. Formerly Christianity's greatest offender, he became its greatest defender. Peter was another. Though he denied Christ before He was crucified, Peter later proclaimed Him so zealously that he met his own crucifixion. Unwilling to die in the same manner as his Lord, he asked to be crucified upside down. Peter's wishes were granted, and he stood before the throne of grace as one unashamed of the gospel of Christ.

All who have experienced the pain of reproach will have the chance to see God roll it away if we persist in believing Him. Some of our Gilgals may not be obvious until we reach heaven, but we can be certain they exist. This week we are going to consider the testimony of several believers whose Gilgals are easier to visualize. I have deliberately chosen testimonies ranging from the 1700s to the present. My goals are three:

- To further establish the Gilgal concept
- To help you learn to recognize your own Gilgal
- To encourage you to believe that God still powerfully uses and blesses people of faith ... and to become one of them

We are going to practice my favorite hobby. In fact, I had to double-check with God to make sure this week's study wasn't self-serving! I love to read the biographies and autobiographies of people through the centuries who have loved and served God with all their hearts. I devour books on the lives of the faithful-though-fallible. The testimonies of Saint Augustine, Jan Hus, Martin Luther, Jonathan Edwards, Oswald Chambers, Amy Carmichael, and Charles Spurgeon are just a few. This morning I again told God that I want to be faithful to Him more than anything in the world. Reading about the lives of those who fulfilled such a high calling is like a strong wind against my back as I run my race.

Though we have much in common with Christ's first motley crew of followers, our experiences also vary. You and I haven't seen the living Lord face-to-face as the first disciples did. He did not breathe His very spirit on us while standing bodily before our very eyes. We did not see Christ ascend from the Mount of Olives or witness tongues of fire falling on us at that first post-resurrection Pentecost. Most of us haven't encountered the risen Lord Jesus on the road to Damascus. Yes, their faith was gigantic, but it was also fueled by sight.

At first glance, you and I and all others who have composed the church of Jesus Christ through the centuries may seem to be at a decided disadvantage ... until we read John 20:29. What words ultimately involving us did Christ say to Thomas?

_____

Beloved, take this seriously and personally: Christ Jesus has promised blessing to those of us who have not seen with our own eyes and yet believe. If Christ honored the tenacious faith of the disciples who had seen Him face-to-face, how much more will He honor the faith of those Peter described in 1 Peter 1:8? Paraphrase or record what Peter said.

_____

_____

Be blessed to know that the verb believe (NIV) or believing (KJV) in 1 Peter 1:8 is a present-active-participle. So is the verb love! Because we have never seen yet keep believing who Christ is and what He says, our capacity to love and find joy in Him is inexpressible! I may have to disturb the orthodontist next door again with a shout of glory.

D. L. Moody was a 1 Peter 1:8 present-active-participle believer. Just before he set sail to America in 1867, West London evangelist Henry Varley told him, " 'The world has yet to see what God will do with and for and through and in and by the man who is fully and wholly consecrated to him.' "[1] Moody determined to be that man.

Dwight Lyman Moody certainly didn't have the makings of greatness. He was the sixth child of an unhappy marriage. While his mother was eight months pregnant with twins, his father became ill and died. They lost everything but the house and couldn't afford firewood to heat it. Though Moody left few reminiscences of his young years in Northfield, Massachusetts, he testified to having a terrible fear of death as a child. His mother cared little about theology in Dwight's formative years, so he understandably found little solace. And as for his education:

In total Dwight Moody had, at the most, four years of formal schooling. Like the other boys, he went to the local school periodically from about age six to ten. From then on, he was considered old enough to work and help the family. In any case he had as much schooling as most people received in northern New England during the mid 1800s. The quality of his schooling, or at least his attentiveness to what was available, is open to question. The earliest of his letters that have survived date back to 1854 when he was seventeen. His spelling was phonetic. Punctuation was omitted from most early letters. ... Capitalization was randomly applied ... In brief, his spelling, grammar, and usage were surpassed in inferiority only by his penmanship. All of these skills improved over the years, but the crudeness of his early writing makes one certain that his formal schooling never totaled more than three or four years.[2]

Why mention his lack of education? Because Dwight Moody found Jesus—despite the early childhood void and a bout with Unitarianism. He accomplished the impossible for a man of his societal caliber. He established about 150 schools, street missions, soup kitchens, colportage societies, and other charitable organizations—including Chicago's first street boys' clinic. A shoe salesman who became the preeminent evangelist of his day—a difficult task since it followed the War Between the States. He believed in sharing the gospel of Jesus Christ in word and in deed.[3] As usual, authenticity bore much fruit. Moody not only created the concept of Sunday School outreach but also single-handedly pioneered modern crusade evangelism and set precedents followed by every great revivalist afterward from Billy Sunday to Billy Graham.[4]

In 1891 Moody opened Northfield Seminary for Young Women. In 1881 he opened Mount Hermon School for Boys. In 1889 he founded what is now known as the Moody Bible Institute in Chicago. Late in life D. L. Moody uttered a prophetic statement, which is perhaps his most accurate epitaph: " 'I am thankful to tell you that I have some splendid men and women in the field. My school work will not tell much until the century closes, but when I am gone I shall leave some grand men and women behind.' "[5] Moody Bible Institute alone not only equipped over 35,000 students of every denomination with unparalleled undergraduate Bible education for ministry but also trained a massive army of missionaries who have taken that same gospel all over the world.

One characteristic of this believing man impresses me most: Dwight Lyman Moody was originally uneducated but his unceasing teachability produced a scholar of scholars. Early in his ministry Moody had little use for grace theology. Then a man named Moorhouse visited Chicago and had a transforming effect on him. Moody invited the former pickpocket-turned-evangelist to preach while he was away. On learning that Moorhouse taught God's love for the worst of sinners, Moody retorted, " 'Then … he is wrong.' "[6] Having heard the sermon, Moody's wife, Emma, suggested that Moorhouse could back up every word from Scripture. When Moody returned to church the next Sunday morning, everyone had a Bible.

Later Moorhouse told the young preacher, "Your sword is only partially out of the scabbard." Mr. Moorhouse "taught Moody to draw his sword full length, to fling the scabbard away, and enter the battle with the naked blade" and "love them into the Kingdom." Moody attributed the thawing of his heart to Moorhouse. The teachable preacher developed his own passion for the Word and instituted what many consider unsurpassed discipleship. I am impressed by D. L. Moody's willingness to receive constructive criticism and go forward with such zeal that his weakness ultimately became his strength. Beloved, sometimes our hearts are right, but our doctrine is wrong. What fruit is produced when we agree to be teachable … and perhaps even say we were mistaken!

Did D. L. Moody see his Gilgal? Was the reproach of his uneducated background ever rolled away? I'd say so. Moody hasn't been the only one to challenge Henry Varley's theory. Actually, the world in bits and pieces has gotten to glimpse what God can do with and for and through and in and by someone who is fully and wholly consecrated to Him. That's what this week of study is all about.

Throughout the centuries the eyes of God have ranged " 'to and fro throughout the earth that He may strongly support those whose heart is completely His' " (see 2 Chron. 16:9, NASB). Heroes of the faith are sprinkled throughout New Testament history. Some were the only lamps in the darkest ages. Many were martyred for nothing more than their willingness to take God at His Word. Countless examples will remain unknown to the masses until we get to heaven, when Christ will surely mesmerize us with their stories.

What fruit is produced when we agree to be teachable!

The lives we will consider this week will defy the false belief system that one person makes little difference. Their stories are as diverse as their gifts. The only common denominator is wholehearted commitment and present-active-participle faith in the God who does more than we could ask or imagine. God still causes individual lives to make multiple differences.

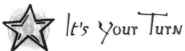 It's Your Turn

1. Write Christ's invitation in Luke 9:23; circle each reference He made to an individual.

_____

_____

_____

As you can see, Christ's invitation was personal. Two parts of a compound word leap from the verse in reference to our lesson today: *any* and *one*. *Any* speaks to me about Christ's ready willingness to lead whoever will follow. We don't have to be particularly gifted, educated, or experienced. *One* reminds me that Christ still extends His invitation to individuals. In ways our finite minds can hardly comprehend, Christ died for millions of ones. Yes, One died for all, but all come as one. Our relationship with Him is intensely personal. Luke 9:23 is written about two persons: the willing follower and his Leader. In this equation one + One = more than we could ask or imagine (see 1 Cor. 2:9; Eph. 3:20).

As I reflect on the words *any* and *one*, a picture comes to my mind from the scene created in John 21:1-8. Read these verses and briefly describe what occurred.

_____

_____

Peter was surrounded by his usual crowd, all fellow followers of Jesus Christ. When Peter saw the resurrected Lord on the shore, however, he couldn't stay in the boat with the rest of them. He swam to shore while the rest followed and towed the net full of fish. Peter was a man overboard. As long as he lived, he remained completely attached to the body of Christ, but no one determined his pace but Jesus. Spiritually speaking, Peter never got back in that boat. Neither did the believers we will study this week.

2. Read 2 Chronicles 16:9 in your Bible. Read in the margin the KJV with *Strong's* definitions. Record any insights you receive.

Strong _____

Heart _____

Perfect (The word *perfect* doesn't mean sinless. Look for further insights into what it means.)

_____

strong
HEBREW STRONG'S NUMBER: 2388
Transliteration: chazaq
Phonetic Pronunciation: khaw-zak'
Part of Speech: v
1) to strengthen, prevail, harden, be strong, become strong, be courageous, be firm, grow firm, be resolute, be sore 1a) (Qal) 1a1) to be strong, grow strong 1a1a) to prevail, prevail upon 1a1b) to be firm, be caught fast, be secure 1a1c) to press, be urgent 1a1d) to grow stout, grow rigid, grow hard (bad sense) 1a1e) to be severe, be grievous 1a2) to strengthen 1b) (Piel) 1b1) to make strong 1b2) to restore to strength, give strength 1b3) to strengthen, sustain, encourage 1b4) to make strong, make bold, encourage 1b5) to make firm 1b6) to make rigid, make hard 1c) (Hiphil) 1c1) to make strong, strengthen 1c2) to make firm 1c3) to display strength 1c4) to make severe 1c5) to support 1c6) to repair 1c7) to prevail, prevail upon 1c8) to have or take or keep hold of, retain, hold up, sustain, support 1c9) to hold, contain 1d) (Hithpael) 1d1) to strengthen oneself 1d2) to put forth strength, use one's strength 1d3) to withstand 1d4) to hold strongly with

heart
HEBREW STRONG'S NUMBER: 3824
Transliteration: lebab
Phonetic Pronunciation: lay-bawb'
Part of Speech: n m
1) inner man, mind, will, heart, soul, understanding 1a) inner part, midst 1a1) midst (of things) 1a2) heart (of man) 1a3) soul, heart (of man) 1a4) mind, knowledge, thinking, reflection, memory 1a5) inclination, resolution, determination (of will) 1a6) conscience 1a7) heart (of moral character) 1a8) as seat of appetites 1a9) as seat of emotions and passions 1a10) as seat of courage

perfect
HEBREW STRONG'S NUMBER: 8003
Transliteration: shalem
Phonetic Pronunciation: shaw-lame'
Part of Speech: adj
1) complete, safe, peaceful, perfect, whole, full, at peace 1a) complete 1a1) full, perfect 1a2) finished 1b) safe, unharmed 1c) peace (of covenant of peace, mind) 1c1) perfect, complete (of keeping covenant relation)

 faith Journal

Recall our plan to continue drawing stones of remembrance from our life stories throughout the Faith Journal section each day this week. Today we will search for GodStops in the third fifth of our lives. Please review the questions and your answers in the Faith Journal section of week 7, day 5 to recapture your context.

Today the inquiries are based on the third fifth of your life: ages _____ to _____.

What pivotal events, traumas, or life markers occurred during these years? Please document anything of importance on the lines below and approximate your age as accurately as you can. If you recall something specific God did to reveal Himself through these markers that you didn't record in our previous lesson, record it here.

_____

_____

_____

_____

Can you think of any lies you believed during these years that God later exposed to you and replaced with His truth? If so, please explain.

_____

_____

_____

GodStops

BEDTIME MEDITATION

_____

_____

_____

_____

_____

PERSEVERING IMPACT

I stepped over ditches of running, raw sewage trying my hardest to watch where I was going in the dark. The winter chill was likely our only respite from the stench. The experience was surreal. I could hardly believe I was living the moment, but I couldn't stop long enough to absorb it. I was walking through villages I'd only read about, so stunned by the poverty that I was almost numb. We gathered in an open place in the squalid village, and several began to preach, however unlawfully. I was too intimidated to say a word until I saw several women timidly gather at the side of the crowd; then love eclipsed my fear. Never had I been in uglier conditions. Never had I seen such beautiful people. I pulled an interpreter aside and asked him to help me speak to the women who were too afraid to join the crowd. During the course of the evening I lost all fear and shared the gospel with anyone who would listen. I am not always certain that someone with whom I've shared the plan of salvation has really received Christ. That night I was sure that many received eternal life.

My heart was disturbed because I wondered how the new converts would ever grow in their new faith surrounded by Hinduism. I spoke with urgency to one of the ministers on the team. A little later he said, "Come with me. I want you to meet someone." We twisted and turned our way through the village and knocked on a door. A young man welcomed us with obvious expectation. His skin was as dark as the night. The delight of his white, toothy smile was a stark paradox amid the filth in the village. The smell of spicy, hot tea welcomed us home. My minister friend said, "Beth, I'd like you to meet our brother. He is God's man in this village. By word of mouth all here learn that they can come knock on this door. His job is to take them from here." Under the threat of severe persecution, ostracism, and death, I might add. Right before my eyes were Scriptures in the native language on the walls of the shanty and in tracts on a small table.

William Carey's India. He was born in August 1761 during what one writer called the " 'dullest period of the dullest of all centuries.' "[7] Leave it to God to take the dull out of any century. (If we're bored, we may be slightly out of touch with God.) Carey, a young husband, father, and cobbler by trade, was part of a group of believing men whom God began to stir for the nations. Though he prayed for God to evangelize all, his heart was drawn to one. While others talked about going to the nations, William Carey packed his bags and his reluctant wife and children to begin a five-month excursion that finally spilled them like a drink offering on the shore of the Bay of Bengal.

The Careys' first years were torturous. Disease claimed the life of his young son, and his wife sorrowed until she virtually lost her mind. Doubt and guilt nearly overtook Carey, but he continued to rehearse in his memory the certainty of his call to India. He persevered to learn the language and did his best to preach at every given opportunity without one convert for the first years. When Mrs. Carey's mind and body could no longer bear the strain, she died, leaving two children for her grieving husband to raise. Confusion and despair loomed, but Carey refused to cease, believing God for a great work in India.

Little by little, William Carey began developing a very specific strength. God gave him a gift for understanding and translating languages. Those with stronger preaching gifts than Carey joined his work, and he soon realized that his calling lay behind a printing press, not a pulpit. He worked tirelessly until the Bible was translated into six different Indian languages and portions translated into 29 others. At one point the small building housing his printing presses went up in flames, consuming vital works

Today's Treasure

Let us not become weary in doing good, for at the proper time we will reap a harvest if we do not give up.
Galatians 6:9

of translations. He started over. William Carey became the devil's nightmare. Every time Satan knocked him down, the man of God stood back to his feet again, more determined than ever.

William Carey's contributions to India were not just academic and evangelical. He campaigned zealously against barbaric Hindu practices. Not only were wives often burned alive on their husbands' funeral pyres as an offering to the gods, but children were also sacrificed at the yearly festival at Gunga Saugor. Against tremendous opposition Carey fought for godly humanitarianism and won. Even now the statute criminalizing infanticide is called the Carey Edict.[8]

How many of us have been outraged by injustices and the oppression of the helpless and poor but wonder what one person can accomplish? Never forget William Carey. Just one man. He gave everything he had and, yes, at great cost. Many would have given up and accepted defeat. At the very least, they would have finally convinced themselves that they misunderstood God. Because William Carey refused to disbelieve and quit, he marked an entire nation. Two hundred years after his arrival in India, the government issued a postage stamp in honor of his almost endless list of achievements.

Did Carey reach his Gilgal? Did life ever come full circle for this man of God? You bet it did. Perhaps in a thousand ways, but let's not miss one: India may have taken the lives of his wife and child, but how many Indian wives and children were saved because William Carey braved the Bay of Bengal? Only heaven knows.

Carey's most famous principle of action was this: "Expect great things from God, attempt great things for God."[9] The key to successful ministry (in the truest, heavenly sense of the term) is hearing from God, seeking reconfirmation if necessary, then wholeheartedly persevering in what we believe He said. We must persevere in our commitment to Christ, not in our commitment to our commitment. William Carey realized that he had come to the right place but in the wrong role. He was not a great preacher. He was a great linguist. We may be in the right place, Beloved, but we may be in the wrong role. Keep seeking God! He will not mislead you.

When we seek God, we will find Him. And when we find Him, we will ultimately find our callings. When we find our callings, let's persist in them, not attempting to do a thousand things well but fanning our gifts to a flame and pursuing excellence in the few. If we do, Beloved, we will reap! The harvest may not become obvious in our lifetime, but it will surely come. Never, never forget this biblical promise: if we sow the things of the Spirit, we will reap the things of the Spirit (see Gal. 6:8-9). Every time. God is faithful. Thank Him in advance for the harvest each time you sow. The flood may not fall on those seeds until after you see Jesus, but the rain will surely come. Believe God! Tirelessly plant the things of the Spirit in the soil of earth. Let nothing make you quit. Though the harvest tarry, it shall come!

⭐ It's Your Turn

1. Read Galatians 6:9 in your Bible. Read in the margin *Strong's* definitions and record the most meaningful portions of the definitions and any insights they give you.

Weary _____

Well _____

---

weary
GREEK STRONG'S NUMBER: 1573
Transliteration: ekkakeo or egkakeo
Phonetic Pronunciation:
  ek-kak-eh'-o or eng-kak-eh'-o
Part of Speech: v
1) to be utterly spiritless, to be wearied out, exhausted

well
GREEK STRONG'S NUMBER: 2570
Transliteration: kalos
Phonetic Pronunciation: kal-os'
Part of Speech: adj
1) beautiful, handsome, excellent, eminent, choice, surpassing, precious, useful, suitable, commendable, admirable 1a) beautiful to look at, shapely, magnificent 1b) good, excellent in its nature and characteristics, and therefore well adapted to its ends 1b1) genuine, approved 1b2) precious 1b3) joined to names of men designated by their office, competent, able, such as one ought to be 1b4) praiseworthy, noble 1c) beautiful by reason of purity of heart and life, and hence praiseworthy 1c1) morally good, noble 1d) honourable, conferring honour 1e) affecting the mind agreeably, comforting and confirming

Doing _____

Due _____

Season _____

2. In Galatians 6:10, whom does Paul suggest we serve as often as we can in well doing?

_____

3. In what ways are you able to benefit those around you during this season of your life, especially those of the household of faith?

_____

_____

4. Do you feel frustrated over the sowing-and-reaping principle or satisfied and encouraged? All of us have experienced seasons of sowing when reaping seemed nowhere in sight. Share what you are presently experiencing, even if it's frustration.

_____

_____

5. How do the wonderful words of Psalm 126 speak to you about today's lesson?

_____

_____

I love this quotation by Oswald Chambers, and I believe it provides a fitting benediction to this portion of our lesson: "Tenacity is more than hanging on, which may be but the weakness of being too afraid to fall off. Tenacity is the supreme effort of a man refusing to believe that his hero is going to be conquered. … Remain spiritually tenacious."[10]

faith journal

Today we begin our responses to inquiries on the fourth fifth of our lives.

Reflections on the fourth fifth of my life: ages _____ to _____

How would you characterize this period of your life?

_____

_____

doing
GREEK STRONG'S NUMBER: 4160
Transliteration: poieo
Phonetic Pronunciation: poy-eh'-o
Part of Speech: v
1) to make 1a) with the names of things made, to produce, construct, form, fashion, etc. 1b) to be the authors of, the cause 1c) to make ready, to prepare 1d) to produce, bear, shoot forth 1e) to acquire, to provide a thing for one's self 1f) to make a thing out of something 1g) to (make i.e.) render one anything 1g1) to (make i.e.) constitute or appoint one anything, to appoint or ordain one that 1g2) to (make i.e.) declare one anything 1h) to put one forth, to lead him out 1i) to make one do something 1i1) cause one to 1j) to be the authors of a thing (to cause, bring about) 2) to do 2a) to act rightly, do well 2a1) to carry out, to execute 2b) to do a thing unto one 2b1) to do to one 2c) with designation of time: to pass, spend 2d) to celebrate, keep 2d1) to make ready, and so at the same time to institute, the celebration of the passover 2e) to perform: to a promise

due
GREEK STRONG'S NUMBER: 2398
Transliteration: idios
Phonetic Pronunciation: id'-ee-os
Part of Speech: adj
1) pertaining to one's self, one's own, belonging to one's self

season
GREEK STRONG'S NUMBER: 2540
Transliteration: kairos
Phonetic Pronunciation: kahee-ros'
Part of Speech: n m
1) due measure 2) a measure of time, a larger or smaller portion of time, hence: 2a) a fixed and definite time, the time when things are brought to crisis, the decisive epoch waited for 2b) opportune or seasonable time 2c) the right time 2d) a limited period of time 2e) to what time brings, the state of the times, the things and events of time

What are your best memories in this period?

_____

_____

What are your hardest memories?

_____

_____

In retrospect can you see ways that God has redeemed any of your difficult memories from this period of time? If so, how?

_____

_____

Did you have a relationship with God at this time? If so, please describe it.

_____

_____

Whom did God use most to influence or bless your life in His behalf at this time?

_____

_____

GodStops

BEDTIME MEDITATION

_____

_____

_____

_____

_____

_____

A SHILLING OF FAITH

Few lives of faith in recent centuries amaze me more than George Müller's. Perhaps one reason his story is so astounding is that our human tendency is to trust God with virtually anything—our health, our children, our circumstances—before we trust Him with our finances. The mere thought makes us squirm, doesn't it? However, you'll want to stay tuned. Any dose of conviction we have to swallow from Müller's testimony is sweetened by his wonderful story.

George Müller was born in Kroppenstaedt, Prussia, in 1805. His father was a tax collector. " 'My father,' Müller recalled later, 'educated his children on worldly principles and gave us much money, considering our age. The result was that it led my brother and me into many sins. Before I was ten years old, I repeatedly took of the government money which was entrusted to my father till one day, he detected my theft. He had deposited a counted sum in the room where I was and left me by myself for awhile. I took some of the money and hid it under my foot in my shoe.' "[11]

Müller's father not only punished him but also sent him to a religious school, hoping that he would become a Lutheran minister. Despite the teachings, Müller's appetite for sin only increased, and he lived much of his young life dishonestly and immorally. Once after squandering a large amount of money his father had given him, he "broke the lock on his trunk and guitar case, and half-dressed, went to the director's room" and claimed he'd been robbed.[12] Nothing about George Müller's first two decades offered the least hint that he would become a man of astonishing faith.

One of the things I love best about God is His unexplainable choice of servants. Frankly, God either has a lot of grace or poor taste. I join Müller and a host of other proofs. When God determines to use a life, no matter how fast the person runs, God will catch him. After long and furious pursuits and conflicts of wills, you'd think the surrender would always be climactic, but God often uses what seems virtually unnoticeable to one to explosively apprehend another. George Müller attended a meeting where the speaker, a man named Kayser, got on his knees and invited everyone to join him and ask God to work mightily in their midst. Somehow the sight of buckled knees in humble, beseeching prayer stirred Müller's heart, and the Holy Spirit bade entrance.

Müller's attraction to vocational ministry and reliance on prayer began almost immediately. As a young adult he started reading God's Word from a personal rather than strictly educational point of view. Müller then did something completely profound. In fact, he did the very thing this entire series requests. He decided to believe God. He relocated to London and began depending entirely on God to supply his needs. He found Scripture packed with promises of God's provision.

The following verses are listed in Müller's biographies as his lifelines. Read each of them and record the basic premise of each promise.

Matthew 6:25-26 _____

Matthew 7:7 _____

John 14:13-14 _____

George Müller took these Scriptures not only personally but also literally. Very early in his ministry he committed himself to believing God for every financial need he

Today's Treasure

"Ask and it will be given to you; seek and you will find; knock and the door will be opened to you. For everyone who asks receives; he who seeks finds; and to him who knocks, the door will be opened." Matthew 7:7

would ever have. Müller and his small family lived meagerly and simply; yet he believed God to give him the opportunity to minister heartily without being on someone else's payroll. He fell under the personal conviction that God wanted Müller to make his needs known to his Heavenly Father alone. Certainly, God does not always require this. Often He meets needs by appointing the person to make his or her need known. Not for George Müller. God not only requested that Müller make his needs known to Him alone but also called Müller to be an active giver of alms. In other words, Müller was to ask nothing but give much. Seem a bit harsh? Beloved, behold the beauty of God's ways: When He gives much, He requires much, and when He requires much, He gives much! Because His young servant clearly heard Him and obediently responded, George Müller experienced one miracle after another in the course of his life.

Müller ministered tirelessly, founding the Scriptural Knowledge Institution to educate believers, distribute Bibles, and evangelize the lost. He knew that the same God who willed the institution into existence would supply every provision. The needs were endless … and so was the money. Often the pound or shilling came not a moment too soon but always through means the Müllers would recognize as their Heavenly Supplier alone. Never was a provision too late. Müller wrote this on January 21, 1835: " 'I received, in answer to prayer, five pounds for the Scriptural Knowledge Institution. The Lord pours in, while we continue to pour out.' "[13] Müller received, and Müller gave. The writer of one biography explained, "George had struck a partnership with God and had promised to dispense whatever the Almighty provided."[14]

In the course of his life George Müller asked much of God but never to squander money on his own lusts. He was certain that God had called him to serve his generation, first through the Scriptural Knowledge Institution and then through the orphanages for which he is best known. The expenses were endless, but George Müller knew that all the resources of heaven and earth belong to God alone. This is the part of his story I find most fascinating: Müller viewed prayer as a withdrawal from God's heavenly bank account into kingdom work on earth. "George had such confidence and trust in the Lord that he counted his requests as good as accomplished when he prayed. He often thanked God for the sum as though already in hand."[15]

Müller himself wrote, " 'From the moment I asked until the Lord granted it fully, I never doubted that He would give every shilling of that sum. Often I praised Him in the assurance that He would grant my request. When we pray, we must believe that we receive according to Mark 11:24, "What things so ever ye desire, when ye pray, believe that ye receive them, and ye shall have them." ' "[16]

Through his many years of ministry Müller kept various records of the needs, his requests, and the ways God met them. The occasions and numbers are staggering. George Müller partnered with God in the utterly impossible. He could have practiced the same safe mediocrity as masses of Christians, but because he decided to believe God instead, Müller lived the great adventure. Don't think for a moment that he didn't experience heartache. Surely most painful on their list of trials, the Müllers buried a deeply loved son. George Müller could easily have decided that a God who would not heal his son after such faith and obedience was not worth serving. Instead, he continued to love, trust, and serve Him for the rest of his days. Before his death George Müller recorded these words: " 'The greater the trial, the sweeter the victory.' "[17]

When the earthly tallies were taken, the Scriptural Knowledge Institution boasted 121,683 pupils and circulated 281,652 Bibles and 1,448,662 New Testaments all over the world and in many languages. In 1897 Müller totaled the finances God brought to the institution as an answer to prayer at 1,424,646 pounds, 6 shillings, and

9 pence.[18] God also funneled untold resources of heaven into Müller's beloved orphanages. God alone can tally the worth of the one who became known around the world as the "father of the orphans."[19]

George Müller made it to Gilgal: full circle from being a thief bound by the stronghold of money to being one of the most faithful stewards ever to draw from the bank account of God.

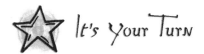 ## It's Your Turn

1. Psalm 81:10 is listed as one of George Müller's life verses. Read the verse. Then write it below in your own personalized version.

_____

_____

2. Now let's read the context in Psalm 81:7-14. Which of these verses speaks most powerfully to you right now and why?

_____

_____

3. According to these verses, what is God willing to do when we bow to Him alone and have no other gods?

_____

_____

4. George Müller's story strikes me as ironic. Because he grew to have so little attachment to money for personal gain, he had absolutely no hesitation when asking God for it to further His kingdom. Many of us have a bad taste in our mouths about the subject of faith and money because we've seen so many abuses through media. What a tragedy to let the abuses keep us from practicing believing prayer for the right uses of our finances! When money is not a god to us and we have a need or godly desire, our Father welcomes our petitions and our acknowledgment that He is the giver of all good things. Many of us have unhealthy relationships with God about our finances. I can't think of a better time to ask Him to hear our hearts and heal any skewed thinking about Him and money. Describe your feelings on the subject.

_____

_____

_____

_____

5. George Müller gave these final words on prayer: " 'It is not enough to begin to pray, nor to pray aright; nor is it enough to continue for a time to pray; but we must patiently, believingly continue in prayer, until we obtain an answer; and further, we have not only to continue in prayer unto the end, but we have also to believe that God does hear us and will answer our prayers. Most frequently we fail in not continuing in prayer until the blessing is obtained, and in not expecting the blessing.' "[20] Can you think of something God gave you after you engaged in enduring, believing prayer? If so, please share.

_____

_____

_____

faith Journal

Today we continue with inquiries based on the fourth fifth of your life: ages ____ to ____.

What pivotal events, traumas, or life markers occurred in these years of your life? Please document anything of importance on the lines below and approximate your age as accurately as you can.

_____

_____

_____

_____

_____

_____

Can you think of any lies you believed during these years that God later exposed to you and replaced with His truth? If so, please explain.

_____

_____

_____

_____

_____

A PAIR OF FATHERS

He loved basketball. He was good at it, too. As captain, he led his team to the Yankee Conference championship for a big win in his senior year. He was accustomed to winning games, not souls. The thought of pastoring a church had never occurred to him. His father-in-law, a pastor, traveling evangelist, and trainer of preachers, was an unofficial overseer of several small independent churches. " 'There's a church in Newark that needs a pastor,' he commented one day. 'They're precious people. Why don't you think about quitting your job and stepping out on faith to see what God will do?' "[21]

He insisted to his father-in-law that he had neither qualifications nor a clue about how to pastor a church. The man of experience responded, "When God calls someone, that's all that really matters. Don't let yourself be afraid."[22] I'm nearly laughing aloud at the thought of many who are horrified at the mere suggestion that God could call them through an in-law. Yes, indeed. The Lord can issue a call through any mouth He pleases.

Before this young Caucasian man knew it, he was standing in front of a tiny, all-black congregation in one of the most challenging spots in urban America. He dove for dear life into a systematic study of Scripture and tried his hardest to learn how to communicate God's Word. In the meantime, God was orchestrating a bigger plan. I'll give you one guess how God told him when He was ready for the young man to know about it. God told his father-in-law, who then phoned his son-in-law. Would he please preach for four Sunday nights in a multiracial church he supervised?

Bewildered, the son-in-law made his way to a shabby, two-story building with a sanctuary in serious need of paint and a capacity for fewer than two hundred people. Not that size was a problem. Most of the seats were empty. Before he knew what hit him, he somehow agreed to pastor the church. The congregation showed its support by dropping in attendance to fewer than 20 people. Welcome to the Brooklyn Tabernacle … and to the story of an unlikely candidate for titanic ministry.

When the Cymbalas' first mortgage payment begged to be paid, the checking account had dwindled to almost nothing. Jim remembered reading George Müller's testimony of countless times he'd prayed for financial-ministry needs to be met, and miraculously they were. He likewise prayed, then checked the mail slot at the front door of the church. He found only bills and flyers. He sat at his desk with his head down and sobbed before God. Cymbala called out to the Lord for more than an hour, when suddenly a thought came to him. He remembered that the church also had a post-office box. Filled with fresh confidence, he walked to the post office only to find the box empty. Downcast in spirit, Jim returned to the church. When he unlocked the door, an unstamped envelope without a word written on it was lying on the foyer floor. His hands shook as he opened it. Inside were two 50-dollar bills. Added to the small checking account, the amount was enough to pay the mortgage.

One of my favorite pictures of this man's story happened at that very moment. Right there in an empty and worn Brooklyn Tabernacle, Jim Cymbala began shouting all by himself, "God, You came through! You came through!" Hallelujahs leapt from his soul. In a church since known for unsurpassed music and worship, a service of purest praise took place between a man and his God. I believe sometimes the emptiness around us can echo a single voice all the louder. I've grown increasingly convinced that God honors public zeal only when it is matched or surpassed by our zeal for Him in private.

Though we love "happily ever after" stories, they are rarely more than fiction. Cymbala's mortgage crisis was only the beginning of a man crying out in desperate

Today's Treasure

"This is to my Father's glory, that you bear much fruit, showing yourselves to be my disciples."
John 15:8

need for God to come through. The Spirit seemed quenched in the services. More discouragement followed. During one service Cymbala was so overtaken by the darkness that seemed to engulf them that he couldn't preach another word. He asked his wife, Carol, to play something on the piano and the few participants to come to the altar for prayer. They did as he asked. Cymbala dropped his head into his hands, and sobbed from the pulpit. In his own words, a tide of intercession arose.[23] A young usher suddenly confessed that he'd taken money from the offering plate. It was the first breakthrough. Innumerable others followed.

In his marvelous best-seller *Fresh Wind, Fresh Fire* Cymbala made a statement I've recalled countless times in the past several years: "I discovered an astonishing truth: God is attracted to weakness. He can't resist those who humbly and honestly admit how desperately they need him. Our weakness, in fact, makes room for his power."[24]

Beloved, how are we making room for God's power? Any thoughts?

_____

_____

Jim Cymbala also discovered something else that greatly ministers to me. He learned that God didn't want him to try to act like someone he wasn't: "God has always despised sham and pretense, especially in the pulpit. The minute I started trying to effect a posture of poise, God's spirit would be grieved."[25] Oh, how that encourages a woman who wrote "Tone down" on her speaking notes for years (to no avail) and would rather have been horsewhipped than watch herself on videotape. My mentors, preachers, and teachers did not flail themselves all over the place while they spoke the way I do. Sometimes I'm even embarrassed for me! But I can't seem to stop when the Spirit of God hits me. I've finally come to the conclusion that my demonstrative zeal is simply the way the Spirit often looks on me. (Who knows why?) On the other hand, someone God uses in a different way would appear completely inauthentic in a similar flail. God calls each of us to be genuine articles. Not on-sale imitations.

The continuing story of Jim and Carol Cymbala and the Brooklyn Tabernacle will undoubtedly go down in church history. If Christ tarries, one day in a future century a desperate young man or woman in ministry might be encouraged to offer God a first real prayer of faith based on Cymbala's example, just as he responded to George Müller's. On second thought, why should such a heritage of faith wait a century? Why not respond to some of the examples God has placed before us now?

How does following an example differ from the kind of imitation we talked about a moment ago?

_____

Since the time the Spirit of Christ resurrected the Brooklyn Tabernacle virtually from the dead, it has become a beacon of hope to many other congregations that long for a fresh wind to blow in their midst. God continues to make countless barrier-crossing contributions to the kingdom through the Cymbalas. God has given Jim favor with all sorts of denominations and ethnicities to share what he has learned. (And mind you, most of it was the hard way.) I have heard him in person and have had the honor of speaking at a conference held in his church. What I find most remarkable is his very humble, almost timid demeanor as he first approaches the pulpit. Then he prays, and the Spirit falls like … well, like a fresh fire.

Without fail, Jim Cymbala teaches the priority of knowing, believing, and practicing the Word of God and stretching ourselves in faith. His other primary contribution has come to the body of Christ through the call to prayer. If pressed to give an answer to what he believes God has most honored in their approach, I believe Jim Cymbala would tell us about the prayer meeting held every Tuesday night. People gather for the sole purpose of crying out to God in prayer, and intercessions fill the church with a sweet aroma that He appears to find irresistible. How many prayer meetings have crowds lacing the sidewalks trying to get in? Beloved, God doesn't attend only the Brooklyn Tabernacle. I'd like to suggest what I think Jim Cymbala might suggest. God is willing to come anywhere people are truly willing to have Him … on His terms. I'd say the Brooklyn Tabernacle found its Gilgal. An otherwise empty church was filled with one solitary voice proclaiming, "God, You came through!" The growing congregation chose to remain empty of every other agenda but His. And He just kept coming.

Dear One, are you getting the picture? Anyone can be a mighty warrior in the kingdom of God, and goodness knows we are occupying planet Earth during a time of great spiritual war. We are seeing the same keys to explosively powerful lives over and over: learn how to wield the sword of the Spirit, raise the shield of faith, and pray, pray, pray! Let's admit our weaknesses, cease our imitations, follow good examples, and position ourselves for miracles. Never forget that the greatest miracle of all occurs each time one human heart is wholly offered to Jesus.

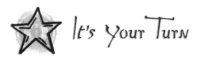 It's Your Turn

Each of the following Scriptures involves intercessory prayer. First read them in an NIV or in a similar reader-friendly translation, if you have one, to get a clear picture of the role of intercession. Then read the *Strong's* definitions in the margin and record any insights you receive into the power and practice of intercession.

2 Corinthians 1:9-11 insights: _____

_____

Trust (v. 9) _____

Deliver (v. 10) _____

Read Romans 15:30. Underline in the margin the English transliteration of the Greek word for "strive together." The prefix *sun* means *together*. What English word can you see tucked in the middle of the Greek transliteration? _____ Sometimes when we enter deep intercession for someone, we literally agonize with the person in prayer. When was the last time you agonized in prayer on behalf of someone? Briefly explain the circumstances.

_____

_____

trust
GREEK STRONG'S NUMBER: 3982
Transliteration: peitho
Phonetic Pronunciation: pi'-tho
Part of Speech: v
1) persuade 1a) to persuade, i.e. to induce one by words to believe 1b) to make friends of, to win one's favour, gain one's good will, or to seek to win one, strive to please one 1c) to tranquillise 1d) to persuade unto i.e. move or induce one to persuasion to do something 2) be persuaded 2a) to be persuaded, to suffer one's self to be persuaded; to be induced to believe: to have faith: in a thing 2a1) to believe 2a2) to be persuaded of a thing concerning a person 2b) to listen to, obey, yield to, comply with 3) to trust, have confidence, be confident

deliver
GREEK STRONG'S NUMBER: 4506
Transliteration: rhoumai
Phonetic Pronunciation: rhoo'-om-ahee
Part of Speech: v
1) to draw to one's self, to rescue, to deliver 2) the deliverer

strive together
GREEK STRONG'S NUMBER: 4865
Transliteration: sunagonizomai
Phonetic Pronunciation: soon-ag-o-nid'-zom-ahee
Part of Speech: v
1) to strive together with one, to help one in striving

Over the past year I have agonized in prayer with a sister over an ill child. Recently, God has blatantly revealed Himself through various blessings in their family. To the degree I had agonized, I got to rejoice. I wept with joy over the latest news. Share the most recent or most memorable time you experienced the profit-sharing of incoming answers after the agony of intercession.

_____

_____

Intercession does not always involve agonizing in prayer, but when we get a chance to see God move, getting to be part of the celebration is worth all the work! The next reference was written by the same inspired writer, the Apostle Paul. This time we'll see no agony in intercession. Be sure to record how he described this act of intercession.

Philippians 1:3-6 insights: _____

_____

Fellowship (v. 5) _____

Can you think of someone for whom you often pray with joy? Share who it is and the reason praying for him or her brings you such joy.

_____

_____

Finally, read Jesus' specific words to His Father in John 11:41-42 prior to raising Lazarus from the dead. What confidence did Jesus have when He prayed?

_____

How different do you think your prayer life would be if you decided to believe with unwavering confidence that your Heavenly Father actively hears you?

_____

_____

God's Word tells us Christ always lives to make intercession for us (see Heb. 7:25) and the Holy Spirit intercedes for us according to God's will (see Rom. 8:27). We don't have to ask Him to intercede because He continually exercises His intercessory role in our lives. We are invited to go straight to the Father in the name of the Son and make our petitions known.

What did Christ tell His disciples in John 16:26-27?

_____

May we press on to new levels of God-given, Christ-enabled praying! While you're so close to John 15:7-8, read the words aloud and ask God to make your theology a much greater reality!

Faith Journal

Today we continue with inquiries based on the most recent fifth of our lives: ages _____ to _____ (your age at present).

How would you characterize this period of your life? Please write a paragraph description.

_____

_____

_____

_____

Describe the biggest blessing in this fifth of your life.

_____

_____

_____

Describe the biggest challenge in this fifth of your life.

_____

_____

Has God revealed Himself in any way through that challenge? If so, how?

_____

_____

Because you have involved yourself in an in-depth Bible study for nine weeks, you obviously have a relationship with God. How would you describe your relationship with God at this point, and how has it changed over this fifth of your life?

_____

_____

_____

What has most dramatically changed your spiritual life over this current fifth? Be specific if possible.

_____

_____

_____

GodStops

B E D T I M E   M E D I T A T I O N

_____

_____

_____

_____

_____

_____

_____

_____

_____

DAY 5
HUMBLE BOASTS

I have enjoyed this week immensely. I so hope it wasn't just for me! Which testimony spoke the most to you personally and why?

_____

_____

_____

Today's Treasure

As it is written: "Let him who boasts boast in the Lord."
1 Corinthians 1:31

When I read life stories like those we've considered this week, I cannot help falling more in love with Jesus. I love His style. I love how He often chooses the least likely people to do the most inconceivable things. No segment of Scripture expresses God's reasoning on this matter more beautifully than 1 Corinthians 1:18-31. For this reason I'm going to ask you to take Your Turn first today. Then the commentary will follow.

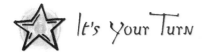 It's Your Turn

Please read 1 Corinthians 1:18-31 in your Bible. Contemplate the meanings of the following words. Underline pertinent parts of the definition and record any insights you gain.

VERSE 22: Paul wasn't paying the Greeks a contrasting compliment when he said they sought wisdom. They placed the highest premium on intellectualism and philosophy. Wisdom was itself the end they desired to achieve. God desires that we seek His Word chiefly so that we can know its divine Author.

VERSE 23: **stumbling block;** (*the second number: <G4625>)* Transliteration: skandalon Phonetic Pronunciation: skan'-dal-on ("scandal"); Part of Speech: n n; 1) the movable stick or trigger of a trap, a trap stick 1a) a trap, snare 1b) any impediment placed in the way and causing one to stumble or fall, (a stumbling block, occasion of stumbling) i.e. a rock which is a cause of stumbling 1c) fig. applied to Jesus Christ, whose person and career were so contrary to the expectations of the Jews concerning the Messiah, that they rejected him and by their obstinacy made shipwreck of their salvation 2) any person or thing by which one is (entrapped) drawn into error or sin*

VERSE 24: **called;** *Transliteration: kletos; Phonetic Pronunciation: klay-tos'; Part of Speech: adj 1) called, invited (to a banquet) 1a) invited (by God in the proclamation of the Gospel) to obtain eternal salvation in the kingdom through Christ 1b) called to (the discharge of) some office 1b1) divinely selected and appointed*

VERSE 24: **power;** *Transliteration: dunamis; Phonetic Pronunciation: doo'-nam-is; Part of Speech: n f; 1) strength power, ability 1a) inherent power, power residing in a thing by virtue of its nature, or which a person or thing exerts and puts forth 1b) power for performing miracles 1c) moral power and excellence of soul 1d) the power and influence which belong to riches and wealth 1e) power and resources arising from numbers 1f) power consisting in or resting upon armies, forces, hosts*

VERSE 24: **wisdom;** *Transliteration: sophia; Phonetic Pronunciation: sof-ee'-ah; Part of Speech: n f; 1) wisdom, broad and full of intelligence; used of the knowledge of very diverse matters 1a) the wisdom which belongs to men 1a1) spec. the varied knowledge of things human and divine, acquired by acuteness and experience, and summed up in maxims and proverbs 1a2) the science and learning 1a3) the act of interpreting dreams and always giving the sagest advice 1a4) the intelligence evinced in discovering the meaning of some mysterious number or vision 1a5) skill in the management of affairs 1a6) devout and proper prudence in intercourse with men not disciples of Christ, skill and discretion in imparting Christian truth 1a7) the knowledge and practice of the requisites for* godly and upright living 1b) supreme intelligence, such as belongs to God 1b1) to Christ 1b2) the wisdom of God as evinced in forming and executing counsels in the formation and government of the world and the scriptures

---

VERSE 27: **chosen;** *Transliteration: eklegomai; Phonetic Pronunciation: ek-leg'-om-ahee; Part of Speech: v;* 1) to pick out, choose, to pick or choose out for one's self 1a) choosing one out of many, i.e. Jesus choosing his disciples 1b) choosing one for an office 1c) of God choosing whom he judged fit to receive his favours and separated from the rest of mankind to be peculiarly his own and to be attended continually by his gracious oversight 1c1) i.e. the Israelites 1d) of God the Father choosing Christians, as those whom he set apart from the irreligious multitude as dear unto himself, and whom he has rendered, through faith in Christ, citizens in the Messianic kingdom: (Jas 2:5) so that the ground of the choice lies in Christ and his merits only

---

VERSE 28: **base;** *Transliteration: agenes; Phonetic Pronunciation: ag-en-ace'; Part of Speech: adj;* 1) ignoble, coward, mean, base, of no family, that is: low born

---

VERSE 28: **despised;** *Transliteration: exoutheneo; Phonetic Pronunciation: ex-oo-then-eh'-o; Part of Speech: v;* 1) to make of no account, despise utterly

---

VERSE 29: According to this verse, why does God choose unlikely candidates?

VERSE 30: **righteousness;** *Transliteration: dikaiosune; Phonetic Pronunciation: dik-ah-yos-oo'-nay; Part of Speech: n f;* 1) in a broad sense: state of him who is as he ought to be, righteousness, the condition acceptable to God 1a) the doctrine concerning the way in which man may attain a state approved of God 1b) integrity, virtue, purity of life, rightness, correctness of thinking, feeling, and acting 2) in a narrower sense, justice or the virtue which gives each his due

---

VERSE 30: **sanctification;** *Transliteration: hagiasmos; Phonetic Pronunciation: hag-ee-as-mos'; Part of Speech: n m;* 1) consecration, purification; 2) the effect of consecration; 2a) sanctification of heart and life

---

VERSE 30: **redemption;** *Transliteration: apolutrosis; Phonetic Pronunciation: ap-ol-oo'-tro-sis; Part of Speech: n f;* 1) a releasing effected by payment of ransom 1a) redemption, deliverance 1b) liberation procured by the payment of a ransom

Verse 31: "As it is written: _____."

Oh, Beloved, I want to stop for a moment and talk about the powerful enemy of all true ministry: pride. I do not speak of it to condemn, because I have been the greatest offender in my hard-hearted, self-righteous past. When God knew we had gone as far as we could go without my taking an in-depth look at my own pitiful flesh, He shattered my pride and confidence like a sledgehammer through a looking glass. I would give almost anything to save someone else the humiliation I endured. I have no words to express my gratitude for the work He ultimately accomplished, but for years I was haunted by a torturous question: couldn't there have been an easier way? Finally and sadly I accepted the answer: apparently not. My God loves me too much not to have chosen another way if it would have sufficed.

Dear One, God wants to bear much fruit in every one of our lives. He wants to infuse our prayer lives with inconceivable power. He wants to stun us with affirmative answers. He wants to leave the marks of the cross we carry in His name on our promised lands and our surrounding spheres of influence. He wants to completely alter our family lines and, if He tarries, raise up one godly warrior after another in the wake of our faithful lives. God longs to do all of these things in any life who will let Him, but He will not tolerate any of our attempts—however subtle and falsely modest—to share His glory. God is jealous of nothing more than His own glory. God opposes the proud and gives grace to the humble. His Word tells us that we can either humble ourselves (see 1 Pet. 5:5-6), or He can humble us (see Dan. 4:37).

I am so convinced that God will respond to our willingness to surrender to present-active-participle believing lives that I have a concern. When He starts showing off, God forbid that we grow proud. Faith that grows proud ceases to be faith. It begins to be a god. And what a tragedy after such humble beginnings: big on God and small in its own eyes. Keep a constant check on it, Beloved. Satan has a way to counterfeit every genuine attempt to obey God. One of the ways he tries to counterfeit a faith-filled believer is to tempt her to take a tithe of the glory when God's power begins to be more frequently evidenced.

God knew He had plans to show me some pretty profound evidence of His activity. To ensure that I would never be tempted to think highly of myself, He temporarily extended the devil's leash where I was concerned. For a while I thought he was going to hang me with it. Let me assure you, it wasn't pretty. I have asked God not to let me live a moment longer than I can remember the pit from which He rescued me and the terror of my own flesh nature. If you've not already had such a lesson, I beg you to learn it from those of us who have. Humble yourself! Unless you physically cannot, make a practice of literally getting on the floor, facedown and prostrate, before God on a regular basis. Every time you have a smug sense of self-righteousness, buckle your knees before God buckles them for you. I have often said what some have not wanted to hear: we, the children of God, can either bend our knees, or eventually He will break our legs … in one form or another. He is Lord. Let me say it louder: HE IS LORD!

He is also a Lord who loves nothing more than to raise up the humble and astonish them with His wonderful works. I could have continued sharing examples of unlikely lives interrupted by the power and presence of God for weeks. Brother Andrew, for instance, a Dutch factory worker God transformed into our world's consummate Bible smuggler. He organized the smuggling of over one million Bibles into China and innumerable Bibles into many other forbidden lands. I'm not suggesting we all start carrying Bibles into illegal territories. I'm suggesting we each believe God to fulfill His choice calling in our lives. God protects what He ordains.

A few months ago I got to hear Heather Mercer speak of her experiences as a prisoner in Afghanistan. Afterward I had the priceless opportunity to sit beside her and visit during dinner in an area restaurant. After spending a little while with her, I was impressed by the same thing that I appreciated so much about the book she and Dayna Curry coauthored (*Prisoners of Hope*, a must-read!). They are very candid about their struggles to maintain their faith and composure under such stressful and frightful conditions. They do not glamorize the mission field, nor do they dare imply that those with enough faith will always experience a Rambo-like rescue.

As any of us who are in touch with the mission field know, some missionaries are rescued through death into the portals of heaven. The Apostle Paul spoke of this kind of rescue when he knew that the time had come for his departure (see 2 Tim. 4:18). God will indeed deliver us. Sometimes from our peril. Sometimes through our peril. Timing is everything to God in matters of life and death. Frankly my friends, when our testimony is complete, we're outta here no matter how premature it seems (see Rev. 11:7). God alone is wise. Oh, to capture the passion of the former enemy of the gospel, who finally said, "To me, to live is Christ and to die is gain" (Phil. 1:21). He lived in the comfort of the blessed "whatever."

I have had the unspeakable privilege of getting to know many missionaries who serve on foreign fields. I am the grateful recipient of my childhood church's love for missions. My current church also has no greater vision than the Great Commission (see Matt. 28:18-20), so I've been happily immersed in missions from all sides. I love missionaries. And not just romantically and remotely. Close up and personally, sometimes sitting in a hotel room hearing horror stories that raise the hair on the back of my neck. They are my heroes. They are not superhuman. They are willing. Some of them are thriving, and some of them are really hurting.

Recently, I read an interview in *Shine* magazine with my friend and highly respected brother in Christ, author Bruce Wilkinson. Michelle Toholsky, the editor in chief, asked Wilkinson if he thought most Christians today aren't "really living out the fullness of the Christian life." He responded, "I don't think any of us are, and I'm not either. About two or three years ago, I was in a meeting with about 55 Christian leaders who had thousands of missionaries around the world who reported to them. I asked them to give me the three reasons why they felt their work in different countries wasn't working—why it wasn't really breaking through. Overwhelmingly, the number one answer was unbelief."[26]

Wilkinson reported coming away from that meeting with the realization that his primary sin was also unbelief. God confronted me in the same sin five years ago when He first began drilling my mind with those two words: "believe Me!" I don't think Bruce and I are the only ones. I am convinced that the most flagrant sin in the body of Christ today is unbelief. Our generation of believers is paralyzed by it. It's time for faith to come back in style in the church of Jesus Christ. Leaders first.

We have many missionaries participating in this Bible study. If you would allow me the privilege, I'd like to address these dearly loved heroes of mine for a moment. You are welcome to eavesdrop because you might need the encouragement yourself.

Dear Servant, God has called you. He has summoned you just as He did the children of Israel in Isaiah 43:10:

"You are my witnesses," declares the Lord,
  "and my servant whom I have chosen,
so that you may know and believe me."

Believe Him, Beloved. More than you believe your own apparent fruitfulness or lack of it. Satan is after your faith more than anything else you possess. "Above all, taking the shield of faith, wherewith ye shall be able to quench all the fiery darts of the wicked" (Eph. 6:16, KJV). Grab your shield from the enemy's hand and raise it high. Repeat those five statements of faith until you start saying them in your dreams. Start praying Scripture over your challenges, believing God for miracles, and thanking Him in advance for a harvest one hundredfold.

I'd like to share one more fitting story before we conclude our eighth week of study. You who are missionaries know it better than I. When Hudson Taylor arrived in Shanghai in 1854, he was starry-eyed with dreams just as many of you were when you went to the mission field. He was also hit by a tidal wave of crushing realities. The opposition. The hardships. The language. The challenges of working with other missionaries. Few converts. The food! Sound familiar? On his deathbed Hudson Taylor couldn't have imagined in his wildest dreams the harvest he helped plant. Many analysts believe the Chinese church, albeit underground, is the fastest growing in the entire world. I want to be stationed where I can witness Hudson Taylor's face when he sees millions of Chinese gather around the throne on that great and glorious day. Every nation, tribe, and tongue—indeed, every people group, dear missionary, including the one assigned to you—will gather, waving palm branches and proclaiming, " 'Salvation belongs to our God' " (Rev. 7:10)!

Only one thing is impossible with God: it is impossible to believe Him in vain.

𝄞 faith Journal

Today we conclude our responses to inquiries about the most recent fifth of our lives: ages _____ to _____ (present). What pivotal events, traumas, or life markers occurred in these years of your life? Please document below anything of importance.

_____

_____

_____

_____

Now allow me to ask you an appropriate question for our conclusion to this week of study. Have you lived long enough and followed God long enough to experience a Gilgal of your own? Remember, we've characterized Gilgal as a place where any one of three things happens:

- We realize that God has rolled away our reproach.
- God has proved us victorious in a do-over (an opportunity to go back and get something right).
- God has taken us full circle in a significant way.

We could have several Gilgal experiences in a lifetime, or we might not recognize them until we reach heaven. I simply want to give you a chance to personalize the concept. You are as precious to God as D. L. Moody, William Carey, George Müller, Jim Cymbala,

Heather Mercer, Dayna Curry, and Hudson Taylor have ever been. Mind you, the way He takes each of us full circle doesn't have to seem significant to anyone else. If it's significant to you, it's significant to God. If you've experienced a Gilgal of any kind, please share it.

_____

_____

Thank you for your attentiveness to the Faith Journal section these past two weeks. The events and experiences you've recorded will be very important in our final week.

GodStops

BEDTIME MEDITATION

_____

_____

_____

_____

_____

———

[1] Henry Varley, as quoted in Lyle W. Dorsett, *A Passion for Souls: The Life of D. L. Moody* (Chicago: Moody Press, 1997), 141.

[2] Doresett, *A Passion for Souls,* 35–36.

[3] George Grant and Gregory Wilbur, *The Christian Almanac: A Dictionary of Days Celebrating History's Most Significant People and Events* (Nashville: Cumberland House, 2000), 367.

[4] Ibid., 737.

[5] D. L. Moody, as quoted in Doresett, *A Passion for Souls,* 412.

[6] Ibid., 139.

[7] As quoted in Mary Drewery, *William Carey: A Biography* (Grand Rapids: Zondervan Publishing House, 1978), 7.

[8] Grant and Wilbur, *The Christian Almanac,* 541.

[9] Ibid.

[10] Oswald Chambers, *My Utmost for His Highest* (Uhrichsville, OH: Barbour Publishing, 1994), February 22.

[11] George Müller, as quoted in Bonnie Harvey, *George Müller: Man of Faith* (Uhrichsville, OH: Barbour Publishing, 1998), 9.

[12] Ibid., 13.

[13] Ibid., 55.

[14] Bonnie Harvey, *George Müller,* 55.

[15] Ibid., 68.

[16] George Müller, as quoted in Harvey, *George Müller,* 69.

[17] Ibid., 152.

[18] Ibid., 143.

[19] Ibid., 144.

[20] Ibid., 153.

[21] Jim Cymbala with Dean Merrill, *Fresh Wind, Fresh Fire: What Happens When God's Spirit Invades the Heart of His People* (Grand Rapids: Zondervan Publishing House, 1997), 13.

[22] Ibid.

[23] Ibid., 19.

[24] Ibid.

[25] Ibid., 20.

[26] Michelle Toholsky, "Men! Men! Men! Living with Them, Never Living Without Them," *Shine,* July–August 2002, 43

Believing God When Victory Demands Your All

1. No matter who or what rises up against you, God's _____ _____ every other (see Josh. 10:1).

   Adoni-Zedek means _____ of _____.

   • God will ultimately take over and complete every earthly _____ of _____.

   Ephesians 1:20-21 says that God "seated Him at His right hand in the heavenly realms, far above …

   every _____ that can be given, not only in the _____ _____

   but also in the one to come."

2. For children of God, a perfect setup for catastrophic _____ is also the perfect setup for

   miraculous _____. The strikes against Joshua and the Israelites were both mental and

   physical and could have been presumed _____.

   • Mental: See Joshua 9:1-4,14-18. Consider all the opportunities to lose this battle mentally:

   How _____   How _____

   Whose _____   Our own _____

   • Physical: They had an _____ march and an _____ battle.

   • Spiritual: They could have presumed God's attitude to be "You got _____ _____ this

   mess; you get _____ _____."

3. Our Father delights in exalting, ambitious _____.

4. When God requires and receives our _____, He'll return a _____.

5. God requires so much of us at times so that we can experience the unmatched _____

   of partnering in divine _____ (see Ps. 47).

Believing God When Victory Demands Your All

GOD IS WHO HE SAYS HE IS

Moses set out with Joshua his aide, and Moses went up on the mountain of God. Exodus 24:13

I can hardly believe my eyes. We've reached the final stretch of our faith walk together —our last week of study. Notice I did not say our last week of believing God. My dear fellow sojourner, we've only begun believing God. We have the rest of our lives, whether our days are few or many, to be increasingly intentional about noting and confessing unbelief; asking Christ to help our unbelief; receiving the living, active Word of God; believing and therefore speaking. As we begin our last five miles together, we will echo some very important principles and inject them further into the marrow of our belief system.

One of the most important principles is this: present-active-participle believing God doesn't happen on special occasions or on sudden demand. Present-active-participle believing God is a lifestyle. It is a daily, deliberate choice. Present-active-participle believing God awakens in the morning and says, "My Lord and my God, I thank You for another day to know You and believe You. Whatever means You may choose to increase my faith today, I commit myself to that glorious end" (see Isa. 43:10). After He sings us to sleep at night, may our Father be able to look at the Son on His right and say, "She believed Me today." And He will credit it to our account as righteousness.

The key word for our final week of study is *all*. In video session 9 we talked about challenges that will undoubtedly arise in our lives when God has every intention of bringing us complete victory, but He ordains that the process will demand our all. All. Such a small word means so much. Never in history has the concept of giving everything to one chief end been so challenged. We have never been more fragmented or lived in a society that demanded more pieces of us. How can a person who is giving a thousand pieces of herself to innumerable demands and desires ever know wholeness? The Lord Jesus Christ offers us the one and only way to wholeness: giving ourselves wholly to Him, inviting His healing, and trusting Him to apportion our energies, gifts, and talents in their most effective ways. Every fish. Every loaf. Withholding nothing. We give Christ our all. And with it He does the impossible.

I want to see the kinds of things Joshua and the children of Israel saw, and I want to practice the kind of faith that invites God to act. Yes, God demanded everything they had at Gibeon, but what He gave in return was astounding. Today we are going to look at the birthplace of Joshua's radical belief. Each day this week we will hammer down one of the statements in our pledge of faith one last time. We want these concepts abiding so securely within us that we believe and therefore speak them for the rest of our lives.

Please write the first statement in our pledge of faith.

_____

Based on all we've studied together and all you've personally discerned from God, why is this statement the most important of all?

_____

_____

Without a doubt Joshua believed God could do what He said He could do (statement 2). Joshua also believed that he was who God said he was—no small challenge, considering he became Moses' successor. He couldn't possibly have led the children of Israel without faith to believe he was who God said he was (statement 3). Furthermore, Joshua believed he could do anything God told him to do. He evidenced his faith by lacing up his sandals and walking in radical obedience (statement 4). If we know anything, we know that God's Word was alive and active in Joshua. Indeed, the Word on his tongue was God's primary game plan for Joshua's success (see Josh. 1:8; statement 5).

Before Joshua could walk in the reality of statements 2–5, however, he committed himself steadfastly to present-active-participle faith in statement 1. He had to know God was who He said He was, or nothing else mattered. Today Your Turn will be interwoven with mine in order to best achieve today's goals.

⭐ It's Your Turn

Please read Exodus 24:1-18, trying your best to picture every scene. Briefly describe the events recorded in each of the following passages.

Exodus 24:1-8 _____

_____

_____

Exodus 24:9-12 _____

_____

_____

Exodus 24:13-18 _____

_____

_____

What is Joshua's involvement in this chapter? _____

_____

_____

Aren't you glad we live under the new covenant (see 2 Cor. 3:6; Heb. 8:8)? Each of us has a perpetual invitation to climb the mountain of intimacy with God to pray, worship, and hear Him speak through His Word. The scenes captured in Exodus 24 speak volumes . Allow me to walk through them with you briefly. I hope you allowed the mental image to form of Moses sprinkling the people with blood. Please picture it even to the point of repulsion if you must. After sacrificing young bulls, Moses sprinkled blood on the altar exactly as the children of Israel may have expected. However, I don't think they ever expected him to start splashing the blood on them.

Why in the world did Moses do such a thing? Carefully look at the context, and you'll see. What had just happened in Exodus 24:7?

_____

The people of Israel made a promise—literally agreed to a covenant—they had no power to keep. They could no more do everything the Lord had said and obey all the commands of His Word than we can. They had to be covered (through sprinkling) by the blood. Like ours, theirs was a blood covenant. By faith in the work of the cross, we have been sprinkled by the blood of Christ. No further sacrifice will ever be needed. The blood of the Lamb secures our covenant.

We see from the context that Joshua was Moses' _____ (see Ex. 24:13).

I'm reminded again that every leader who is great in God's eyes is a servant. We can probably assume that Joshua stood close to Moses as he sprinkled the blood all over the people. For all we know, Joshua may have held the bowl and refilled it when it was empty. You can be pretty certain that because Joshua was Moses' aide, the blood was sprinkled all over him. The next thing we know, Moses, Aaron, Nadab, Abihu, and the 70 elders went up and saw the God of Israel. Keep in mind that they saw His glory and, obviously, some of His surroundings. Had they seen His face, they would have died (see Ex. 33:20).

What did they see, according to Exodus 24:10? _____

_____

We do not know whether Joshua was with Moses and the others listed in verse 9. His presence as Moses' aide may have been assumed. We do know that Joshua accompanied Moses in verse 13. How far he proceeded up the mountain with Moses is unclear, but we know he went farther than anyone else. Verse 15 tells us that a cloud covered the mountain, and the glory of the Lord settled on it.

What did the glory of the LORD look like to the Israelites (see v. 17)? _____

If the glory of the LORD appeared like that to the Israelites down below, can you imagine how it appeared to Joshua? He was second only to Moses.

How many days were Moses and Joshua in their positions on the mountain before God spoke (see v. 16)? _____

I ache for the body of Christ in our generation to learn how to tarry before God and expectantly wait for Him to speak. I'm desperate to learn it for myself. If we did, what revelation we would receive! We cannot have a drive-thru relationship with God and expect to behold His glory. Joshua didn't get a to-go order of God. He dined with Him for days.

Now read Exodus 33:7-11, describe the events, and identify Joshua's involvement.

_____

_____

Take a good look at a key word in verse 7. The NIV uses the word *anyone*, and the NASB and KJV use the word *everyone* in references to those inquiring of the Lord in the tent of meeting. Please don't miss the intimation that anyone or everyone who wanted to inquire of the Lord could go to the tent. Yet what do we see them doing? As Moses entered, they stood back and watched him from a distance. We are people of the new covenant—people to whom God has offered a "surpassing glory" (2 Cor. 3:10). Yet, like the children of Israel, much of the body of Christ still stands back and watches those they consider truly anointed draw near God's glory. Dear One, you are anointed (see 1 John 2:27). Never settle for a secondhand relationship.

Joshua wasn't satisfied with a distant glory. He wasn't satisfied to live his relationship with God secondhand through that of Moses. Joshua learned his lessons well. He knew that Moses' God was his God. The purpose of today's lesson is to determine the birthplace of Joshua's remarkable faith and to find the basis of statements 2–5 in his belief system. Now we have our answer: Joshua's great faith was born in the presence of God. Joshua knew God was who He said He was because he knew God. He was convinced of statements 2–5 because he banked his whole life on statement 1.

Please read 2 Timothy 1:12 in the KJV. Why was Paul unashamed? Please write his answer word for word.

_____

_____

Recall the verse that launched our study. Isaiah 43:10 says,

> "You are my witnesses," declares the LORD,
> "and my servant whom I have chosen,
> so that you may know and believe me."

Circle the words that 2 Timothy 1:12 and Isaiah 43:10 have in common. (Overlook any difference in verb tenses.)

know

GREEK STRONG'S NUMBER: 1492
Transliteration: eido, oida
Phonetic Pronunciation: i'-do, oy'-da
Part of Speech: v

1) to see 1a) to perceive with the eyes 1b) to perceive by any of the senses 1c) to perceive, notice discern, discover 1d) to see 1d1) i.e. to turn the eyes, the mind, the attention to anything 1d2) to pay attention, observe 1d3) to see about something 1d31) i.e. to ascertain what must be done about it 1d4) to inspect, examine 1d5)to look at, behold 1e) to experience any state or condition 1f) to see i.e. have an interview with, to visit 2) to know 2a) to know of anything 2b) to know, i.e. get knowledge of, understand, perceive 2b1) of any fact 2b2) the force and meaning of something which had definite meaning 2b3) to know how, to be skilled in 2c) to have regard for one, cherish, pay attention to (1 Th. 5:12)

believed

GREEK STRONG'S NUMBER: 4100
Transliteration: pisteuo
Phonetic Pronunciation: pist-yoo'-o
Part of Speech: v

1) to think to be true, to be persuaded of, to credit, place confidence in 1a) of the thing believed 1a1) to credit, have confidence 1b) in a moral or religious reference 1b1) used in the NT of the conviction and trust to which a man is impelled by a certain inner and higher prerogative and law of soul 1b2) to trust in Jesus or God as able to aid either in obtaining or in doing something: saving faith 1bc) mere acknowledgment of some fact or event: intellectual faith 2) to entrust a thing to one, i.e. his fidelity

persuaded

GREEK STRONG'S NUMBER: 3982
Transliteration: peitho
Phonetic Pronunciation: pi'-tho
Part of Speech: v

1) to persuade 1a) to persuade, i.e. to induce one by words to believe 1b) to make friends of, to win one's favour, gain one's good will, or to seek to win one, strive to please ne 1c) to tranquillise 1d) to persuade unto i.e. move or induce one to persuasion to do something 2) be persuaded 2a) to be persuaded, to suffer one's self to be persuaded; to be induced to believe: to have faith: in a thing 2a1) to believe 2a2) to be persuaded of a thing concerning a person 2b) to listen to, obey, yield to, comply with 3) to trust, have confidence, be confident

Dear One, the more we know God, the more we will believe Him, and the more we choose to believe Him, the more we will get to know Him. This is the cycle that replaces "believe little, see little; believe less, see less." The know-believe cycle is the one we want to pedal for the rest of our days! We birth faith by knowing the One we believe, and we walk faith by believing the One we know.

Now read the definitions of the following words from 2 Timothy 1:12 in the margin and record the pertinent or most insightful meanings.

Know _____

Believed _____

Persuaded _____

The God to whom you commit yourself and everything that concerns you is huge. He is the omnipotent Maker of heaven and earth. He is the One who sees. He is the One who knows. He is the One who acts on behalf of His children. He is the Mighty Warrior. He is the compassionate Father. He is the Way, the Truth, and the Life. He is the coming King. He is love. He is light. He is good. He is right. He is your soul's delight. He is … whatever you need. He alone is wise. In Him alone life makes sense, and apart from Him all is chaos.

Each morning when you turn your face toward heaven, before you make your first petition, start confessing who He is. Call Him by as many names and titles as He brings to mind and praise Him for His immutable attributes. Say to your soul, "Behold and believe!"

The God of Abraham, Isaac, Jacob, Moses, Joshua, Gideon, Samson, David, John the Baptist, Mary of Magdala, Mary of Bethany, Peter, James, John, and Paul is your God. The same yesterday, today, and forever. A God so holy, powerful, and present that when He revealed Himself to Ezekiel in the Old Testament and John in the New, both dropped like dead men. He is the magnificent One, full of splendor, beautiful beyond comprehension. The I Am That I Am throughout every generation. Whoever He was, He is. Who He was to them, He is to you. Start taking Him up on His Godness. When you have no idea what to believe Him for in a given situation, just believe Him to be huge.

Come, holy God, and be Thyself.

faith Journal

In this section each day of our concluding week, we are going to do something very special and, hopefully, creative. We will draw and label a time line representing our life experiences and unique faith journeys. Over the previous two weeks, we reflected on five chronological segments of our lives. This week's exercise will allow us to see the parts as they fit into the whole and watch how God can work and reveal Himself through any circumstance. Over these five days, we will diagram on a time line the rocks of remembrance from each fifth of our lives. We will mark the spots where we've discovered God in our pasts. Please participate fully, for this exercise profoundly affects our conclusions.

Carefully follow these instructions. You will need three blank, 8½-by-11 sheets of paper, tape, and a ruler or another straight edge. For perfectionists, I suggest using a pencil for a first draft, then copying the finished work in ink on three fresh pages.

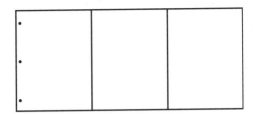

- Tape three 8½-by-11 sheets of paper together vertically. Then turn them over so that you are writing on the side without the tape.

- Draw one horizontal line across the center of all three sheets, leaving approximately a two-inch margin on each end. You'll need the room at the top and bottom of the page to supply your information. When the time comes, I suggest switching back and forth from top to bottom to have as much room as possible to record information. Place a bold dot at the beginning of the line and write the date of your birth and where you born. Please place an ellipsis (...) on the other end to represent your future.

- Using a ruler or another straight edge, divide your line with short perpendicular marks into five even increments to represent each fifth of your life, as illustrated below.

- Now record the calendar year for each new increment. I'll choose a fictitious character we'll call Mary as our example. She is 35 years old, so her fifths will be divided into increments of seven years. Date yours according to your own age.

- Reread your Faith Journal entries from week 7, days 1 and 2. Then diagram any pivotal events from your first fifth with symbols of your creative choice and brief labels of explanation. I've provided below several symbols for experiences we have in common. For all others, make up your own or just use words.

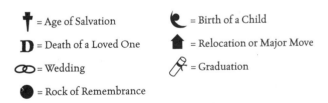

- Place a bold dot on the line at any point you drew forth a rock of remembrance (remembered God) in your first fifth and label it with a descriptive word or phrase. (Remember, today we are filling in the first fifth only.) Write brief phrases of general intervention below. I hope you will plot the requested information on your diagram, but you are welcome to be as detailed and involved from that point as you'd like. Examine "Mary's" example of the first fifth of her life below and her descriptive phrases on the following page.

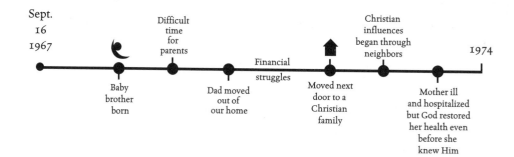

Very difficult years due to separation of my parents
Dealt with low self-esteem, fear, and insecurity
Not taken to church
In the midst of it, God revealed Himself through—
• a very nice Christian neighbor;
• Bible School I occasionally attended in the summer with her;
• a sense of God through nature.

This time line will become a treasure to you if you let it and possibly a treasure to your loved ones. Like most things, you will get as much out of the exercises as you put into them. Tomorrow we'll diagram the second fifth of your life.

BEDTIME MEDITATION

_____

_____

_____

_____

_____

_____

_____

_____

GOD CAN DO WHAT HE SAYS HE CAN DO

As much as I have loved every Bible study with which God has graced my life and given me, I have known almost from the beginning that this one is unique. My purpose is to call people to grow in the love and knowledge of God through in-depth attention to His Word. This series, however, has an additional, very pointed purpose. I believe it is a part—however small—of a worldwide call to revival.

I am convinced that God is calling the body of Christ to a vast revival of a very specific nature: a revival of biblical faith. I see a fresh emphasis springing up all over the believing world. This faith revitalization is birthed through an eye-opening realization and authentic repentance of the far-reaching plague of unbelief. It will then gain further momentum of the Holy Spirit's outpouring through the intentional pursuit of balanced New Testament faith-practice. This balance may be difficult to maintain, but it is not difficult to define: balanced New Testament faith-practice must be Scripture-driven and God-centered.

In general, the body of Christ has seen little faith-practice in the past century, and too much of what has been seen is human-centered. Our repulsion over the abuses is not going to hold up in the court of God as a reason we failed to exercise faith. Those who have genuinely tried to practice biblical faith deserve applause even if some were unintentionally out of balance. At least they tried!

If God were to give the worldwide church of Jesus Christ a grade today, like the seven churches in Revelation, I fear we'd receive an F for faith. Most of us—and certainly I—have been tightly chained, smugly satisfied, and dangerously arrogant through unbelief.

Over the past years God has challenged me and empowered me to change. Never in my entire history with God have I received more blatant approval from Him over a newly directed approach. I still research the Word with the same fervor and pursue sound scholarship, but now I intentionally and often verbally add my faith to it. In other words, I actively say, "God, infuse these words not only into my heart and mind but also into the marrow of my belief system. Bring these words to life in me today. Help me not only to learn them but also to walk by faith in them. Help me believe You." Even when I've missed the mark of sound application, I've sensed Him saying, "You're on the right track, child. Stay after it! Keep practicing belief, and you'll learn more and more about My desires as you go."

One of my new mottoes has become: if I err, let me err on the side of belief. God looks on the heart. I'd rather Him see misguided actions from a believing heart than safe-and-sound actions from an unbelieving heart.

By no means do I claim to have discovered equilibrium in a proposed practice of faith. Balance is a never-ending challenge in anything involving the human race. But in addition, an overanalysis of faith-practice would only legalize and suffocate the very thing it meant to police. This revival of faith—of which we're a small part—will undoubtedly weave across the steadfast plumb line of God's intended interpretation. A continual commitment to the pursuit of balance, however, will help steer it back on course again and again.

Think about the very nature of faith. How is it defined in Hebrews 11:1?

Today's Treasure

LORD, *I have heard of your fame; I stand in awe of your deeds, O* LORD. *Renew them in our day, in our time make them known; in wrath remember mercy.* Habakkuk 3:2

worketh, do
Greek Strong's Number: 1754
Transliteration: energeo
Phonetic Pronunciation:
en-erg-eh'-o
Part of Speech: v
1) to be operative, be at work, put forth power 1a) to work for one, aid one 2) to effect 3) to display one's activity, show one's self operative

will
Greek Strong's Number: 2309
Transliteration: thelo, ethelo, theleo, etheleo
Phonetic Pronunciation: thel'-o, eth-el'-o, thel-eh'-o, eth-el-eh'-o
Part of Speech: v
1) to will, have in mind, intend 1a) to be resolved or determined, to purpose 1b) to desire, to wish 1c) to love 1c1) to like to do a thing, be fond of doing 1d) to take delight in, have pleasure

pleasure
Greek Strong's Number: 2107
Transliteration: eudokia
Phonetic Pronunciation:
yoo-dok-ee'-ah
Part of Speech: n f
1) will, choice 1a) good will, kindly intent, benevolence 2) delight, pleasure, satisfaction 3) desire 3a) for delight in any absent thing easily produces longing for it

The words *hoped for* and *unseen* should quickly suggest that we aren't likely to make an exact science of faith. The less evidential nature of walking by faith rather than by sight has its obvious risks. One of the inevitable questions each person challenged to believe God has to answer is whether she is willing to risk being wrong. Faith may not be palatable to perfectionists for this very reason. Thankfully, I gave up on perfectionism a long time ago. One positive result of past failure is that you surrender the pursuit of perfection and, if you've gained any sense, replace it with the pursuit of God's redemption. Nothing is more redemptive than faith in God. You learn that failure may be painful, but it's rarely fatal. After coming to grips with the high premium God places on our faith, I refuse to give up a life practice of believing God just because I accidentally swerve off the road a few times in my faith journey. Hebrews 11:6 says that faith pleases God, not perfection.

If my proposal is right and God is calling our generation to awaken to the sin of unbelief, to repent, and to start believing God, then He is preparing to do something huge. How do I know? Because God is intensely practical. God never calls us to do anything for nothing. Philippians 2:13 makes a statement with profound implications: "it is God who works in you to will and to act according to his good purpose." This is a perfect time to interject Your Turn.

 It's Your Turn

Please read Philippians 2:13 in the KJV. Then read *Strong's* definitions in the margin of the following words and record insights about them.

Worketh _____

Will _____

Do _____

Where have you already seen the original word in this verse? _____

What insight does the repetition give you? _____

_____

Pleasure _____

Philippians 2:13 conceptualizes God's wonderful practicality. One reason God works in us is so that we can work for Him. When various spokespeople and lay people who are seeking God in very different places hear the same biblical principles as a fresh revelation, we are wise to perk up our ears. In all likelihood God is saying something vital … and timely. As I prepare to conclude my remarks on the second statement of our pledge of faith, I'd like to emphasize what I suggested in video session 3.

Before I do, please write the second statement in our pledge of faith.

_____

In video session 3 we talked about the two extreme teachings in the body of Christ about miracles. I gave each teaching a name and presented the two views on opposite ends of the stage on easels. Do you remember what they were? Check the two.

❑ 1. sensationalism   ❑ 2. heresy   ❑ 3. pharisaism   ❑ 4. cessationism

I hope you remembered the session and marked 1 and 4. We defined sensationalists as those who tend to prioritize what God can do above who He is. We defined cessationists as those who believe miracles ceased, for all practical purposes, after the establishment of the early New Testament church. Though I love the entire body of Christ and am committed to unity, I believe the Word as a whole supports neither extreme. I suggested that although the present day is not characterized by signs and wonders, God certainly still performs miracles. I've seen them firsthand.

What does this review have to do with today's lesson? Do you remember when I suggested that even most cessationists believe that God will again perform various signs and wonders in the last days? I'd like to conclude my thoughts on our second statement of faith by theorizing that God is purposely working a fresh faith in His body of believers because He is about to perform a fresh work, one that has been calendared in heaven since time began. And, yes, one that will involve signs and wonders as He extends His final saving and judging revelations to planet Earth. You and I may or may not see the kinds of characterizing signs and wonders His Word predicts, but we are to begin preparing by adjusting our faith to the swelling work God is planning to perform. We must leave the generations that come behind us a heritage of faith and an invitation to go further still. The closer the calendar creeps to Christ's return the more faith Christians will need to stand firm and to serve Him in ways fitted to the times.

I'm anticipating the following question: does God need our faith to act, since He already has the events of the last days planned? Of course not. His purpose from the moment He created humanity was to invite man to partner with his Maker in His work. Simply put, faith partners with God. Faith also invites God. Swelling faith can hasten swelling works of God because frankly, He favors the invitation. With all my heart I believe God wants us to ask Him to reveal Himself more blatantly on earth so that many might be saved, others delivered, others helped, and still others healed. How many thousands die daily? How many millions are starving? Imprisoned? Despairing? Beloved, the time has come to ask God for miracles!

Paraphrase Today's Treasure into a prayer to God from your heart.

_____

Though I don't believe we are in the final days, I am convinced the last days are hastening on us. The fact that this study came from a worldwide Internet Bible-study opportunity is staggering evidence of escalating end-time events. Daniel 12:4 (KJV) predicts the vast increase in travel and knowledge. The prophecies in 2 Timothy 3:1-5 about human character in the last days are a terrifying indictment on our current culture. Please read these verses.

Which characteristics in these verses seem most obvious to you in your culture?

_____

For the life of me, I can't pinpoint a single one that doesn't fit. Beloved, the months are rapidly blowing off the kingdom calendar. God has a twofold agenda in the last days that I suggested a few paragraphs ago: salvation and judgment. He is determined to reach every people group with the true testimony of Jesus Christ before His Son's return (see Matt. 24:14), and He must ultimately judge an earth replete with sin for the sake of His great name, as prophesied in the Book of Revelation. A mighty outpouring of the Holy Spirit, profoundly spectacular revelations, and miracles of mercy and terror will occur in the final days. We are told that these signs will come like birth pains. I believe those birth pains have already started and we are presently witnessing scattered evidence of all those characteristics. Our world is plagued by cancer, AIDS, and various unexplainable viruses. Weather patterns are changing. Violence is raging. Lines are being drawn.

The news is far from being only negative. The numbers of believers surrendering to missions is exploding. Lay people are hungering to know the Word of God. The body of Christ is drawing its Sword—God's Word—for spiritual war. God is pouring out His Spirit on college students in ways I've never seen before. What I and others like Mary Graham of Women of Faith, Kay Arthur, and Anne Graham Lotz have witnessed among women has been nothing less than a miracle of God. True worshippers, both men and women, are rising in every denomination. Don't let anyone tell you that nothing positive is happening in Christ's true church. But now something else must happen. We must have an authentic revival of biblical faith.

The body of Christ must begin preparing now by increasing and adjusting its faith accordingly so that each generation is exceedingly equipped as the day of the Lord draws near. We must be like the men of Issachar in 1 Chronicles 12:32.

What does Scripture say about them? _____

_____

We too need to understand the times. Our world is in an uproar. The fury of Satan escalates. The return of Christ hastens. And Luke 18:8 raises a compelling question: " 'When the Son of Man comes, will he find faith on the earth?' " Each generation must be prepared to be the one inhabiting planet Earth when Christ comes. If He comes in ours, will He find faith?

Please review your responses to inquiries into the second fifth of your life in the Faith Journal sections of week 7, days 3 and 4. Diagram each pivotal event and any rocks of remembrance on your time line. Also record general descriptive phrases below the line as shown in "Mary's" example in week 9, day 1. In tomorrow's lesson you will proceed to the third fifth of your life.

_____

_____

_____

_____

_____

_____

_____

_____

GodStops

BEDTIME MEDITATION

_____

_____

_____

_____

_____

_____

I AM WHO GOD SAYS I AM

We are devoting our concluding week of study to injecting our hearts and minds one last time with each statement in our pledge of faith. We want our pledge to abide so securely that we can draw our shield of faith in the split second between the enemy's launching a fiery dart and the point of impact. According to Ephesians 6:16, our shield of faith "can extinguish all the flaming arrows of the evil one." Don't forget that the word *all* is one of our key words this week. Do you realize the magnitude of the promise in that marvelous verse? Satan can't fling a single flaming arrow at you that believing God cannot extinguish. No wonder the KJV says to raise our shield of faith above all. Dear One, you have the makings of a mighty warrior in Christ. All you have to do is use your weapons.

Today's Treasure

When Peter saw this, he said to them: "Men of Israel, why does this surprise you? Why do you stare at us as if by our own power or godliness we had made this man walk?" Acts 3:12

Today we're taking a last look together at the third statement in our pledge of faith.

Please write it here. _____

Therefore be imitators of God, as beloved children. Ephesians 5:1

dear
GREEK STRONG'S NUMBER: 27
Transliteration: agapetos
Phonetic Pronunciation:
   ag-ap-ay-tos'
Part of Speech: adj
1) beloved, esteemed, dear, favourite, worthy of love

children
GREEK STRONG'S NUMBER: 5043
Transliteration: teknon
Phonetic Pronunciation: tek'-non
Part of Speech: n n
1) offspring, children 1a) child 1a1) a male child, a son 1b) metaph. 1b1) the name transferred to that intimate and reciprocal relationship formed between men by the bonds of love, friendship, trust, just as between parents and children 1b2) in affectionate address, such as patrons, helpers, teachers and the like employ: my child 1b3) in the NT, pupils or disciples are called children of their teachers, because the latter by their instruction nourish the minds of their pupils and mould their characters 1b4) children of God: in the OT of "the people of Israel" as especially dear to God, in the NT, in Paul's writings, all who are led by the Spirit of God and thus closely related to God 1b5) children of the devil: those who in thought and action are prompted by the devil, and so reflect his character 1c) metaph. 1c1) of anything who depends upon it, is possessed by a desire or affection for it, is addicted to it 1c2) one who is liable to any fate 1c2a) thus children of a city: it's citizens and inhabitants 1c3) the votaries of wisdom, those souls who have, as it were, been nurtured and moulded by wisdom 1c4) cursed children, exposed to a curse and doomed to God's wrath or penalty

One of our online sisters wrote in to the community page to say she'd been practicing her five statements as fast as she could say them. When she said the third statement slowly and thoughtfully, she got the words right, but when she said it quickly, she caught herself saying, "I am who I say I am." Several others immediately responded that they had caught themselves doing the same thing. You see, we tend to default the fastest to what we believe the deepest or what we've believed the longest. That's why we must keep nailing these concepts down until what's deepest in our belief system is God's Word!

Can you think of several reasons why believing we are who God says we are is one of the hardest of the five statements for us to actively accept? List some of those reasons.

_____

_____

_____

Here's one of my reasons: at least God acts as if He is who He says He is, making this truth vastly more believable. I, on the other hand, acted entirely differently from who God said I was for many years, making this fact considerably harder for me to believe. You too? We've stumbled once again on the primary reason we act so differently from who we are once we know what God's Word says about us: unbelief. I didn't start acting like who God said I was until I committed myself to believing it.

Today we're going to begin by looking at Ephesians 5:1, and we're going to follow it up tomorrow with Ephesians 5:2. Read Ephesians 5:1 KJV in the margin. Using *Strong's* definitions, paraphrase the meaning of the following words.

Dear _____

Children _____

I love the NIV translation of this phrase even more: "as dearly loved children … live." Every time I read Ephesians 5:1, I picture God sending us out of the door of our secret place with Him and into the world, saying, "Now go and act like the dearly loved child you are today. And not just anyone's dearly loved child. Keep in mind today that your Father created that world and told the sun to come up again this morning. I'll be sitting right here on My throne all day long. Keep checking in with Me and let Me know what you need. You have My cell number." God's cell number? You didn't realize you have it? Of course you do. It's Jeremiah 33:3.

Write that verse. _____

_____

From time to time during our study I've mentioned that I have a few concerns for those of us who really decide to make believing God a lifestyle. One concern I mentioned is that we never distort the concept and become sign seekers. Another is that we remain humble when we see God answer prayer and never judge another person for a less active faith-practice. Like any life of devotion, the present-active-participle believing life can have its complications. This is where the flip side of the third statement in our pledge of faith becomes vital: to live in victory, we must not only know who we are; we must also know who we are not.

Needless to say, the list of things we are not is endless, but one is paramount. Keep the following fact very straight in the days, months, and years ahead as you practice present-active-participle faith: you are not God. You are His child. Why this warning? Beloved, if you truly make a lifestyle of believing God, your fruit is going to start showing, and so is the power of your prayer life. All of a sudden people around you will start trying to make you responsible for God's actions. Trust me. I've been there. Scripture has a good name for what some people try to make a person of active faith: false christs. People are so desperate to find Christ that they are willing to manufacture Him from a mortal with any vague resemblance.

My first brush with what I'll call the false-Christ syndrome happened when I was in college and in a friend's wedding. I was the most spiritual person she knew at that time, which means she didn't get out much. How in the world any form of witness survived my defeat and hypocrisy is beyond me. Her wedding was scheduled to be outside, and the sky was practically falling with rain. When I arrived and started to make myself comfortable, she took one look at me and growled, "Don't even think of sitting down. Get over there and start praying for that rain to stop!" Boy, did I! God felt sorry for me and stopped the rain, but His unwillingness to rebuke the humidity still left my friend aghast at our hair. I laugh about it now, but I've since been placed in some positions that weren't nearly as funny.

You and I have each experienced times when we've prayed our hardest for several people to be healed of physical illness. One is delivered on earth. The other is delivered in heaven. We've also prayed for people struggling to makes ends meet. One gets a job. Sometimes the other loses her home. Some people reason that God does what He wants and that our prayers mean nothing. But the truth of God's Word differs starkly. The believing prayers of those who pursue a sanctified walk with Jesus Christ are powerful and effectual. So why does God sometimes bring such different results from the same depth of earnest, believing prayer?

- We don't know.
- We're not supposed to know.
- We're not responsible for the One who does know.
- We are not God. We are His children.

We must be careful not to allow people to make us feel responsible for getting something from God or for explaining His mysterious actions. If we do, we are letting them make us false christs, and we have escorted them not only into inevitable disappointment but also into God-offending idolatry. We can learn volumes from Jesus' first followers, who were surely in these kinds of positions constantly. As we established in week 3, they also didn't get everything they asked. I think God knows that human hearts and minds can't handle it. Yet the disciples continued believing and receiving for the rest of their days. May we follow suit. Peter and John left us a wonderful example (see Today's Treasure). They could have written a manual called *How to Handle a Miracle*. Go ahead and take Your Turn.

marvel ye
GREEK STRONG'S NUMBER: 2296
Transliteration: thaumazo
Phonetic Pronunciation:
    thou-mad'-zo
Part of Speech: v
1) to wonder, wonder at, marvel
2) to be wondered at, to be had in admiration

earnestly
GREEK STRONG'S NUMBER: 816
Transliteration: atenizo
Phonetic Pronunciation: at-en-id'-zo
Part of Speech: v
1) to fix the eyes on, gaze upon
2) to look into anything 3) metaph. to fix one's mind on one as an example

holiness
GREEK STRONG'S NUMBER: 2150
Transliteration: eusebeia
Phonetic Pronunciation:
    yoo-seb'-i-ah
Part of Speech: n f
1) reverence, respect 2) piety towards God, godliness

 It's Your Turn

Please read Acts 3:6-13. Briefly describe what occurred in these verses. _____

_____

_____

_____

_____

Read verse 12. Using *Strong's* definitions in the margin, record any insights you gain from the words.

Marvel ye _____

Earnestly _____

Holiness _____

Based on these definitions, write several major points you think Peter and John might have made if they had coauthored a manual called *How to Handle a Miracle*.

_____

_____

_____

_____

_____

Like Peter and John, let's know who we are not. We are not God. Give up trying. And give up asking anyone else to try. Our part is to believe God. His part is to be God and to do what is ultimately and eternally best. He alone knows the ultimate objective to which He aligns every divine act on behalf of His children. All are dearly loved. All are intricately planned for. God never sits on His hands.

When we receive what we ask, let's not dream of taking credit. When we get to participate in a miracle, let's avoid ever letting another person marvel at us or admire us. If we take credit when we receive what we ask, not only will we offend God and mislead people, but we will also place ourselves in the position to take credit when we don't get what we earnestly ask. I am reminded of a bumper sticker I once saw: "There is a God. You are not He." Acts 3:12 is key. Read it again. None of us possess enough power or godliness to perform a miracle on our best day.

A segment of Paul's writing provides us a fitting conclusion. Goodness knows he could have written *How to Handle a Miracle 2*. He experienced and witnessed one miraculous delivery after another and saw God work wonders through Paul's own mortal hands. On the other hand, he also experienced shipwrecks, beatings, lashings, imprisonments, thorns, and the mysteries of one being healed and another remaining sick. When I encounter the mysteries of God afresh and the unexplainable ways He works so evidently on one hand and less evidently on the other, I am reminded of the Apostle Paul's words in Romans 11:33-36. I hope you're in an environment where you can read the words aloud.

I'm crazy about you, Child of God. Aren't we glad we are children and He is God? "Oh, the depth of the riches of the wisdom and knowledge of God!" (Rom. 11:33).

✎ faith Journal

Please review your responses to inquiries on the third fifth of your life. You will find these in the Faith Journal sections of week 7, day 5 and week 8, day 1. Diagram the third fifth of your time line with the information you supplied.

_____

_____

_____

_____

_____

_____

🔥 GodStops

BEDTIME MEDITATION

_____

_____

_____

_____

_____

I CAN DO ALL THINGS THROUGH CHRIST

Today's Treasure

The only thing that counts is faith expressing itself through love.
Galatians 5:6

The fourth statement in our pledge of faith is one of the true miracles of the believing life. We—joint heirs of Jesus Christ—are capable of doing things we simply cannot do. Today It's Your Turn will be interspersed throughout mine for the most effect. I love the complementary ideas in the following two verses. Please write the teachings of each verse.

John 15:5 _____

_____

Philippians 4:13 _____

_____

Simply put, without Him we can do nothing. With Him we can do everything. And just imagine. Sometimes we actually stop and think about which one we ought to choose. "Let's see. Should I choose nothing or everything?" I'm sorry, but I can think of no scholarly way to say it. Only one word comes to my mind: *duh*. Sometimes brilliance is not the human strong suit.

I may waver from time to time over the third statement in our pledge of faith, but I'd have to have serious mental issues to doubt our fourth. I live out of my own league almost all the time. Every now and then I'll be speaking in a large arena and have a sudden shift from spiritual thoughts to a natural thought that strikes me with indescribable terror: "What on earth are you doing on this stage, and why is everyone staring at you as if you know what you're talking about?" Last summer I took Melissa with me to the Christian Booksellers Convention. We stood in lines to get people's autographs, and we elbowed each other when we walked past an author or an artist we recognized. I don't know how to explain it, but I don't feel like an author. I just feel thankful to be saved and relieved to be out of the pit. All the rest is a miracle of a God who wanted to make sure He got all the credit when Blonder-than-she-pays-to-be had sense enough to get in out of the rain.

If you've walked with Jesus long, I know you have your own examples. What are a few things you've done in the strength of Christ that you knew with all your heart you could not naturally do?

_____

_____

_____

Never discount the miracle of the enabled unable. Through this miracle we become living, breathing 2 Corinthians 4:7s. What does this wonderful verse identify as God's goal?

_____

Can we all agree, then, that God is greatly glorified when we are each enabled to do what we're unable? Good. Because today we are going to discuss what is arguably the biggest earthly challenge "unables" like us have in common—loving people we don't feel like loving. Please read Today's Treasure. I realize that what I'm about to ask you to do will seem redundant, but studies show that we retain much more of what we write with our own hand.

Please write Today's Treasure here. _____

_____

This week is our last opportunity to nail down our five-statement pledge of faith. My deep desire is that we wrap up each statement with a few last thoughts of importance that God Himself would have us consider. As we share our final discussion on present-active-participle belief that we can do all things through Christ, I can think of nothing He desires more than to empower us to love … when we don't.
Faith expressing itself through love. What in the world does that mean? Please look up Galatians 5:6. Read *Strong's* definition in the margin of the word *worketh*, the KJV translation of the NIV's phrase *expressing itself*, and write the meaning.

_____

What do you think the verse means now that you've researched the word?

_____

_____

If we place 2 Corinthians 5:7 and Galatians 5:6 side by side, we can come up with two divine life challenges that, if accepted, catapult us onto a path infinitely higher than this world's self-centered interstate of mediocrity: We live by faith. We love by faith.
   We have dedicated nine weeks to the challenge to live by faith. For the remainder of today's lesson and for our final shared thoughts on statement 4, we are going to hear the call to love by faith. In our previous lesson we viewed Ephesians 5:1 and reminded ourselves that God is God and we are His dearly loved children. At all costs we must avoid accidentally getting those roles confused. Faith is not getting God to behave like an obedient child and do what we want Him to do. Faith is believing God will do what He says He can do and what we discern He desires to do.

Let's read Ephesians 5:1 again, then add and emphasize verse 2. Please look up these verses in the KJV. In your own words, what is the life challenge of Ephesians 5:2?

_____

_____

What does the word *walk* mean, according to the *Strong's* definition?

_____

worketh
GREEK STRONG'S NUMBER: 1754
Transliteration: energeo
Phonetic Pronunciation: en-erg-eh'-o
Part of Speech: v
1) to be operative, be at work, put forth power 1a) to work for one, aid one 2) to effect 3) to display one's activity, show one's self operative

walk
GREEK STRONG'S NUMBER: 4043
Transliteration: peripateo
Phonetic Pronunciation: per-ee-pat-eh'-o
Part of Speech: v
1) to walk 1a) to make one's way, progress; to make due use of opportunities 1b) Hebrew for, to live 1b1) to regulate one's life 1b2) to conduct one's self 1b3) to pass one's life

The One who adopted us into His royal family has called us to live according to our legacy. We are to literally live love. Fuzzy thought, isn't it? But check the verse again. The very nature of love is sacrificial. In fact, if we're not presently feeling the squeeze and sacrifice of loving, we're probably exercising a preferential, highly selective, self-centered human substitute.

Not only have we been called to live a sacrificial love. At times we may also expend untold self-sacrificing efforts for years and even for the rest of our lives without seeing any apparent fruit. God has called us to love even when—

- we don't want to;
- we don't feel like it;
- we get nothing obvious in return;
- they don't deserve it;
- they're not worth it;
- they don't even know it;
- it makes no difference.

Unless you're not getting out enough, I am sure God is confronting you with the challenge to love someone right now who brings out most of those feelings in you. Without using names or dishonoring someone, please describe several of your present challenges to love.

_____

_____

Mind you, loving sacrificially does not equal subjecting ourselves to untold abuses. God doesn't call us to sacrifice our sanity. He calls us to sacrifice our selfishness.

You and I have been constantly challenged over the past nine weeks to believe what God says over what we've contrarily seen or experienced.

faileth
GREEK STRONG'S NUMBER: 1601
Transliteration: ekpipto
Phonetic Pronunciation: ek-pip'-to
Part of Speech: v
1) to fall out of, to fall down from, to fall off 2) metaph. 2a) to fall from a thing, to lose it 2b) to perish, to fall 2b1) to fall from a place from which one cannot keep 2b2) fall from a position 2b3) to fall powerless, to fall to the ground, be without effect 2b3a) of the divine promise of salvation

What do the first three words of 1 Corinthians 13:8 say?

_____

Please read *Strong's* definition of *faileth* in the margin. What does it mean?

_____

No need to look up the word *never*. It means exactly what you think it means: never. Not once. Not ever. According to the Book of Truth, when we love in Jesus' name and for the sake of His sacrificial legacy, that love absolutely cannot fail. Each of us has to decide whether we are going to believe God's Word or our eyes and emotions. This is where loving by faith comes in. We've got to know that our every effort to love sacrificially never fails—

- to get God's priority attention (see Mark 12:28-30);
- to ultimately and undoubtedly be rewarded;
- to have a profound effect, whether in the other person, in the circumstance, or in us.

Love by faith. Love our enemies by faith. Love our neighbors by faith. Love fellow believers by faith. Love our family members by faith. Love our spouses by faith. Love our in-laws by faith. Love a rebellious teenager by faith. Love our betrayer by faith. Love an ill and bitter parent by faith. Love by faith, not just by feeling.

Please read afresh the aggravating words of 1 Corinthians 13:4-13. The reason I find them aggravating is because—in our human capabilities— they represent the impossible dream. All those *always* and *nevers*. I don't know about you, but I never always do anything.

Please list the characteristics of this love we are called to exercise.

_____

_____

_____

Beloved, the reason it sounds impossible to humans beings is because it is. The kind of love 1 Corinthians 13:4-8 describes is divine. To grasp its availability, we have to see it in tandem with the preceding chapter, which describes supernatural enablings for the supreme purpose of making God conspicuous in us.

What does 1 Corinthians 12:7 say? _____

_____

_____

No, love is not a spiritual gift. If it were, we would all conveniently claim not to possess that particular gift. Rather, love is a supreme and priority calling—the fruit of the Spirit of Christ within us that surfaces when we are filled (see Gal. 5:22-23; Eph. 5:18). The chief reason we find loving so painful, aggravating, and fruitless is because we keep trying to love with our own emotions' pitifully small resources. Romans 5:5 is my favorite Scripture to pray when I am challenged to love someone. This Scripture begs for an index card. How do we receive this love in order to extend this love?

Please read the *Strong's* definitions for the following words in the margin. Paraphrase the meanings.

Ashamed _____

Shed abroad _____

Hearts _____

Any insights? _____

_____

_____

ashamed
GREEK STRONG'S NUMBER: 2617
Transliteration: kataischuno
Phonetic Pronunciation:
kat-ahee-skhoo'-no
Part of Speech: v
1) to dishonour, disgrace 2) to put to shame, make ashamed 2a) to be ashamed, blush with shame 2b) one is said to be put to shame who suffers a repulse, or whom some hope has deceived

shed abroad
GREEK STRONG'S NUMBER: 1632
Transliteration: ekcheo, ekchuno
Phonetic Pronunciation: ek-kheh'-o
or (by variation), ek-khoo'-no
Part of Speech: v
1) to pour out, shed forth
2) metaph. to bestow or distribute largely

hearts
GREEK STRONG'S NUMBER: 2588
Transliteration: kardia
Phonetic Pronunciation: kar-dee'-ah
Part of Speech: n f
1) the heart 1a) that organ in the animal body which is the centre of the circulation of the blood, and hence was regarded as the seat of physical life 1b) denotes the centre of all physical and spiritual life 2a) the vigour and sense of physical life 2b) the centre and seat of spiritual life 2b1) the soul or mind, as it is the fountain and seat of the thoughts, passions, desires, appetites, affections, purposes, endeavours 2b2) of the understanding, the faculty and seat of the intelligence 2b3) of the will and character 2b4) of the soul so far as it is affected and stirred in a bad way or good, or of the soul as the seat of the sensibilities, affections, emotions, desires, appetites, passions 1c) of the middle or central or inmost part of anything, even though inanimate

Agapao love is a daily commitment of the will to vacate the heart's premises of its own preferential affections and make its chambers fleshy canteens for the liquid love of God. Yes, it's still a challenge, but it's no longer the impossible dream. We live by faith. We love by faith. Faith and love are inseparable housemates that offer hospitality to hope. When we lose our faith to love, we lose the energy to love. Then we lose our hope.

Beloved, when all is said and done, living is for loving. So these three remain: faith, hope, and love. But the greatest of these is love. This is our daily hope: faith expressing itself through love.

✦ faith Journal

Please review your responses to inquiries on the fourth fifth of your life in week 8, days 2 and 3. Diagram all pivotal events and rocks of remembrance on your time line and add any general descriptions in the space below the line.

_____

_____

_____

_____

_____

_____

GodStops

BEDTIME MEDITATION

_____

_____

_____

_____

_____

GOD'S WORD IS ALIVE AND ACTIVE IN ME

I've spent much of the morning in and out of grateful tears. Even now I sit and shake my head and burn with tears at the inconceivable kindness of my God. Perhaps you feel as I do: I cannot fathom how a holy God could have such stubborn love, boundless mercy, and tenacious redemption toward the sons and daughters of men. Why in this world He would allow me—such a former failure and pit dweller—the privilege to partner with Him and with you in this journey of faith is infinitely beyond me.

I need you to hear me on this one: this series is a miracle of God. I had no initial intention of writing homework. My original plan was to simply teach a 10-session lecture series on faith. I am so glad God did not tell me in advance. Had He, I think I would have melted into a heap on the floor. The concept of homework couldn't have come to me at a more exhausting time. I was just wrapping up *Beloved Disciple: The Life and Ministry of John* after an extremely intense 1 1/2 years of research, writing, and taping. The vision for the lecture series on believing God was a fire within me, but I never pictured writing daily homework. For me, writing demands much more intensity and energy than speaking.

My editors at LifeWay were the first to talk about homework assignments to accompany the video-driven Internet series. Their intention was never to heap on a consecutive series after I'd had no rest. They are wonderful people who wanted to best serve participants who had grown to expect homework. They only wanted to know whether I minded their compiling assignments from various authors and writings on faith. Once I knew they had a vision for an accompanying written study, my first intention was to write a skeleton foundation they would fill in with quotations from other referenced sources. I nearly had cardiac arrest when God gently broke the news to me that I was going to write the material myself.

"I don't have the mental strength, Lord."

"I do, Child."

"I'm physically exhausted, Lord."

"That's OK. I'm not."

Like no other series I've ever written, all I did was muster the strength to put two hands on the keyboard of a computer. I don't mean to be mystical. I'm not claiming divine authorship for this work. I just need to make sure you understand that the glory must go to God if anything at all has been accomplished through this series.

The basic teachings of the video series were concepts God has developed over the past five years of my life as He challenged me to start believing Him. The written work, however, was at times as new to me as to you. Some of what you've learned, I simultaneously learned as it went on the computer screen. My hands at times seemed to be on automatic pilot. I did not know how I would ever make it to the end. Over and over and sometimes in tears I kept saying, "I believe You for this homework, Father. I believe we'll finally make it to week 9, day 5." And here we are.

If you look back, you'll see how much shorter the commentary was at first. My intention was to be very brief because my mind was so exhausted. The more I wrote, the more momentum the Holy Spirit built. You'll probably agree that it's a good thing I'm stopping now, or this study might have droned on for the next 15 years.

Enough has been said.

Now it's time for Him to be alone with you. And alone with me. Oh, how I look forward to sitting in His presence, basking in just knowing I am my Beloved's and He is mine! My plan now is to believe Him for some rest. What follows that rest is His

Today's Treasure

God was manifest in the flesh, justified in the Spirit, seen of angels, preached unto the Gentiles, believed on in the world, received up into glory.
1 Timothy 3:16 (KJV)

(This Scripture is believed by most scholars to be the Apostle Paul's recitation of a hymn of New Testament creed sung by the early church.)

call. One thing I can promise you. For the rest of my days, Beloved, I'm believing God. And yes, I just did the hand motions. Tricky while typing.

I love music. Over the weeks of this series the notes of one song in particular have danced on the scores of my mind to the voice of the incomparable Rich Mullins. By the way, in case you're unfamiliar, you don't casually listen to the late Rich Mullins' songs. You analyze them while they analyze you. So take your time here.

I believe in God the Father
Almighty Maker of Heaven and Maker of Earth
And in Jesus Christ His only begotten Son, our Lord
He was conceived by the Holy Spirit,
Born of the virgin Mary,
Suffered under Pontuis Pilate,
He was crucified and dead and buried.

And I believe what I believe
is what makes me what I am
I did not make it,
no it is making me
It is the very truth of God
and not the invention of any man

I believe that He who suffered
was crucified, buried and dead
He descended into hell and on the third day,
He rose again
He ascended into Heaven
where He sits at God's mighty right hand
I believe that He's returning
To judge the quick and the dead
of the sons of men
I believe in God the Father
Almighty Maker of Heaven and Maker of Earth
And in Jesus Christ His only begotten Son, our Lord
I believe in the Holy Spirit
One Holy Church
The communion of Saints
The forgiveness of sins
I believe in the resurrection,
I believe in a life that never ends
And I believe that what I believe
is what makes me what I am
I did not make it,
no it is making me
It is the very truth of God
and not the invention of any man.[1]

Creed. Rich Mullins knew that God makes a man who he is, but how much that man believes what God said in many ways makes the man what he is. My desire at this moment is to behold the beauty of his words. Let's not miss it by splitting doctrinal hairs over his exact wording. As a people who have taken this journey of fresh belief together, let's sit here and reflect for a moment, gather the meaning to our breast, and nod. We have stated the same concept perhaps a hundred different ways over the past nine weeks. Most succinctly, believing God is what closes the gap between our theology and our reality. Maybe what we believe doesn't so much make us *what* we are as *how* we are. Undoubtedly, how we're doing at any given time in our spiritual walk will depend on who and what we're believing. I did not make it. No, it is making me.

Long before Rich Mullins was scheduled for arrival on planet Earth, the New Testament church had its own song of creed. Read the hymn again in Today's Treasure. Picture your earliest brothers and sisters in their gathering places singing the words with passion and conviction, bearing triumphant smiles or sacrificial tears on their faces. See Peter and John, Mary the mother of Jesus, Mary of Magdala, and all the others. The church was under terrible persecution. Christians were dying for the very belief system they hailed in that song.

Picture the Apostle Paul singing those very words with all his might while the wounds of 39 lashes were still wet on his back. I wonder whether this hymn was among those he and Silas sang from inside the prison after they had been severely flogged (see Acts 16:23). Acts 16:25 tells us the other prisoners were listening intently to them. Paul was such an evangelist that once he knew he had their attention, I would not be at all surprised if he sang them a song of sound biblical doctrine.

Whatever they sang, suddenly a violent earthquake shook the very foundations of the prison. At once all the prison doors flew open, and everybody's chains came loose (see Acts 16:26).

Paul believed what Christ believed. It's what made him what he was. He did not make it. No, it was making him. It was the very truth of God and not the invention of any human. No whip could beat it out of him. From his last imprisonment the apostle Paul wrote that though he was chained, God's Word is not chained (see 2 Tim. 2:9). Indeed, it is not. God sends forth His Word, and it never returns void, unchaining the soul of every person with the courage to believe it. Beloved, as we go our separate ways, may we commission one another to spend our lives devouring His Word. We have only one certain way of knowing that—

- God is Who He says He is;
- God can do what He says He can do;
- I am who God says I am;
- I can do all things through Christ.

The way we know these truths is expressed in our fifth statement: God's Word alive and active in us. Breathe it. Believe it. Speak it. Live it. Love it. And brace yourself for it.

"The Bible is not a book for the faint of heart—it is a book full of all the greed and glory and violence and tenderness and sex and betrayal that befits mankind. It is not the collection of pretty little anecdotes mouthed by pious little church mice—it does not so much nibble at our shoe leather as it cuts to the heart and splits the marrow from the bone. It does not give us answers fitted to our small-minded questions, but truth that goes beyond what we even know to ask."[2]

As we draw to our conclusion, let's look up 1 Timothy 3:15-16 together. A portion of it is stated in Today's Treasure, but I'd like for you to read the whole passage. What does verse 15 tell you about the church?

Dear One,

Thank you. Oh, how I thank you. I will never forget this ride as long as I live. I conclude this series with more affection, appreciation, and devotion for the true church of Jesus Christ than I have ever felt before. I teach a very interdenominational weekly Bible study on Tuesday nights in Houston, so I've come to love diversity dearly. We still have one cultural aspect in common, however, that keeps us from being a true microcosm of God's ultimate concept of church. We are all from south Texas. A peculiar people if you've ever met one. Even where we are denominationally different, we are culturally similar.

The Internet dimension of *Believing God* changed all that. We have shared the indescribable privilege of having church the way Christ loves having church. The way we'll have it through all eternity. Every color and kind. Any nation who would. As Rich Mullins sang, God has "One Holy Church." And we, Beloved—and all our brothers and sisters throughout the world who have looked to the grace-work of Christ on the cross for salvation—are that church. I am head over heels about you.

If I don't see you here, I'll see you there. Until then, no more business as usual. From here to eternity, we're present-active-participle believing God. Stay a verb. Live out loud. And wake up a few nouns.

Believing God,

Beth Moore

 *faith Journal*

Conclude your time line, Dear One! Review your responses to the inquiries on the last fifth of your life, which you journaled in week 8, days 4 and 5. Please have your time line with you as we share video session 10. It will be important to us in our concluding time together. Today please use this section to articulate the primary way God has revealed Himself to you throughout this nine-week faith walk.

_____

_____

_____

_____

_____

_____

GodStops

BEDTIME MEDITATION

_____

_____

_____

_____

_____

_____

[1]"Creed" by Rich Mullins and Beaker, 1993 BMG Songs, Inc. (ASCAP) and Kid Brothers of St. Frank Publishing (ASCAP), A Liturgy, A Legacy and a Ragamuffin Band (Nashville: Reunion, 1993). All rights on behalf of Kid Brothers of St. Frank Publishing administered by BMG Songs, Inc. Used by permission.

[2]Rich Mullins, as quoted in James Bryan Smith, An Arrow Pointing to Heaven (Nashville: Broadman & Holman Publishers, 2000), 43.

Believing God for the Rest of Your Days

As we conclude our corporate study of faith, let's take one last glance at the portraits that hang on the walls of the Hall of Faith and then read Hebrews 11:32–12:3. Let's stand at the wall and gaze at the space in the heritage of faith that awaits our pictures. Today and perhaps for the rest of our lives, we will see ourselves as—

_____.

Part 1: Defining a Race Well Run

The original word for *fought* is *agonizomai* meaning "to _____ for victory in the _____

_____ ... to _____." The original word for *fight* is *agon* meaning _____.

A. Sometimes we _____ our way to the finish line. Other times we _____ our way to the finish line.

B. We run our race well not by _____ to wrestle but by _____ the faith.

   • *finished:* "not merely to _____ it but to bring it to perfection or its destined _____,

   to _____ it through."

Part 2: A Few Facts to Help Us Keep the Faith

A. Faith always _____. We will receive at least the following three results:

   • The _____ of God (Heb. 11:6)

   • The _____ of God (Eph. 1:18-20)

   • The _____ of God (John 11:38-40)

B. Faith soon _____. Second Timothy 4:6 (KJV) says, "the time of my departure is at hand."

   ephistemi: epi—by, near, upon; *histemi*—to stand.

C. Above all things, faith must present-active-participle believe _____ _____ (Ps. 62:11-12).

Conclusion:

   • The call to intercession (Eph. 3:17b-18)

   • The commission to faith

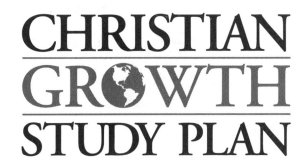

CHRISTIAN GROWTH STUDY PLAN

In the **Christian Growth Study Plan (formerly Church Study Course)**, this book *Believing God: Experiencing a Fresh Explosion of Faith* is a resource for course credit in the subject area Bible Studies of the Christian Growth category of plans. To receive credit, read the book, complete the learning activities, show your work to your pastor, a staff member or church leader, then complete the following information. This page may be duplicated. Send the completed page to:

Christian Growth Study Plan
One LifeWay Plaza; Nashville, TN 37234-0117
FAX: (615)251-5067; Email: cgspnet@lifeway.com
For information about the Christian Growth Study Plan, refer to the Christian Growth Study Plan Catalog. It is located online at www.lifeway.com/cgsp. If you do not have access to the Internet, contact the Christian Growth Study Plan office (1.800.968.5519) for the specific plan you need for your ministry.

Believing God
COURSE NUMBER: CG-0815

PARTICIPANT INFORMATION

Social Security Number (USA ONLY-optional)
Personal CGSP Number*
Date of Birth (MONTH, DAY, YEAR)

Name (First, Middle, Last)
Home Phone

Address (Street, Route, or P.O. Box)
City, State, or Province
Zip/Postal Code

Please check appropriate box: ❑ Resource purchased by self ❑ Resource purchased by church ❑ Other

CHURCH INFORMATION

Church Name

Address (Street, Route, or P.O. Box)
City, State, or Province
Zip/Postal Code

CHANGE REQUEST ONLY

☐ Former Name

☐ Former Address
City, State, or Province
Zip/Postal Code

☐ Former Church
City, State, or Province
Zip/Postal Code

Signature of Pastor, Conference Leader, or Other Church Leader
Date

The Commission to faith

Lord, today I accept my calling
not to perfection or performance.
My calling is to faith.
I have been chosen for this generation.
I have a place in the heritage of faith.
I'm going to stop wishing and whining
and start believing and receiving.
What Your Word says is mine.
I won't let others steal my hope.
I won't argue with a Pharisee.
I will believe and therefore speak,
for You, my God, are huge.
Nothing is too hard for You.
Our world needs your wonders.
Rise up, oh Lord!
Please renew Your works in our day.
I confess the unbelief of my generation
and ask You to begin Your revival of faith
in my own heart.
For You are who You say You are.
You can do what You say You can do.
I am who You say I am.
I can do all things through Christ.
Your Word is alive and active in me.
Satan, hear me clearly:
My Father is Maker of heaven and earth.
You are under my feet,
because today and the rest of my days,

I'm believing God!